D1738245

LANGUAGE, LITERACY, AND COGNITIVE DEVELOPMENT

The Development and Consequences of Symbolic Communication

The Jean Piaget Symposium Series
Available from LEA

OVERTON, W. F. (Ed.) • The Relationship Between Social and Cognitive Development

LIBEN, L. S. (Ed.) • Piaget and the Foundations of Knowledge

SCHOLNICK, E. K. (Ed.) • New Trends in Conceptual Representation: Challenges to Piaget's Theory?

NIEMARK, E. D., DeLISI, R., & NEWMAN, J. L. (Eds.) • Moderators of Competence

BEARISON, D. J. & ZIMILES, H. (Eds.) • Thought and Emotion: Developmental Perspectives

LIBEN, L. S. (Ed.) • Development and Learning: Conflict or Congruence?

FORMAN, G. & PUFALL, P. B. (Eds.) • Constructivism in the Computer Age

OVERTON, W. F. (Ed.) • Reasoning, Necessity, and Logic: Developmental Perspectives

KEATING, D. P. & ROSEN, H. (Eds.) • Constructivist Perspectives on Developmental Psychopathology and Atypical Development

CAREY, S. & GELMAN, R. (Eds.) • The Epigenesis of Mind: Essays on Biology

BEILIN, H. & PUFALL, P. (Eds.) • Piaget's Theory: Prospects and Possibilities

WOZNIAK, R. H. & FISCHER, K. W. (Eds.) • Development in Context: Acting and Thinking in Specific Environments

OVERTON, W. F. & PALERMO, D. S. (Eds.) • The Nature and Ontogenesis of Meaning

NOAM, G. G. & FISCHER, K. W. • Development and Vulnerability in Close Relationships

REED, E. S., TURIEL, E., & BROWN, T. (Eds.) • Values and Knowledge

AMSEL, E. & RENNINGER, K. A. (Eds.) • Change and Development: Issues of Theory, Method, and Application

LANGER, J. & KILLEN, M. (Eds.) • Piaget, Evolution, and Development

SCHOLNICK, E., NELSON, K., GELMAN, S. A., & MILLER, P. H. (Eds.) • Conceptual Development: Piaget's Legacy

NUCCI, L. P., SAXE, G. B., & TURIEL, E. (Eds.) • Culture, Thought, and Development

AMSEL, E. & BYRNES, J. P. (Eds.) • Language, Literacy, and Cognitive Development: The Development and Consequences of Symbolic Communication

BROWN, T. & SMITH, L. (Eds.) • Reductionism and the Development of Knowledge

LANGUAGE, LITERACY, AND COGNITIVE DEVELOPMENT

The Development and Consequences of Symbolic Communication

Edited by

ERIC AMSEL
Weber State University

JAMES P. BYRNES
University of Maryland

2002

LAWRENCE ERLBAUM ASSOCIATES, PUBLISHERS
Mahwah, New Jersey   London

Lawrence Erlbaum Associates, Inc., Publishers
10 Industrial Avenue
Mahwah, New Jersey 07430

Cover design by Kathryn Houghtaling Lacey

Library of Congress Cataloging-in-Publication Data

Language, literacy, and cognitive development : the development and consequences of symbolic communication / edited by Eric Amsel, James Byrnes.
    p. cm.
    Chapters of this book were originally presented at the 28th Annual Symposium of the Jean Piaget Society held from June 11-13, 1998, in Chicago, Ill.
    Includes bibliographical references and indexes.
    ISBN 0-8058-3494-X (cloth : alk. paper)
    1.   Language acquisition. 2. Communication. 3. Literacy. 4. Cognition in children. I. Amsel, Eric. II. Byrnes, James P. III. Jean Piaget Society. Symposium (28th : 1998 : Chicago, Ill.) IV. Jean Piaget Society.

P118 .L373 2002
401'.93—dc21

                                                                                          2001051291

Books published by Lawrence Erlbaum Associates are printed on acid-free paper, and their bindings are chosen for strength and durability.

Printed in the United States of America
10   9   8   7   6   5   4   3   2   1

Contents

v

Preface

For many years, scholars in diverse fields have grappled with questions centering on human symbol skills. Such skills include the ability to encode, manipulate, and express sounds, gestures, notations, and other intrinsically meaningless entities that are conventionally imbued with the power to stand for objects, events, actions, and other meaningful states of affairs. The human capacity to elevate vocalizations, movements, or artifacts into meaningful private mental codes and socially communicative forms is a remarkable achievement that has defied well over a century of examination of its formal nature, origin in the species, and development within the person. Questions as to the formal nature, phylogenetic origin, and ontogenetic development of symbol skills are conceptually interrelated. Indeed, answers to questions about the nature, origin, and development of human symbol skills have defined various standard paradigms, including nativism, empiricism, and constructivism.

The goal of the present book is to reexamine these long-standing questions about human symbol skills. To rein in the issues somewhat, however, we have decided to focus on the subsample of issues that address symbolic communication. That is, we examine human symbol skills, but de-emphasize issues of their representation and manipulation in order to highlight the significance of the ability to communicate symbolically. By symbolic communication we mean understanding others or expressing oneself with symbols, whether that involves communicating linguistically, mathematically, or through another symbol system expressed in speech, gesture, notations, or through some other means. That is, we focus on the instruments for communication (the nature and format of symbols and systems in which they are embedded) as distinct from the messages communicated (i.e., the propositional content).

Our strategy is to explore the significance of communicating symbolically as a means for understanding human symbol skills. Symbolic communication may play a central role in the representation and manipulation of symbols, processes that seem to have gotten more attention than communication has. The process of communicating with symbols, perhaps to oneself, or to a real or hypothetical other, may be a central element in explanations of what information comes to be symbolically represented and how those symbols are mentally manipulated. The upshot is that there may be a much more interesting and dynamic relation between communicating, representing, and manipulating symbolic forms that is worthy of full and careful consideration across a variety of symbolic communicative means and modes.

In the present volume, we bring together prominent researchers and theorists whose work contributes substantially to the refinement and understanding of the questions regarding symbolic communication in all its forms, but particularly speaking, gesturing, reading, and writing. These authors are known for studying a range of empirical issues regarding the significance of symbolic communication. A number of contributors were invited because of their theoretical and empirical interests in the nature and consequences of forms of symbolic communication that are acquired spontaneously. By spontaneously acquired forms of symbolic communication, we mean that such forms may be acquired with environmental input, but without the need of carefully orchestrated, consciously intended, and formally structured attempts by parents or teachers to directly teach or train the forms to children. Katherine Nelson and Lea Kessler Shaw examine a range of evidence dealing with symbolic communication and its role in children's acquisition of language and for conceptual development. Nancy Budwig provides evidence of the progressively adequate grammaticalization of linguistic practices between mother and child, particularly with regard to complex linguistic forms expressing mental states. Susan Goldin-Meadow presents a review of evidence addressing gestures as a means of communication, exploring both its use by deaf children who spontaneously use gestures as a primary means of communication and hearing adults who use them as a secondary communicative outlet. Keeping with the theme of language, Dedre Gentner and Jeff Loewenstein examine the role of symbolic communication for children's analogical reasoning, arguably a central mechanism in their understanding and representing the world.

Going beyond spontaneously acquired symbolic communication skills, other contributors have addressed symbolic communication with formally learned notational systems. These contributors examine symbolic communication with formally trained literacy skills. David Olson examines research and theory addressing the question of the impact of communication and on thought of acquiring reading and writing skills. Richard Lehrer and Leona Schauble provide a rationale for and evidence of elementary school-aged children's use of inscriptions to communicate and analyze aspects of the physical world and its impact for their mathematical and scientific reasoning. Finally, Colette Daiute discusses her theoretical and empirical findings regarding elementary school children's communication to create a social context in which they write stories together and improve their written skills.

Even this brief review of the range of work on symbolic communication reveals potential parallels between spontaneously acquired linguistic systems as expressed in speech or gestures and formally taught notational systems for reading and writing. Whereas the former formalizes communicative practices, the latter formalizes speech, and each alters thought, including thoughts about the communicative process itself. This book examines these and other parallels for cognition and development of spontaneously acquired and formally learned symbolic communication systems.

Our focus on the development and consequences of communicating with symbols, whether spontaneously acquired or formally learned, brings up three specific issues that we have asked our chapter authors to consider:

The Contribution Issue. How does symbolic communication in all its forms (speaking, gesturing, reading, and writing) contribute to cognitive development? Does the act of communicating with symbols transform thinking beyond merely communicating an intended message?

The Special Status Issue. Is there a uniformity of explanations of the nature and consequences of symbolic communication across different communicative systems? Is it necessary or useful to distinguish particular forms of symbolic communication (e.g., spoken language, notational systems) for purposes of explaining its nature or its consequences for cognition and development?

The Origin Issue. Is it necessary or useful to evoke innate constraints of one form or another or processes to explain the acquisition of a particular form of symbolic communication (e.g., the whole-object constraint in spoken language)? Are some other forms of symbolic communication completely free of specific constraints? What if any aspects of symbolic communication are universal?

The examination of issues and search for parallels between spontaneously acquired and formally learned symbolic communication systems are not typical in the literature as attention is usually given to the uniqueness of each acquisition at the age it is made. Infants' and toddlers' acquisition of language is seen in the context of other skills, symbolic and otherwise, acquired by infants and toddlers, and children's learning skills for reading and writing notations and inscriptions are examined in the context of other academic and nonacademic skills. We believe that a clearer and deeper understanding of symbolic communication will be realized by an examination of and comparison between the nature and consequences of children's acquisitions of different symbolic communicative systems. The examination of such issues and search for such parallels is the basis for the opening chapter by Ellin Scholnick and the concluding chapter by Eric Amsel and James Byrnes. In Scholnick's opening paragraph, she introduces each chapter more completely than was done here and examines how each one explores similar issues, which she characterizes metaphorically as a partnership between representational systems of thought, language, and notations. In our concluding chapter, we identify broad and general themes in each chapter and expand on Scholnick's partnership metaphor to examine the nature and consequences of symbolic communication in distinct contexts.

As noted, the overarching theme of the book is to go beyond traditional accounts of human symbol skills to examine the development and consequences of symbolic communication. The three traditional accounts are briefly reviewed in thumbnail sketches, particularly addressing how each addresses the development of symbolic communication and its consequences for cognition and development. Piaget's stance on the nature of symbolic communication and its developmental significance is open to several distinct interpretations. For example, some claim that Piaget espoused Cognitive Determinism (i.e., that language is merely a reflection of thought, cf. Byrnes & Gelman, 1991). They base this claim on portions of influential works such as *The Early Growth of Logic in the Child.* Others, however, point to Piaget's early works on morality and later works on the four factors of cognitive development in which he argued that social exchange promotes intellectual advances. Still others could use his work in the 1970s on explanation, consciousness, and success to argue that he would espouse a transformational role for symbolic communication. In the latter studies, Piaget claimed that when children attempt to explain the surprising results of actions to themselves, they elaborate their structural understandings. Thus, it is overly simplistic to pigeonhole Piaget's stance in terms of a particular classical framework. Nevertheless, it could reasonably be said that Piaget spent far less time on the topic of symbolic communication than he spent on other topics such as conservation, equilibration, and structuralism. One can only speculate how his stance would have evolved had he devoted more attention to it.

Vygotsky claimed that symbolic communication is of major significance in the child's acquisition of knowledge. Vygotsky suggested that symbolic communication is a particularly important means for the child to fully appreciate the nature of symbolic thought, with the most important being speech but with other forms (e.g., symbolic play) also having important roles. For Vygotsky, language as a means of symbolic expression serves a representational function once internalized. Beyond spoken language, other formats for symbolic expression (notably logic and mathematics) also become internalized and contribute to cognitive functioning.

Chomsky argued that unlike any other aspect of human cognition, spoken language could not be acquired via general purpose learning mechanisms such as operant conditioning or reflective abstraction. The specific learning mechanism is nonetheless so abstract that different channels of linguistic expression (speech, sign language, etc.) appear similarly constrained. Interestingly, arguments like Chomsky's regarding language have been made about other means of symbolic communication, including logic and mathematics.

ACKNOWLEDGMENTS

The Chapters of this book were originally presented at the 28th Annual Meeting of the Jean Piaget Society held from June 11 to 13 in Chicago, which was organized by the editors. We want to express our appreciation to the executive committee and board of directors of the Piaget Society who graciously allowed us to forge an unusual symposium. The topic of the 28th Annual Symposium on the Jean Piaget Society, "Language, Literacy, and Cognitive Development," was not without controversy, and we appreciate the support of then-president Michael Chandler and the members of the board of directors for providing us an opportunity to explore new and important theoretical and empirical directions in cognitive development. We would also like to thank Saba Ayman-Nolley for her tremendous work as local arrangements chair for the 1998 symposium. The good cheer and helpful comments of the Lawrence Erlbaum Associates Executive Editor Judi Amsel and her assistant Bonita D'Amil were also appreciated.

REFERENCES

Byrnes, J. P., & Gelman, S. A. (1991). Perspectives on thought and language: Traditional and contemporary views. In S. A. Gelman & J. P. Byrnes (Eds.), *Perspectives on language and thought: Interrelations in development* (pp. 3-27). New York: Cambridge University Press.

Part I

INTRODUCTION

Chapter 1

Language, Literacy, and Thought: Forming a Partnership

Ellin Kofsky Scholnick
University of Maryland

This is a chapter about connections. It discusses a question to which this symposium was addressed. Thinking, language, and conventional notations can be deployed for the same task, representing knowledge. How are these systems of representation linked? The question is central. Humans are symbolic creatures. Their interactions in the world are often filtered and shaped by interwoven public and private representational systems. Within the tapestry, one symbolic system may be layered on another, as when thoughts about an event are described in words that are sculpted into an essay. Even within symbol systems, elements represent each other. For example, purposes are described metaphorically as paths (Lakoff & Johnson, 1980). Language, thought, and literacy not only represent the world and the self, they represent each other. Each system has distinctive properties and components that are themselves woven together, but the systems coil and thread through one another. Although each system has a distinctive texture, the strength of the human fabric derives from the way the various threads are knit together. Within this cloth, it is often hard to distinguish the warp from the woof or the constraints of the notational system from the structure of the events represented. Literacy builds on and expresses prior conceptual and linguistic notions. Conversely, the use of specific notational systems influences how events are conceptualized and described.

This characterization of three representational media, as interacting systems representing themselves, each other, and the world, is controver-

3

sial. Discussions of language, thinking, and notational systems are usually framed within two intersecting debates. Is the better explanatory framework derived from formal analyses of syntax and logic or from the social structure of discourse (Nelson, 1999)? The search for a consistent model to encompass diverse symbolic capacities takes place within a larger scientific and epistemological dispute reflected in the choice of metaphors for describing human functioning (Lakoff & Johnson, 1999). The mainstream view of language, thinking, and various forms of literacy is computational. Each is a separate symbolic system subdivided into distinct components, such as syntax, semantics, and phonology, or domains, such as space and biology (Spelke & Newport, 1998). All share certain formal properties. They are composed of a set of elements and potential relations, and are governed by rules of combination, substitution, and transformation of elements and relations. The major analytic task is to characterize the architecture of these systems. Within the computational metaphor, the internal connections across systems and the external connections to the world occur through association and mapping. These mappings are made possible by their common digital or mathematical format. The language of thought and the structure of the world are inherently computational (Gardner, 1985; Pinker, 1997). The symbol system of logic and mathematics underlies our entire representational apparatus. Cognition and language are software programs written in a notational code.

Many of the chapters in this book dispute the computational, analytic framework because it impedes finding a common rubric to deal with diverse forms of notation, which are clearly historical and cultural products, and the language and thinking that notational systems encode. Qualitative transformations of each system that result from their interaction are also difficult to acknowledge and explain (see Karmiloff-Smith, 1992, for an exception). This chapter begins by outlining the problems the computational metaphor poses for the study of interacting, layered symbolic systems, each with the potential for symbolizing one another. I then propose a different metaphor and use it as a framework for discussing the contents of this volume.

HIDING CONNECTIONS

The computational model of cognition is heavily influenced by analytic philosophy with its attempts to convert cognition into either linguistic or mathematical symbol manipulation (Lakoff & Johnson, 1999). Cognitive science's adoption of the computer metaphor pushed abstraction of cognition and language even further by characterizing them as products of an abstract, analytic, independent mind (Bloom, 1998; Lakoff & Johnson,

1999; Overton, 1998, 1999a). In contemporary cognitive science, development is merely the refinement of already constructed systems and the application of these systems to the world of experience that is already formatted to conform to the mind's machinery (e.g., Spelke & Newport, 1998). The metaphor does not lend itself to answering central questions about internal, external, and temporal connections among symbolic systems; for example, (a) How are the various mental processes that are so seamlessly joined in behavior integrated in the mind? How are representational and other bodily systems related? (b) How is the child situated in the cultural and social world that the child is trying to represent and that provides models of representation? (c) What explains development of each symbol system separately or in concert?

The Modular Mind: Internal Connections

Language is such a rich medium that it poses a temptation. In order to understand it, we need to analyze it and we assume that the products of the analysis describe how the system actually works. Each system is reduced to simpler components. Language is partitioned into syntax, phonology, semantics, and pragmatics, each with distinctive characteristics. The semantic system bears little resemblance to the structure of phonology or the rules of communication. The mapping of words onto representations of the world appears very different from the mapping of articulatory movements onto sounds or sounds onto written letters (Maratsos, 1998). Moreover the systems appear at different times, starting with detection of the phonological and prosodic features of language and moving to adept, persuasive prose. Vocabulary and communicative skills change throughout the life span, whereas command of the phonological and grammatical structure of one's native tongue rarely changes radically after middle childhood (Maratsos, 1998).

Those who yield to the temptation partition the mind in separate modules and domains (Fodor, 1983). A dissociative research strategy highlights children with communicative disorders who, nevertheless, manage to perform cognitive tasks, or children with cognitive deficits who, nevertheless, manage to speak. The division of the mind leads to endless debates about the primacy of language in cognitive growth and cognition in linguistic growth (Gelman & Byrnes, 1991). Components of language are also split off from each other, and knowledge is parceled into separate bundles. Consequently, it is puzzling how children combine the parts and map sound onto meaning, syntax, and communicative acts (Bloom, 1998; Maratsos, 1998) and why they have so much difficulty with analyzing words into sounds during the course of learning to read (Olson, 1994). A modular approach dissociates processes that often need to be integrated and often pays undue attention to those components of a system that are most conducive to a modular perspective. Thus, the pragmatics of communication are de-emphasized.

The Abstract Child: External Connections

Stripped-Down Situations. The computational model of knowledge also perpetuates the myth of an abstract child undertaking a solitary journey to discover the nature of the world (Scholnick, 1999a, 2000). Consequently, researchers often devise experimental situations with impoverished linguistic and contextual cues in order to determine how children understand grammatical distinctions or learn new vocabulary (Bloom, 1998). Abilities that are honed to handle particular contexts are studied in decontextualized environments. The data from these tasks are problematical because the child sounds much more mature in ordinary discourse than in the laboratory. Children skillfully use mental state vocabulary well before they master false belief tasks (Nelson, 1999; Nelson, Hensdale, & Plesa, 2000). Children who perform well in one laboratory situation fail to transfer their knowledge or skill to a slightly altered situation (Gentner & Markman, 1997). Yet, in everyday discourse, children overgeneralize rules (Pinker, 1999).

The Structure–Function Split. Within the computational metaphor, the child is characterized as a miniature scientist or linguist (Gopnik & Meltzoff, 1996; Pinker, 1994). Just as the physicist contemplates nature and derives pure knowledge of the world, the child acquires knowledge of language or scientific domains merely to grasp some underlying pattern. The knowledge the child intuits resembles what adults or linguists understand. The child may even employ the same analytic skills and methodology that the linguist or scientist uses. The analogy is a false one because science is never pure. The problems that science explores are partially determined by the social structure of the scientific enterprise and the resources societies devote to explorations of particular areas that are deemed of political and economic importance (Foucault, 1972; Harding, 1998).

Descriptions of the child as theoretical physicist/linguist also ignore important facets of the embodied child who uses symbols to accomplish vital ends and becomes an adept symbolizer in the course of accomplishing these ends (Bloom, 1998; Overton, 1999b). The separation of knowledge of linguistic structure from mere communicative skill (Chomsky, 1988) fails to explain how children learn that language can serve multiple functions and how children learn to exploit language to serve these functions. Pragmatic knowledge is separated from true language as if syntax and meaning were the products of the rational mind, whereas communication and imagination are simply practical applications that do not change understanding of the basic foundational categories (Lakoff & Johnson, 1999). The excessive abstraction in current theories of language also creates the artificial problem of putting the child back into language acquisition (Bloom, 1998). Because language occurs in an embodied individual, changes in language affect how children express emotions and conceptualize the self. Changes in emotional state or self-regulation affect what we say and how we say it.

The Isolated Child. The strategies of abstracting the child from the everyday environment and language from use are linked to dissociating language from society. The more one postulates that knowledge is represented as a high level abstraction, the less likely it is that this abstract analysis can be acquired through experience. Therefore, the basis for the abstraction has to be "wired" into the individual, and it becomes harder for people to map internal abstractions to concrete uses. Abstractions are isolated from their social content and social context. The search for linguistic universals or universal processing mechanisms leads to a divorce of language from its historical/cultural roots. Yet a hallmark of human intelligence is its adaptability to specific situations. Language is an indispensable medium of social and cultural transmission about effective methods of adaptation (Tomasello, 1999).

The notion of an "isolated child" does not allow spoken language and literacy to be placed within the same framework. Notational systems vary across historical eras and cultures, and even domains. Current explanations of the acquisition and application of inscriptional systems are incompatible with neonativist explanations of language and conceptual change (Spelke & Newport, 1998). Unless literacy is simply a veneer laid over language and thinking or an instrument designed for different purposes than thinking or speaking, the theoretical task of explaining how spoken language is mapped onto written language is formidable.

Alternatively, if language and thought are transformed or strengthened by literacy, then language and thought are not so abstract and modularized after all (Karmiloff-Smith, 1992). Each can be influenced by literacy, a sociocultural invention. If children's linguistic prowess is enhanced by academic instruction in childhood, perhaps their linguistic skill bears the imprint of earlier exposure to society and culture. Language is designed to convey culture. Language is designed for social communication. Why aren't social influences and the sociocultural messages operative from the beginning? Admittedly, individuals build on inherent human cognitive and linguistic proclivities that guide initial learning (Nelson, 1996). However, even within the same linguistic community, people differ in their styles of expression and the use to which they put language. Ignoring these individual differences and the experiences that create them produces an incomplete picture.

The Static Child: Temporal Connections

The model of the miniature linguist/scientist constructing or refining intuitive theories restricts explanations of mechanisms of change to mapping, parameter setting, or theory revision guided by innate procedures (Gopnik & Meltzoff, 1996; Spelke & Newport, 1998). These mechanisms are not straightforward. Mapping is a complex process requiring putting the right experiences into the right correspondences. It is not clear, if the child works independently, how the child finds the right connection without some guiding predispositions (Maratsos, 1998). Mapping often requires fine-tuning, a complex skill in its own right (Gentner, chapter 4, this volume). Adults do not just map more things, they map them differently from children. Similarly, theory revision is a skill, honed through practice and knowledge of a domain (Kuhn, Amsel, & O'Loughlin, 1988).

The computer metaphor does not lend itself to an organic model of growth. Qualitative changes occur that transform a novice into an expert or an illiterate into a reader. The successive acquisition of concepts, language, and literacy cannot easily be explained by mapping.

PARTNERSHIPS WITHIN THE SELF
AND ACROSS PEOPLE AND TIME

A more promising way of looking at the connections among symbol systems is a partnership in which distinct systems with unique characteristics coalesce around particular tasks. The systems share common goals, but may divide the labor, support each other, and even change one another and their relationship as they interact. Describing the connections among language, thinking, and notation as a coalition overcomes the limitations of modular systems, disconnected children, and static performance.

Partnerships focus attention on the internal connections among the three symbolic systems. The metaphor rests on two assumptions: (a) human representational systems symbolize the world, the self, and one another in multiple, overlapping ways; (b) multiple redundant cues are available in the external world for learning the meaning of words, the structure of sentences, the content of concepts, and methods of reasoning (Scholnick, 1999b; Woodward & Markman, 1998). Consequently, there are numerous inroads into understanding and diverse potentials to link notation, language, and thinking. Because the systems overlap, each system can refine representations generated by the others. Partnerships imply contributions from distinct individuals with distinct strengths and perspectives that can be recruited to solve diverse tasks. Partners can support one another, change one another, and produce products that are qualitatively different from what individuals could create independently.

Because partnerships are social, the metaphor highlights a different sort of connection to the outer world than the computer metaphor. Computers are input devices sensitive to a particular form of input and capable of producing a specified form of output. Partnerships are more fluid and flexible and it is often difficult to discern the separate contribution of inner and outer representations to understanding (Oyama, 1999). External memory aids may help retrieval of events. Cultural forms of representation permeate our thinking and language.

Developmental change may also result from the give-and-take of representational interactions. People in relationships change one another. As connections are established, individual modes of interaction are intertwined. Representational systems change by forging partnerships. Language builds on the representational capacity of the individual and enriches it with a communicative function and connective structure. Thought changes once language enables the cultural transmission of concepts and metacognitive control. Conversely, new knowledge transforms communication. As in human relationships, the interaction of language, concepts, and literacy changes partners as they adapt to one another and work together on tasks. Flavell (1972) called this bidirectional transformation *reciprocal mediation*.

Partnerships can produce and explain qualitative change. A blending of resources produces a novel system with greater representational power and a wider scope than its separate constituents. Symbol systems are synthesized to perform overlapping functions by the process of putting thoughts into words to communicate them to other minds or reciprocally by the process of interpreting others' speech in terms of personal meanings. Individuals eventually approach each task of thinking, conversing, or writing, as theoretician-linguist-authors (Nelson, 1996).

The authors in this volume differ in the extent to which their work fits a partnership metaphor and how they characterize the nature and role of each participant in handling a set of common tasks. They focus on the role of different components of cognition, language, and notation in different task settings. Hence, they differ in the degree to which they connect the three representational systems and the nature of the connections among the systems. They also differ in the dynamics of the connections, particularly whether the interchange is unidirectional or bidirectional. The succeeding sections and Table 1.1 summarize these differences.

TABLE 1.1
Internal and External Partnerships

Chapter	Topic	Mental Relations	Social Relations
Goldin-Meadow	Organizing thought for communication	• Thought without language • Thought contradicting language • Thought expressed in gestures • Gestures aiding thought	• Parents and children using different communicative systems • Verbal instruction enabling thought to be expressed linguistically • Parent provides opportunities for comparisons
Genter & Loewenstein	Forming analogies between knowledge bases	• Language aids analogy • One knowledge base organizes a second, which then reorganizes the first	
Olson	Reading and writing shape language	• Literacy makes language metarepresentational	• Sociocultural tools • Formal instruction
Nelson & Shaw	Development of language and literacy	• Language structures thought • Literacy restructures the entire representational system	• Social relations constitute thought, language, and self • Language and literacy as cultural tools
Budwig	Using language to express internal and interpersonal ideas	• Language and thought influence each other	• Development of self in relation
Daiute	Writing narratives	• Affect, thinking, self-expression are interrelated	• Children form social relationships • Children adopt and subvert cultural forms • Teachers provide cultural tools • Mentation is always socially situated
Lehrer & Schauble	Generating mathematical models to explain evidence	• Mutual influences of mathematical thought, inscriptional tools	• Teachers work in zone of proximal development • Students prompt growth in one another • Cultural tools help communication

COMPUTATIONAL ACCOUNTS

Goldin-Meadow. Two chapters in this book, each describing the influence of language on thought, stem from the computational model. Goldin-
Meadow (chapter 5, this volume) attacks two related claims: (a) language
and thinking necessarily coincide, and (b) linguistic structure shapes
thought (Vygotsky, 1986; Whorf, 1956). She examines an area where
thought and language ought to overlap, thinking that is organized for
speaking, and points to two instances of dissociation: children who are isolated from a linguistic communicative context, and children whose verbal
and cognitive representations are contradictory.

The first case involves deaf children born to hearing parents who do
not use a conventional sign language to communicate with their children.
Nevertheless, the children invent gestural systems that serve the same
functions as language: representation of present and absent events, self-
regulation, and communication of desires. The invented gestural system
also reveals many of the categories that underlie a conventional grammar.
Children distinguish actors from recipients of the action, and actions from
objects or actors, and they encode these linguistically. They assign each
grammatical case to a distinctive word order (not the one used in conventional English) and use inflectional markings.

These data suggest to Goldin-Meadow that children do not need to be
socialized into language. The parents of these deaf children do not use the
same systematized and stable gestural system to communicate with their
offspring. Instead the deaf child, like all children, brings innate conceptual and linguistic categories to bear on the act of communication. The
syntax of gestures arises because "human communication—even when not
guided by a conventional language model—evokes categories of this sort."
Consequently, children isolated from influences of a cultural-historical
tradition embodied in the structure of a particular language can construct
a viable communicative system. One communicative, public representational system substitutes for another. There are multiple ways to communicate, and the deaf child draws on a means that the hearing child does
not need to exploit as fully. Although this case does not appear to be a
partnership, there are some possibilities. Goldin-Meadow describes how
communicative pressure and conceptual structure produce a gestural system but she does not explore how the resulting system might alter the
original representations. Communication is depicted as unilateral, but
the parents are transmitting information to their children that may alter
the content or form of the child's subsequent messages.

The second case involves children in a cognitive transition that is fostered by gestures rather than language. The dissociation of language and
thought is less extreme than for deaf children. Nonconservers, faced with

conservation tasks, can use language to encode and express their understanding. They need not create a new vocabulary, syntax, or communication strategy. But the children juggle two perspectives, nonconservation notions they can verbalize, and new, less systematized conservation ideas expressed in gestures. They cannot use language, which presents ideas successively, to display two simultaneous conflicting perspectives. They cannot even label their nascent concepts. Instead they use gestures to display ideas inaccessible to speech. These children, who express conflicting gestural and linguistic representations, are in a volatile cognitive state that is a precursor to change. They are open to *verbal* instruction.

Three symbol systems—language, gesture, and thought—overlap in their representational function and in content. Goldin-Meadow's analyses do not appear to fit an internal partnership model because language is not necessary for thinking and the structure of specific languages does not determine cognitive growth. Cognition exploits the unique properties of gesture to "creep around" the conventional, culture-specific language children have at their command. The interchange between language and thought seems to be absent. Yet, a close examination suggests more cooperation and interchange than Goldin-Meadow acknowledges. The partnership is achieved by a third representational system, gesture, which can support, supplement, and substitute for language. That system expresses thinking and paves the way for cognitive change.

The nonconserver will soon bring thought and speech into alignment and gesture may create the bridge between the other two representational systems. The children who expressed conservation gesturally were most amenable to verbal instruction. How might gestures facilitate growth? Goldin-Meadow notes that gesture carves the world differently from language and, consequently, draws attention to different aspects of situations. Once gestures make unnoticed relationships salient, the relations can be redescribed in conventional speech. Iconic gestures serve the same function in cognition as language does, supplying an ancillary representational device. Gestures may enable the problem solver to hold two ideas in mind and choose the one not spoken about. Gesture may make ideas more accessible and memorable because they are encoded in two representational systems. Gestures may serve as cognitive props drawing on noncompeting cognitive resources during demanding tasks. As the needed concepts and skills become automatized, they can be recoded linguistically. Finally, because gestures communicate thoughts, observers can respond linguistically and clarify content. Thus gestures serve some of the functions as language and each can influence the other and cognition.

Gentner and Loewenstein.   Like Goldin-Meadow, Gentner and Loewenstein (chapter 4, this volume) examine the relationship between language and thinking from a cognitive science perspective. They come to a different conclusion about the dynamics of the relationship between language and thought and they are interested in a different aspect of development: extracting abstract, flexible, transferable concepts and rules. Hence, they are concerned with connections and relations. In a cognitive science perspective, knowledge acquisition occurs through a process by which the external world is mapped onto internal representations and these, in turn, are mapped onto one another (Lakoff & Johnson, 1999). Gentner asserts that the process of mapping is neither automatic nor static nor unidirectional. Analogical skill and domain knowledge change in the course of application of analogical thinking. Her description of analogical thinking exemplifies a partnership.

One form of partnership is internal to the analogy itself. In an analogy, knowledge about a familiar base domain is mapped onto a target domain in order to make that domain more comprehensible. For example, purposes are likened to journeys. Gentner has developed a computational model of analogies that begins by searching for identical properties in the base and the target domains (e.g., travel and achieving a goal require motion). Eventually, identical relations are sought out (e.g., reaching difficult goals and distant locations requires more time and effort). Reasoners begin with local matches and then try to align more and more properties with more and more relations, hoping to find consistency across domains in features and relations among features. Mappings are based on comparison of two knowledge bases and also inferences that the familiar relations in the base domain also hold for the target. Mapping proceeds by creating broader and deeper alignments. After the initial alignments are found, they are tested. Once the base has structured the target, the two domains work as partners. The original domain is modified because aspects of the target may make neglected features of the base more salient. Putting two things into relation heightens the relation itself. Each domain is an instance of an abstract relation, and thinking becomes more relational. For example, the categories from which we build concepts are based on detected similarities and relations. As individuals notice higher order relations when they search for analogies, those higher order relations become the tools of categorical thought. In this promotional interchange, analogies cast disparate phenomena into a common representational format. These formats then become lenses for forming further analogies and higher order generalizations.

Consequently, one domain structures another and each influences thinking. Additionally, one representational system can aid another. The seeker of analogies has two problems, finding an entry into a new domain and switching from the very obvious perceptual similarities to deep, relational alignments. Language helps in both regards. Analogies arise by comparing a target with a base. When a blueprint and a model plane are in proximity, children have the opportunity to compare the two layouts. Labels put objects in "symbolic juxtaposition" and prompt individuals to notice similarities. Calling roses and daisies "flowers" induces children to search for their similarities. Relational terms, such as "distant" goals, also enable individuals to notice the more subtle connections among properties, and to retain the connections. Using a relational term or a description of the base helps reify the pattern and ready it for further use. Once the representations are redescribed at a more abstract level, the individual can make new mappings. Language becomes the prop and engine for abstract, flexible, transferable thinking. Gentner and Loewenstein note that "symbolic comparison operates *in tandem* with experiential comparison to foster the development of abstract thought." I argue that conceptual development may also influence our terminology, our meaning system, and the way we use language.

SOCIAL INFLUENCES

The partnership metaphor applies both to interactions among representational systems and interchanges between internal and external resources in the development of symbolization. The external resources are provided by interpersonal support and by cultural tools of expression in the form of language and literacy. Goldin-Meadow downplays external input when she argues that mastery of a conventional symbol system is unnecessary for the development of communication and cognition. Gentner and Loewenstein allude briefly to the role of parents in arranging the comparisons that form the foundation for analogical thinking. They also note that different languages may highlight different properties and relations. The other chapters of the book are written within a functionalist and sociocultural perspective and most include analyses of conventional notational systems as well as language and thought.

Olson.   Like Gentner and Goldin-Meadow, Olson assesses the impact of one representational system on another. Goldin-Meadow evaluated influences of language and gesture on thought. Gentner and Loewenstein examined the role of one conceptual system in representing and structuring another, and language as a connective tissue and pointer during mapping. Internal connections among language and thought are high on Olson's agenda, too, as is the mapping process. Like Gentner and Goldin-Meadow, he is not concerned with interpersonal influences on the growth of representation. But, unlike the two cognitive scientists, he discusses the acquisition of literacy. Consequently, he draws markedly different conclusions about the influence of conventional communicative systems. Like Goldin-Meadow and Gentner, he acknowledges that writing, relational language, and gesture facilitate the storing of ideas and serve as computational props, but he argues that writing has an additional role. The ideas and strategies coded in notational systems are the product of a long cultural evolution. Acquiring a notational system enables the child to take advantage of this evolution to make rapid cognitive advances.

Olson goes further by claiming that the invention of notational systems opened up new possibilities for language and thought. Gentner charts how a familiar structure first organizes a new domain and then, how that newly discovered organization may refine or recast the old structure, making it more generalizable. Olson accords even more power to the new representational system because it embodies an already established and elaborated structure. The acquisition of an alphabetic script requires the child to segment speech into its phonemic and lexical constituents and to become aware of abstract rules of word and letter combination. The child does not simply map written words onto speech or letters onto phonemes. The child must first use the mold of writing to carve out words and sentences from speech and to understand the concept of a word. Writing, in which one symbol system represents an earlier symbol system, changes the old system by creating new categories, and creates awareness of both the representational device and the original representational system. Thus writing is metarepresentational. The child uses writing to structure language, thinking, and the world. Writing enables dissection and analysis of concepts and thought. Literacy produces the abstract, universal, modular child—the little linguist and theoretician—proposed by cognitive scientists. "Written words, decontextualized, serve as the objects of philosophical reflection . . . and the centerpiece of the Western intellectual tradition" (Olson, chapter 6, this volume).

An external system, embodying social, historical, and cultural advances, casts earlier language and thought into a new mold. But Olson also acknowledges that speech is not an invention of a writing system, nor is the child's mind putty to be shaped through literacy. Writing must mesh with the structure of speech and the child's conceptual system. The child actively and gradually constructs understanding of the units of language, the rules of language, and the nature of representation. The struggle to bring these systems into alignment calls attention to both their unique properties and their common representational function. This growing metalinguistic and metaconceptual awareness prompts and transforms the thinking-speaking-writing system the child employs. Olson's analysis incorporates one aspect of a partnership. The mastery of each representational system reorganizes the other systems and produces a combination in which roles are intertwined. In their interactions, Olson gives a paramount role to writing in contributing to our linguistic and intellectual history. In actuality, new ideas continue to push our notational systems. The new millennium is more likely to be characterized as a digital than an alphabetic era. Olson's chapter describes "What Writing Does to the Mind" but the mind is still inventing new words, new notations, and new functions for both. Potentially, there are partnerships.

Nelson and Kessler Shaw. Whereas Olson focuses on the role of literacy mainly as a vehicle for cultural transmission, the remaining chapters also include the influence of social interactions with adults and peers on the acquisition of diverse representational systems. Nelson (1996, 1999; Nelson, Hensdale, & Plesa, 2000) has staunchly criticized explanations based on the divided, abstract, static child who unearths implicit linguistic structures and conceptual frameworks and then faces a totally different task of acquiring conventional notational systems. From the outset she characterizes language acquisition as "entry into a socially shared symbolic system, which serves as a means of communication within a community." Drawing on Wittgenstein's (1953) insight that learning a language is entering a form of life, Nelson and Kessler Shaw (chapter 2, this volume) chart the acquisition of an experiential semantics that enables children to develop a social and an inner life.

Nelson and Kessler Shaw describe conversational partnerships in which the infant's interlocutors provide a structured world for the baby to represent and the child is tuned to notice the repetitive patterns that unfold in functionally relevant routines. The developmental sequence—from social interchanges to shared attention to socially shared symbolic dialogues to systematic knowledge encoded through notational systems—begins with a public self that is progressively interwoven with the private representational self that emerges. Consequently the growing cognitive and linguistic systems are embodied, situated, and interrelated.

What is the nature of the partnership? In this chapter (but see Nelson, 1996, 1999), Nelson and Kessler Shaw analyze word meaning, and with it, the dual problems of finding a means to represent internally the external world, while also finding a medium to express these internal representations to an external audience. Because Nelson and Kessler Shaw emphasize social interactions, the content they account for, from which other structures and systems will be derived, is social, goal-oriented events. The words that interest them are not labels for objects, but for actions, places, and subjective states.

The authors describe how thought and language become intertwined to create a new, more powerful representational system. But in the social relationship of child and society and the semantic relationship of inner concept and outer expression, there are privileged partners—language and society. The child possesses some innate conceptual proclivities to understand social events and to abstract regularities within these events. These event structures, of great interest to the child who participates in them, are also the basis for linguistic structure. Once language is acquired, it supplies the impetus and tools to systematize and refine concepts. Communicative language constitutes thought. Even the capacity to think about personal mental processes, and perhaps hone those mental processes through the process of self-examination, draws heavily on social and linguistic resources. Thus Nelson and Kessler Shaw begin where language and thought intersect, in communicating about event regularities and intriguing transient events. Language, acquired from social interactions, provides the symbols and frames common to each process and the means of discerning the elements and structures unique to each system as well.

Budwig. The remaining chapters describe more reciprocity between representational systems. Like Nelson and Kessler Shaw, Budwig's (chapter 3, this volume) analysis of language acquisition assumes an embodied, socially situated child. She proposes a functionalist view of language and thought in which language serves simultaneously as a means for inculcating the child into a culture and for expressing ideas. Children learn language by noting the situations in which particular linguistic forms are used and then adapting those forms to new meanings children construct. Thus two interchanges underlie Budwig's analysis, an internal connection between form and function, and an external interchange between the children and their conversational partners.

Many researchers study the child's lexicon as a window into the child's representation of the external world. However, Budwig's interest in the embodied child leads her to examine children's understanding of internal states, like desire, and personal constructs, like agency. She notes that different functional situations are associated with specific syntactic forms, like the deployment of pronouns or passives. "I broke the mirror" expresses more agency than "The mirror broke." Children simultaneously learn new aspects of the self and a language of self-expression. New functions arise as the child learns more about the self as the source of agency. They also acquire new syntactic forms to encode agency. Budwig tracks how children use already mastered syntactic constructions to express new meanings before they acquire the conventionally appropriate means of expression. New meanings first inhabit old forms. As these forms are deployed for several purposes, the child's need for differentiation leads to the adoption of new forms. These new forms, first used to express old meanings, can draw attention to and become vehicles for expressing new ideas. There is a constant interchange between new ideas, which push for expression through the appropriate syntax, and forms of speaking that need new interpretations. Note the parallels to Gentner's analysis and also Werner's (Werner & Kaplan, 1963).

Budwig emphasizes the influence of conceptual growth in this interchange, and she describes language as simply a window to thought. Cognition appears to be the privileged partner. However, Budwig notes that words are the tools through which the social and cultural worlds are described, evaluated, and reproduced. Thus language can influence concepts. Words are the means by which speakers convey their belief systems. They are part of a triangle including syntax and communication. For each side of the triangle, new inputs on one side first link to old outputs and then produce new, differentiated outputs that are integrated into a more refined system. Language, thought, and communication co-articulate one another.

Meanings and syntax operate within a social situation, so partnerships are the context and cause of development. Children initially express desires that other people are asked to satisfy. Soon children realize that they can satisfy their own needs, but they act within situations that adults control. Consequently, children must negotiate permission for their actions. Simultaneously, parents, knowing that harmonious partnerships involve mutual consent for actions, subtly use the language of desire to control the situation. Adults ask the children if they want to do what parents want them to do. Children learn the language of agency and control from conversational partners as children become capable of entering into relationships. Communication is the process by which new functions inhabit old forms, and new forms become the vehicle for more precisely expressing and understanding old functions. In trying to clarify communicative intent and to express their own desires, parents foster development.

Daiute. Like Budwig, Daiute (chapter 8, this volume) analyzes the interpersonal interactions that produce transformations in the knowledge base and in the self, but Daiute examines older children learning to write. Daiute explores how peer interactions change children's mastery of the narrative form, their understanding of themselves as writers and collaborators, and their personal relationships. She is less interested in how language, writing, and thinking interact within the child, and more concerned about how social interchanges foster literacy. Moreover, she observes children's acquisition of narrative, a form of literacy embodying a cultural tradition of conveying interpersonal events.

I have suggested that forging a partnership is an apt metaphor for development. Daiute examines the mechanics of the source of the metaphor. In a partnership, contributors may provide inspiration to each other to produce something new that may stimulate further growth. Partners also edit each other and stimulate awareness of strategies and quirks in communication. Interchanges also draw attention to two audiences, the conversational partner with whom one exchanges ideas, and the reader for whom one narrates. Writing embedded in social interactions is infused with affect that may increase engagement in the task. Enjoyable social interactions may stimulate the playful imagination that contains the seeds of growth. Thus Daiute claims that interpersonal affective interaction shapes cognition by investing ideas with meaning.

Daiute's analysis is influenced by feminist theories (Rosser & Miller, 2000). She rejects the idea that children are simply apprentices who learn to reproduce cultural forms of narratives by absorbing adult instruction. The apprentice–novice relationship is too hierarchical. Children question and resist wholesale adoption of cultural scripts and tools because they want to put their own stamp on them. Daiute's descriptions come closer to partnerships than apprenticeships because she observes children going beyond current ways of thinking, speaking, and writing, to provide new and different models that can transform the culture.

The young writers she describes are the antithesis of isolated scientists. This is not surprising because she situates them in a dyad and she gives them a task, writing stories, that draws on their own cultural backgrounds and personal affective experiences. Although the setting is academic, the children use writing to express and gain knowledge of their own and others' subjectivity. In writing, they simultaneously refine a cultural form and their interpersonal understanding. Often, interpersonal connections prompt the development of representations. Daiute's analysis, therefore, does not lend itself to separating language, thought, and literacy, because they are intertwined with each other, with affect, and with the task. Daiute describes her strategy as using relational discourse to illustrate how "knowing, thinking, and learning are inextricably linked to the practices and affects of communication and imagination."

Lehrer and Schauble. Daiute and Olson describe mastery of writing. Lehrer and Schauble (chapter 7, this volume) examine the acquisition of mathematical inscriptions. Modern science employs symbolic devices, such as diagrams and graphs, to depict abstract, hypothetical, mathematical concepts. The concepts and inscriptional devices are closely linked. For example, mathematical understanding requires learning concepts like distributions that are conveyed by frequency plots. How frequencies are plotted may determine how the distribution is described. Lehrer and Schauble agree with Olson that conceptual analysis and abstraction are facilitated by exposure to a conventional inscriptional system. However, Lehrer and Schauble also include bidirectional interchanges between concepts, reasoning, and representations.

Children's inscriptions and conceptions push advances in a spiraling cycle. Conceptual change permits more sophisticated use of mathematical notations. When children define growth in terms of rate of change over time, they are ready for a notational device to chart the changes. The new notation may make these and new, unexpected dimensions salient and permit comparison of data points. Externalizing this knowledge provides the opportunity to detect the patterns and parameters of the data. The child may begin to note differences in growth curves, a new concept for the child. Refinements in representational skill enable new concepts to be depicted, which may then lead to new mathematical ideas and new inscriptional tools. Like Olson, Lehrer and Schauble claim that learning a notational system also produces awareness of the nature of the learned system. Additionally, use of inscriptional representations in diverse contexts promotes awareness of situations where the inscriptional tool is applicable.

The title of the chapter, "Co-constituting Inscription and Thought," describes an internal partnership producing representational change. The chapter also shows how external social networks foster change. Gaining abstract symbolic competence is a protracted process embedded in a social context that provides the symbols and the problems to which the symbols may be applied. Teachers help students learn these representational systems and their appropriate applications. Skilled teachers intervene to hand children tools when the children are ready. They provoke children to reevaluate familiar concepts and tools and to search for new tools and concepts. In turn, children's pointed critiques and questions of teachers and peers prompt deeper and richer understanding. Both students and teachers grow in the interchange. As children learn to model the world mathematically, their teachers are learning about learning and teaching.

REVISITING THE PARTNERSHIP

This chapter introduces a partnership metaphor. The volume fleshes it out. Conceptual, linguistic, and notational systems can represent the self, the world, and each other. They do not appear simultaneously. Each system represents and interprets the world in a unique format and each may serve unique functions. But there are significant inherent redundancies among the systems because the systems often encode the same content and represent one another. Every chapter discusses the relation among these multiple representational systems. Those relations range from domination to team work to co-construction. Olson and Nelson and Shaw depict the ways one system shapes another in its own image. Olson describes how literacy creates the categories by which language is analyzed. Nelson notes how language shapes thought. Other authors focus on interactions entailing support or substitution. Gesture can serve as a communicative vehicle when language is not up to the task. Gestures act as mnemonic props for problem solving. Relational terms and labels reveal similarities and make analogies more memorable. Verbal descriptions of graphs can facilitate thinking with them.

Bootstrapping is another way one representational system changes another one. A familiar system affords an entry into another. Analogies make the unfamiliar familiar. Budwig proves an illustration. New ideas are expressed in an old linguistic vehicle, and become more amenable to public and private analysis. Other speakers then supply a new, more appropriate linguistic vehicle or children can make differentiations on their own. Sometimes, bootstrapping produces unidirectional change (Carey, 1999). The initial system leads into the new one, which can eventually be understood on its own terms and the bootstrap is discarded. But Gentner and Loewenstein and Lerher and Schauble describe transformational partnerships in which both the system that is entered and the tool that served as entry point are restructured. Moreover, linking two representational systems produces metarepresentational awareness of the properties and powers of each system. Perhaps individuals also become co-representational, and develop into thinker-speaker-transcribers.

Like descriptions of internal relations, analyses of external social and societal influences on inner processes run the gamut. Goldin-Meadow minimizes external influences and argues that children can develop modes of thinking and communicating outside of a conventional symbol system. Gentner also accords little influence to the culture or the social situation except that language can provide pointers to relations or base domains for analogies. Different languages provide different pointers. Tutors may also create the opportunities to make the comparisons that yield analogies.

Other chapters contain examples of dominance relations in the form of social constructionism (Gergen, 1993). Olson describes how cultural tools interpret the world and provide the repository for knowledge in a form the child appropriates. Nelson notes that social interchanges help the child build a theory of mind. Children develop by communicating with conversational partners about the child's situation and internal state and by being exposed to diverse cultural practices. However, both Olson and Nelson acknowledge that the child is not a passive partner in the interchange. The child must be able to assimilate cultural input.

Budwig, Dauite, and Lehrer and Schauble allow the child more creativity. Budwig describes growing interpersonal relations in which the child is developing ideas of agency and control while the adult is trying to cope with managing a relationship in which the child is gaining agency and control. Dauite depicts situations where children work out their relationship with one another and with the cultural narrative form. Children play with and subvert these forms to produce innovations. Lehrer and Schauble describe teaching and learning in collaborative groups. Teachers insert questions and information at critical junctures, when children are ready to learn more. Children also question one another about the problem and the representational format, leading to conceptual, linguistic, and notational change.

How do these analyses contrast with and change our notions of the abstract, static, modular child? They suggest that there are interacting systems of representation that may be harnessed to solve the same task, and that may coalesce to enable generalization, abstraction, and metarepresentation. The capacity for abstraction may grow out of the systems that are socially derived and societally situated. The adoption of cultural tools and engagement in social practices to fulfil social and private ends foster representational competence. Representation processes are dynamic. The content and nature of each representational device changes as each system opposes and supports, and collaborates with one another in mutually transformative partnerships.

REFERENCES

Bloom, L. B. (1998). Language acquisition in its developmental context. In D. Kuhn & R. S. Siegler (Vol. Eds.), *Handbook of child psychology: Vol. 2. Cognition, perception and language* (pp. 309–370). New York: Wiley.

Carey, S. (1999). Sources of conceptual change. In E. K. Scholnick, K. Nelson, S. A. Gelman, & P. H. Miller (Eds.), *Conceptual development: Piaget's legacy* (pp. 293–326). Mahwah, NJ: Lawrence Erlbaum Associates.

Chomsky, N. (1988). *Language and problems of knowledge.* Cambridge, MA: MIT Press.

Flavell, J. H. (1972). An analysis of cognitive developmental sequences. *Genetic Psychology Monographs, 86,* 279–350.

Fodor, J. A. (1983). *Modularity of mind.* Cambridge, MA: MIT Press.

Foucault, M. (1972). *The archeology of knowledge.* New York: Pantheon.

Gardner, H. (1985). *The mind's new science: A history of the cognitive revolution.* New York: Basic Books.

Gelman, S. A., & Byrnes, J. P. (Eds.). (1991). *Perspectives on language and thought: Interrelations in development.* New York: Cambridge University Press.

Gentner, D., & Markman, A. B. (1997). Structure mapping in analogy and similarity. *American Psychologist, 52,* 45–56.

Gergen, K. (1993). *Realties and relationships: Soundings in social construction.* Cambridge, MA: Harvard University Press.

Gopnik, A., & Meltzoff, A. (1996). *Words, thought, and theories.* Cambridge, MA: MIT Press.

Harding, S. (1998). *Is science multicultural? Postcolonialisms. feminisms, and epistemologies.* Bloomington: Indiana University Press.

Karmiloff-Smith, A. (1992). *Beyond modularity: A developmental perspective on cognitive science.* Cambridge, MA: MIT Press.

Kuhn, D., Amsel, E., & O'Loughlin, M. (1988). *The development of scientific thinking skills.* San Diego, CA: Academic Press.

Lakoff, G., & Johnson, M. (1980). *Metaphors we live by.* Chicago: University of Chicago Press.

Lakoff, G., & Johnson, M. (1999). *Philosophy in the flesh: The embodied mind and its challenge to Western thought.* New York: Basic Books.

Maratsos, M. (1998). The acquisition of grammar. In D. Kuhn & R. S. Siegler (Vol. Eds.), *Handbook of child psychology: Vol. 2. Cognition, perception and language* (pp. 421–466). New York: Wiley.

Nelson, K. (1996). *Language in cognitive development: The emergence of the mediated mind.* New York: Cambridge University Press.

Nelson, K. (1999). Levels and modes of representation: Issues for the theory of conceptual change and development. In E. K. Scholnick, K. Nelson, S. A. Gelman, & P. H. Miller (Eds.), *Conceptual development: Piaget's legacy* (pp. 269–291). Mahwah, NJ: Lawrence Erlbaum Associates.

Nelson, K., Hensdale, S., & Plesa, D. (2000). Entering a community of minds: "Theory of mind" from a feminist perspective. In P. H. Miller & E. K. Scholnick (Eds.), *Toward a feminist developmental psychology* (pp. 29–41). New York: Routledge.

Olson, D. (1994). *The world on paper.* New York: Cambridge University Press.

Overton, W. F. (1998). Developmental psychology. Philosophy, concepts, and methodology. In R. M. Lerner (Vol. Ed.), *Handbook of child psychology. Vol. 1. Theoretical models of human development* (pp. 107–188). New York: Wiley.

Overton, W. F. (1999a, April). *Child-centered inquiry: The embodied child as agent of action.* Paper presented at the biennial meeting of the Society for Research in Child Development, Albuquerque, NM.

Overton, W. F. (1999b, June). *Understanding, explanation, and reductionism: Finding a cure for Cartesian anxiety.* Paper presented at the Symposium of the Jean Piaget Society, Mexico City.

Oyama, S. (1999). Locating development: Locating developmental systems. In E. K. Scholnick, K. Nelson, S. A. Gelman, & P. H. Miller (Eds.), *Conceptual development: Piaget's legacy* (pp. 185–208). Mahwah, NJ: Lawrence Erlbaum Associates.

Pinker, S. (1994). *The language instinct: How the mind creates language.* New York: Morrow.

Pinker, S. (1997). *How the mind works.* New York: Norton.

Pinker, S. (1999). *Words and rules: The ingredients of language.* New York: Basic Books.

Rosser, S. V., & Miller, P. H. (2000). Feminist theories and implications for developmental psychology. In P. H. Miller & E. K. Scholnick (Eds.), *Toward a feminist developmental psychology* (pp. 11–28). New York: Routledge.

Scholnick, E. K. (1999a, October). *Knowledge is power.* Paper presented at the Cognitive Development Society meeting, Chapel Hill, NC.

Scholnick, E. K. (1999b). Representing logic. In I. E. Sigel (Ed.), *Development of mental representation: Theories and applications* (pp. 113–128). Mahwah, NJ: Lawrence Erlbaum Associates.

Scholnick, E. K. (2000). Engendering development: Metaphors of change. In P. H. Miller & E. K. Scholnick (Eds.), *Toward a feminist developmental psychology* (pp. 61–83). New York: Routledge.

Spelke, E. S., & Newport, E. L. (1998). Nativism, empiricism, and the development of knowledge. In R. M. Lerner (Vol. Ed.), *Handbook of child psychology: Vol. 1. Theoretical models of human development* (pp. 275–340). New York: Wiley.

Tomasello, M. (1999). *The cultural origins of human cognition.* Cambridge, MA: Harvard University Press.

Vygotsky, L. S. (1986). *Thought and language.* Cambridge, MA: MIT Press.

Werner, H., & Kaplan, B. (1963). *Symbol formation.* Hillsdale, NJ: Lawrence Erlbaum Associates.

Whorf, B. L. (1956). *Language, thought, and reality: Selected writings of Benjamin Lee Whorf.* Cambridge, MA: MIT Press.

Wittgenstein, L. (1953). *Philosophical investigations.* New York: Macmillan.

Woodward, A. L., & Markman, E. M. (1998). Early word learning. In D. Kuhn & R. S. Siegler (Vol. Eds.), *Handbook of child psychology: Vol. 2. Cognition, perception and language* (pp. 371–420). New York: Wiley.

Part II

VERBAL AND GESTURAL COMMUNICATION AND COGNITIVE DEVELOPMENT

Chapter 2

Developing a Socially Shared Symbolic System

Katherine Nelson
Lea Kessler Shaw
City University of New York Graduate Center

The title of this chapter implies a developmental process, the endpoint of which is entry into a *socially shared symbolic system*, which serves as a means of communication within a community. The basic assumption here is that language is constituted of socially shared symbols and exists within socially shared symbolic systems, the use of which may take the individual simultaneously beyond the present into past and future, and beyond the self into a socially shared reality. The system can only operate effectively in communication if it is not only social, used within social environments, but shared; that is, its symbols mean the same thing (more or less) to all users in the same context, and both when speaking and listening (or reading and writing).

The chapter is about word meaning at different levels, more specifically about the acquisition of shared meaning (Nelson, 1985). The question to be addressed here is "How does the child acquire this kind of shared meaning?" The thesis is that the child moves increasingly within concentric circles that lead her to enter the system of meanings shared by the community. Wittgenstein's (1953) aphorism that "to learn a language is to enter a form of life" aptly describes the child's adventure in learning, first, words, and later, modes of discourse. The system of shared meanings and the child's process of acquisition are jointly referred to here as *experiential semantics.*

The concentric circles shown in Fig. 2.1 are designed to suggest that the child is embedded from the outset within a social world that becomes increasingly articulated, definite, symbolic, and systematized. In this view language itself is one of many cultural systems, but one that offers enor-

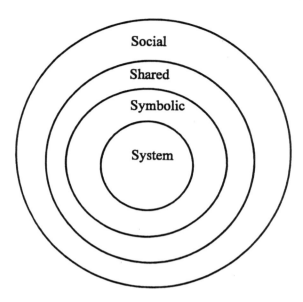

FIG. 2.1. Embedded layers of the SSSS: the Socially Shared Symbolic System.

mous power to the individual who enters into it. Language symbols are asserted to be essentially social, a claim at odds with many conceptions of symbols (e.g., Freud's, Piaget's, or Fodor's), but one that is defended here. They are essentially social because they emerge from within a social matrix where the meanings incorporated in them are shared between individuals (Werner & Kaplan, 1963). Symbols may be formed and used by individuals for personal purposes, but this use is derivative of their social origins, as Vygotsky (1986) believed. These points are basic to the argument presented here.

Our orientation to these problems shares with other developmentalists (Bloom, 1993; Bruner, 1983; Snow, 1986; Tomasello & Kruger, 1992) an emphasis on the importance of the child in the study of language development. This perspective contrasts with the dominant trend in linguistics and related fields—including some in developmental psychology—to declare that language is acquired through special mechanisms that have little or nothing to do with the rest of the child's life, social or cognitive. The child-oriented view instead takes account of social and cognitive development, as well as the interests of the child in communicating within specific social environments. This developmental approach, however broadly accepted for other problem domains, has been widely disparaged by many theorists of language acquisition. Yet it is critical to understanding problems of meaning, which is essentially what is at stake in acquiring language.

The speech-language system *in use* in the child's environment is what must be acquired by an individual child. Thus the question to be addressed is this: How does the child's prior experience in the social-communicative world, together with his or her experiential history, which yields knowledge structures relevant to the language problem, in collaboration with expert language users attuned to the child's interests and needs, enable the development *over time* of the interpretation and production of meaningful speech? This statement of the problem is that of the *acquisition of shared meaning*, termed *experiential semantics*, which puts the emphasis on both learning and conventions for expressing meaning. The conventions constitute the *system*, as used here, which includes all the uses of language, cognitive and communicative. This approach to the matter derives from Wittgenstein's (1953) understanding of language in terms of criteria of use, although the idea of *system* here is closer to Saussure's (1915/1959) idea of *langue* (as opposed to *parole*). The proposal then is that the existing conventions or criteria within a community of speakers constitute a *system of use*. It is an evolved social system that emerges historically from use within successive generations of communities and is reconstituted within each generation ontogenetically by the same process. Such a system includes but is not exclusive to grammar; semantic structures, phonology, and pragmatics are all systematically interrelated. The strong implication is that grammar serves human linguistic needs for exchanging meaning rather than the reverse claim implied in the Universal Grammar tradition (Chomsky, 1965, 1988; Pinker, 1994) that human linguistic expressions are constrained by an independently motivated grammar.

This chapter proceeds as follows: First the terms in the title are discussed, with special attention to the problems of symbols in language learning—where word meanings fit, how they relate to nonverbal experience, and how they change over development. We then discuss a proposal for understanding the process of a child's acquisition of the meaning of words, and then turn to the fourth term—system—and try to make clear why that is a special problem with important cognitive as well as linguistic implications and potentials. We illustrate this section with some new data on mental state terms that speak to all aspects of the SSSS development.

TOWARD A THEORY OF THE DEVELOPMENT
OF EXPERIENTIAL SEMANTICS

Word learning begins in the early months of the second year (and to some extent for some children the latter months of the first year), but extends to the problems of building vocabulary during the school years and indeed throughout life. These problems, widely separated in time, are not, however, broadly different. Although the developmental status of the child changes radically over this period, the problem of the acquisition of word meaning remains similar. How the problem is addressed and solved, and what resources and strategies are brought to bear on it, are what varies psychologically as the child gains greater experience with the language. Meaning acquisition is set up and proceeds in phases that overlap with biologically organized pre-speech and speech acquisition processes. These can be roughly outlined in terms of the four components signified as SSSS. The first two terms are well specified in contemporary developmental theory as basic to language acquisition, and therefore, important as they are, they will be very briefly considered here.

Social

The most basic aspect of the SSSS is that the child is born into and grows within an *interpreted* social world, where the things and events of the world as well as its people are arranged by and are interpreted by adults in speech to children beginning virtually at birth. For example, what and when the child eats, when and where the child sleeps are as subject to social-cultural norms as are the songs and stories that are told, read, and sung. Infants preferentially attend to social stimuli, and those who are deprived of social companionship and comfort suffer both cognitively and emotionally. As Snow (1986), Stern (1985), Trevarthen (1980), and others have demonstrated repeatedly, parents (in our society) tend to treat their children as social partners and conversationalists almost from birth, and children respond with attentive looks, gurgles, smiles, in rhythmic interaction with parental child-directed talk. This practice is presumably as important to the child's entering into meaningful communicative exchanges as is the pre-speech pattern extraction that has been demonstrated recently (Morgan & Demuth, 1996). However, it must be noted that in cultures where mothers do not engage in these practices children may need to extract patterns of conversation from those of adults and children talking together in groups (Heath, 1983; Ochs & Schieffelin, 1984). It is important from the perspective of a social orientation to language development, and from the perspective of experiential semantics, that our theories are universal in the sense that they may apply to varying cultural and social conditions. Thus we recognize that all children live in and experience social environments where talking is part of the milieu, without insisting that the particulars of any social world must be constrained to meet theoretical a priori specifications based on our own social practices.

Shared

By the last half of the first year the child begins to take part in a new interaction pattern, sharing attention to objects with another by following the other's gaze or point, responding to the other's emotional reaction to an event, and imitating another's object-directed actions. This level of *secondary intersubjectivity* (Sugarman, 1983; Trevarthen, 1980; anticipated by Werner & Kaplan, 1963; see also Tomasello, 1995) sets the stage for the pairing of speech and object that begins to bring the child into the sharing of words and things at the end of the first year and the beginning of the second. The first speech forms that the child recognizes and responds to, and that she attempts to produce, are usually simple associates of objects or situations. These "words" may be used in a way similar to a point, for sharing *reference* to objects or events (such as "bath"), or to an aspect of a situation (as in the use of "bye-bye" in the context of departure). There is an important distinction between the use of words in specific contexts or for specific objects, and their shared use (both receptive and expressive) for any object of that kind in varied situational contexts. The first use may be communicative in the same sense that a point is (indicative of shared attention), but such use of a word or gesture rather than a point does not yet constitute a symbol.

By the end of the first year many children are quite attuned to the use of specific forms—words or phrases—in specific contexts for specific uses. Such attunement has been observed both informally and systematically in prior research (Benedict, 1979). More recent research (Woodward, Markman, & Fitzsimmons, 1994; Schafer & Plunkett, 1998) has demonstrated that infants of about 12 to 18 months can form specific word–image associations after a few trials in a laboratory, as measured by increased looking to the specific picture paired with the specific speech form. These studies have systematically demonstrated processes of attention to and analysis of speech and its patterns and correlations with the visual array in the latter part of the first year and the first part of the second. However, the leap from this point into meaningful language requires on the part of the child the integration of these pre-speech skills with pre-speech communicative patterns and conceptual knowledge.

There is a pervasive temptation to take precursor behaviors—such as the assocation of words with objects—as representing underlying competence relevant to more complex achievements, but this obscures the long slow process of development that is necessary for the full flowering of a system of knowledge or skill. Fischer and Bidell (1991) warned about the pitfalls of this kind of leap in a well-articulated chapter presented first at a previous Piaget Society Symposium. The task for developmental psychologists is to track the emergence of the system over time, in this case the symbolic system, and to understand the processes by which it is constructed. Precursors should be recognized as such and not taken as indicators of some hitherto unrecognized competence. Decades of research in and out of laboratories, homes, and playrooms have documented that integration of pre-speech skills, speech patterns, and conceptual knowledge follows diverse developmental pathways into a fully realized symbolic system that is not achieved until the late preschool years.

Symbolic

Symbols are established in use between speakers to express an intended *meaning*. When do children begin to use words as symbols? Given that human languages consist of symbols, are all uses of words symbolic? Indeed, are all words (e.g., *bye-bye* or *pattacake*) symbols at all? Empirical studies have consistently found that there are two fairly well-defined phases of language acquisition typically observed during the second year of life: *first words* and *vocabulary spurt* (Bloom, 1973, 1993; McCarthy, 1954; Nelson, 1973). First word productions are typically observed around the age of 1 year but may occur 2 or 3 months earlier or later. It is usual for children to acquire productive vocabulary slowly over the next 6 months, reaching a total of about 50 words at an average of 19 months. At this time, but not much before, we can say that the child is acquiring symbols. (This point is discussed more fully later.) Thereafter, words accumulate more rapidly (the vocabulary spurt). There are, however, wide variations among children in the appearance of these phases and their timing.

The phase shift from slow accumulation to accelerated vocabulary growth has been the subject of much theoretical speculation, some of it concerned with the possibility of a shift in the function of words from sign to symbol, or (as claimed in Nelson, 1991), to the understanding of "what words do." These matters remain unresolved. Bates and Carnevale (1993) argued that no explanation beyond the mathematical function for rate of acquisition is needed. Yet regardless of the fact that no new contribution to the mathematical function is necessary, the newly rapid accumulation may still have psychological significance, in particular it may indicate a new understanding of meaning potential.

Nelson and Lucariello (1985) proposed that children began with simple associations between words and the situations in which they were used, and termed this phase "*referential*," indicating that children could refer to things with words in their situated here and now context. We claimed a developmental milestone was achieved when they understood that words were used symbolically to stand for concepts, calling this "denotation," based on the distinction Lyons (1977) made between *reference, denotation, and sense.*[1] Sense is a further achievement, however, beginning when

---

[1]Lyons' (1977) use of these terms departed from their use in linguistic philosophy, following Frege (1892/1980) where "sense" meant roughly the *intention*—concept or definition—of the term in contrast to "reference," which meant the thing or things referred to. This distinction was useful in cases where two words might have the same referent but have different

words are recognized as having relations to other words, as in a system of meaning, and I return to it later. The issue first is, when does an associated element become a symbol?

When words are used to represent a state of the world that is not present in the immediate environment, and when they are used with the intention of communicating that representation to another, we may conclude that the word is being used symbolically. Although this test is useful, it is not always easy to apply in practice. The essential point is that words are not necessarily symbols simply by virtue of being words in a natural human language. Words may be used as other kinds of signs. In the semiotic tradition that Peirce (1897/1955) initiated in the last century, symbols are the most abstract of the signs that make up the semiotic repertoire; less abstract signs are icons, such as pictures, which bear a relation of similarity to the signified, and indexes, which are associated in some way with the signified, as smoke is an index of fire. In the case of the child's words, object names may be used first simply as indexes—as associates of the thing named by virtue of their having been experienced together. In this sense they may be used *referentially* to point to a thing in a shared context but not to *stand for* that thing in discourse. This issue underlies the interpretation of both early words in infant vocabularies, and the use of signs by "language-using" primates in natural and human environments.

A symbol is generally understood as a semiotic form that *stands for* or *represents* something. According to Werner and Kaplan (1963) symbols bear knowledge and are thus essentially cognitive. They insisted that symbols were differentiated from mere signs by virtue of representing, not merely eliciting or anticipating action. Ogden and Richards (1923/1946) illustrated the psychological point to this analysis in the semiotic triangle, where the relation between the symbol (word) and object signified is indirect, related through the mental concept (the denotation in Lyons' terminology) of the thing signified. As Fig. 2.2 shows, the bond between word and object is problematic and arbitrary—it is only completed through the mental conception corresponding to the object.

The more important point to be made here is that symbols are inherently social and communicative, not individual. Thus the semiotic triangle

senses, or vice versa. In making a distinction between denotation and sense, Lyons was attempting to cover the linguistic problem that a word can be said to have a meaning in its own right (its denotation, or the concept for which it stands), but that words also are embedded in systems of other words, both in sentences and in semantic fields or domains, and that the relations between words in these structures may determine their meaning, or sense. For example the word *dog* is a common count noun, which relates it to others of that class, determining its possible placement in sentences. It is also an animate noun with certain implications, and it is a hyponymn of *animal* and of *mammal*, which implies many characteristics that would not necessarily be included in the simple concept or definition for *dog*, such as manner of birth. See Nelson (1985) for further discussion.

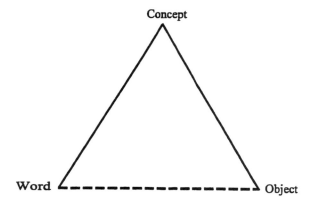

FIG. 2.2.   The basic semiotic triangle (based on Ogden & Richards, 1923).

proposed by Ogden and Richards (1923/1946) (and replicated in Lyons, 1977) is incomplete. It must be connected to another triangular structure, representing the word–concept relation of another speaker (see Fig. 2.3). This conception from the social foundations of language fits very well the Werner and Kaplan view that symbols are established initially by an intentional act between the mother and the child, an act that extends the initial

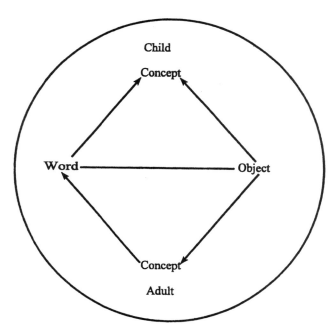

FIG. 2.3.   The extended semiotic triangle showing relation between word and concepts of child and adult within a shared meaning system.

relationship of *sharing* attention. Through naming, the child's concept of the object, for example *dog*, can be set into correspondence with the adult's concept of the dog, providing the basis for referring to the concept in the absence of real dogs. It is important to note that the two concepts may differ, although the words are shared.

From this view the super-triangular relation of word-object-concept1-concept2 provides the motivation for symbolic reference in the first place. As the basic semiotic triangle reveals, there is no necessity for a symbol of the object for the individual alone. The concept points to the object without additional mediation, as Millikan (1998) has recently argued. Symbolic mediation is required, however, to connect one's concepts to others in the social world, not to objects or other nonsocial entities.

This is a claim about what words do: They serve to connect a part of the world as understood by one person to that of another. This is not a proposal that children (or people in general) necessarily strive to make these connections, or to reduce mental discrepancies, although they might do so as they enter into the language games of the community. Rather it is proposed that words function in a particular way, similarly to the Ogden and Richards original claim, but with the added understanding that words communicate between conceptual systems.

At this point we can note what this symbolic level of word learning means for the child who enters into it. As symbols, words relate to the child's pre-verbal experientially based conceptualizations in a new way. Words at this level provide the basis for a new level of *shared* reality; of a *continuing* reality; and of a *context-general* reality. For example, the very use of the word *dog* for new instances of encountered dogs (and not for instances of cows, among other things) means that child and adult agree on this categorization: It is no longer only the child's own conceptualization of this aspect of the world. Moreover, this agreement on the categorization of things continues over time and in many different contexts: Dogs remain dogs wherever and whenever encountered, and naming them confirms that reality. This basis in language has continuing importance as more abstract aspects of the social, personal, mental, and cultural world come to be named and thus shared.

These considerations also imply that the child's pre-linguistic concepts have a different quality from those that serve as symbolic significants, that is, that enter into shared symbolic processes through naming. The latter concepts become cognitively more discrete and stable by virtue of their shared communicative quality. This is true, whether the child hones pre-existing concepts to fit the language or acquires new concepts through the process of word learning itself.

Just as one individual does not need a symbol to form a concept of an object so two individuals do not need symbols to draw attention to things in the immediately present world; they can simply point to what they are interested in, as mother and child do late in the first year and early in the second. The essential function of a symbol is to provide a means of communicating with another about things and relations that *cannot* be pointed to. This function is so vital to us as humans, both socially and individually, that it is strange to contemplate an existence without it.

Readers may object at this point that the claim that symbols are inherently social is not congruent with many uses of the term, for example in Piaget's (1962) use of individual symbol in contrast to conventional signs, or in its use in general in modern cognitive science, where all cognition is assumed to involve symbol manipulation, whether in humans, computers, or other creatures. This social-communicative foundation is, however, in accord with Peirce's semiotic system of communicative signs, and it is also in accord with Vygotsky's theories of semiotic mediation.

One can of course make and use symbols for oneself, as one can and often does use language for oneself. Indeed, the Vygotskian theory of inner speech (Vygotsky, 1986) is precisely built on this move from the communicative to the cognitive. In this sense, however, one is using symbolic language as a tool, in effect talking to oneself as to another person. Moreover, symbol use is facilitative, in fact constitutive of higher order cognition, as Vygotsky also argued. Using words to represent higher order categories and relations takes human thought beyond the levels that other animals can reach. And, as David Olson (1994), among others, has argued, when we can display these words graphically they can take us even farther (see also A. Clark, 1997; Donald, 1991). But that is a later story.

It is highly significant that natural language symbols—words—relate to *conventional* concepts, that is, concepts that are widely used and understood within a society or linguistic group. This is an important corollary of the significance of shared symbols in that it is the social importation of the cultural meaning into the child's communicative schemes that provides entree into societal, rather than narrow interpersonal meaning systems. The child's first words may be understood by close relatives, and in this sense shared, but the system will be thus social dyadic, not cultural. For this reason, the child's initial conceptual organization of the world may need to be reorganized to accord with the uses of words in the language. In effect, the child needs to "re-parse" the world conceptually in response to learning words. Thus the initial over- and under-extensions of the early referential period give way to a more conservative, responsive process of attending to the extensions of words and their constructions in grammar as used by adults, reflecting the conventional meaning systems.

What Kinds of Words?   The process of acquiring a conventional meaning system can be seen most clearly by going beyond object naming as the prototypical word learning process. The importance and implications of this move are threefold:

1. Object names do not provide all of the challenges to the learner of less concrete terms, that is, terms that refer to less concrete aspects of the real world.
2. Children learn many kinds of words that refer to less tangible aspects of reality than object names. Thus, if we are to understand what they are doing we need to examine the full range of word types involved.
3. Focus on objects and object name-learning encourages a focus only on reference and only in a here-and-now context.

There is a strong tendency, not only in developmental psychology but in cognitive science and philosophy, to extend the analysis of object terms to other kinds of nouns and to words in general, but this base is deceptive. The move away from object names is parallel to Wittgenstein's move away from the language of objects and material facts to the language of the non-objective internal states.

The kind of meaning acquisition that object names exemplify does not cover the problems involved for all the kinds of words that children learn and use. Object names are just too simple, Quinean claims to the contrary.[2] Dedre Gentner's (1982) analysis of the advantages of object names for the learner is cogent. She pointed out that, unlike actions and properties, objects are perceptually salient and stable, with well-defined boundaries, thus forming an accessible target for associating with a name. Recent infant research has reinforced this analysis by demonstrating that even young infants see objects as bounded wholes (Spelke, Breinlinger, Macomber, & Jacobson, 1992).

As John Macnamara (1982) put it, objects are things you can pick up or bump into. This characterization vividly illustrates the relatedness of objects to the person (you), and to actions (pick up, bump into). Objects are not only easy to visualize but they have a place in our lives that provides the basis for conceptualizing and generalizing, that is, forming a basis for using symbols to represent them in different contexts, when the objects themselves are not present. Their very concreteness provides the basis for shared attention and in consequence shared conceptualization. This is not to say that the child's conceptualization will be the *same* as the adult's; the

---

[2]Quine's (1960) analysis of referential ambiguity has dominated developmental discussions of word learning for the past 15 years, after Markman and Hutchinson's (1984) seminal article on the topic. However, it can be definitively argued that Quine's analysis does not apply to the situation of children learning words under natural conditions (Nelson, 1988, 1996). Moreover, Quine's argument applies mainly to the theoretical language of science. He also presented a behaviorist model of children's word learning that did not depend on the child's a priori assumption that words apply to whole objects, as present-day theories do. The Quine argument is now well known and will not be reviewed in detail here.

use of the symbol however, may in time bring it closer to the adult's, as the adult's use of the word appears in only those contexts that fit the adult criteria of reference.

Much has been made of the observation that children tend to learn nouns as their first words and as the majority of their first vocabularies (Gentner, 1982; Markman, 1987; Nelson, 1973). It is theoretically important that this is not true for all children (Bates, Bretherton, & Snyder, 1988; Lieven, 1978; Lieven, Pine, & Dresner Barnes, 1992; Nelson, 1973, 1981); nor, as recent research has shown, is it true for all languages being learned, for example, Korean, Japanese, and Chinese (Gopnik & Choi, 1990; Tardif, 1996). Whereas recent discussion has focused on children's learning of verbs in contrast with objects (Tomasello & Merriman, 1995), many other kinds of words represent intangible aspects of experience, social and personal, and some of these are learned at a surprisingly early age. Furthermore, it is misleading to characterize the child's first words as either nouns or verbs. Words are identified as nouns because of the roles they play in sentences, but single word uses cannot be so identified, and children use their single words for a variety of speech functions (Greenfield & Smith, 1976).

Researchers' emphasis on noun learning usually reflects an implicit identification of nouns with object labels, but although object names are nouns in all languages, not all nouns are object labels. In this regard, it is of interest, although seldom noted, that between a quarter and a third of the *nouns* in children's early (2nd year) vocabulary are not object names (as current theories imply) but refer to a variety of non-object entities. Thus the actual proportion of object labels in most children's first vocabularies is much less than a majority, and there are strong individual differences in this respect.

In an analysis of the vocabularies of 45 children aged 20 months (Nelson, Hampson, & Kessler Shaw, 1993), we focused particularly on nouns that were not object names, with the goal of determining what aspects of the social and material world children might be referencing with their early symbolic forms. The data come from a checklist[3] filled out by mothers. We found that 32% of the nouns used productively by the toddlers studied were not object labels, called BLOCS (basic level object category terms), but belonged to a variety of other ontological types—places, events, actions, social situations, person roles, weather phenomena, and so on. Table 2.1 provides examples of these uses. At the bottom of the list are words that were learned by at least half the children by the age of 20 months. This study demonstrated that 1-year-old toddlers were not restricted either to object labels or to action verbs, but from the beginning

---

[3]An early form of the checklist now published (Fenson et al., 1993).

TABLE 2.1
Non-BLOC Noun Types in 20-month Vocabularies

Type	Examples	Number (of 45 children) Using the Type
Location	Park, Kitchen	24
Action	Kiss, Drink	14
Generic	Toys, Animals	14
Event	Party, Lunch	12
Person role	Doctor, Brother	10
Natural Phenomena	Rain, Wind	6
Temporal Entities	Day, Morning	9
Object Parts	Button, Wheel	2
Material	Wood, Playdough	1

Non-BLOC nouns learned by at least half the children by 20 months:
Bath, home, kiss, money, outside, park, toy, walk

BLOC = Basic level object category type.
Table based on Nelson, Hampson, and Kessler Shaw (1993).

learned and used words for a variety of less tangible concepts symbolized by nouns in English.

Why should we study such words? Why not first establish principles for learning object terms and then see if we can adapt those to other kinds of words? This is in fact the preferred strategy in both philosophy (Millikan, 1998; Quine, 1960) and psychology (Golinkoff, Mervis, & Hirsh-Pasek, 1994; Markman, 1991), but the later Wittgenstein taught us otherwise. For psychology, the following reasons seem persuasive:

- Abstract words are common in all vocabularies, including the earliest vocabularies.
- They provide a better test of how word meanings can be learned than object names that have occupied so much of the research attention.
- They allow us to generalize across kinds of words and domains to general processes.
- They may lead to explanations for a number of observations about both early and later lexical acquisition puzzles; for example, over and under-extension, comprehension before production, and its inverse, production without meaning, fast mapping and its limitations, and the extraordinary number of words learned by children from 2 years to 20.
- They encourage us to ask: What do words do for the child? And they provide the answer: Words *stabilize, generalize,* and bring the learner into a *wider world of ideas.*

Note that object concepts do not need to be stabilized, as they apply to stable parts of the world. They also yield general kinds readily on grounds that have been well studied in the psychological literature. But object terms do not really bring the child into a new world of ideas. For that, one needs to move to a level beyond the immediate, and beyond the known event world. One needs to enter the world of the imagined past and future, the not here and not now.

An important and basic question to raise is "How do children learn to use these other words and attribute meaning to them?" To answer this question we need to study the process in the real world of children and their parents as they use the language in everyday settings. Specifically, we need to observe them in what Wittgenstein called "language games," that is, the use of words in specific situational contexts for specific functions. Meaning not only resides in use but must be extracted from use by the learner. Paraphrasing Wittgenstein, for the child, learning language is to enter a shared culture, or shared cultural enterprises.

Analyses of transcripts of mother–child interactions in their homes when the 45 children were between 13 and 20 months of age (from the same study yielding the data shown in Table 2.1) showed that XBLOC terms were used within highly restrictive discourse contexts. For example, *call* as a noun was used only in the "play phone" context, although it was used as a verb in other contexts such as "*call* Daddy for dinner," or "this book is *called* Pat the Bunny." This observation provides an important clue to how these words are learned, which we follow further in later sections. It highlights the fact that the basic problem of acquiring *experiential semantics* is to *abstract meaning from use*.

As a first step toward understanding this process, we can ask: Children learn and use the kinds of words shown in Table 2.1. Do they use these words as symbols? Or are they used as associates, indexes, elicitors of action, for example? Or are they empty of either image or concept, and simply used as pragmatic discourse markers? The data available on these words is insufficient to answer this question, although some of the analyses already carried out suggest limited shared understanding. For example, in one exchange, a mother asked her daughter who was drawing the observer's attention to a bandage, "Where did you get cut last night?" The child replied repeatedly "in the park." This was apparently not the case, and the mother corrected: "On your thumb." The child presumably associated the "where" question with the location word "park," not with the body part "thumb." If such matters can seem so obscure to toddlers, how can we understand what sense they are making of the language they are learning and using by 2 years of age? We cannot simply move on to the point where children seem to know what both we and they are talking about. We need to understand the process by which they reach that point, and focusing on object words and taxonomies simply won't get us far enough.

Words, Discourse, and Events. To the extent that children's initial understandings of the world are in terms of events (Nelson, 1986, 1996), then relations among things in the child's experienced world form the basis for relations among words for children. This is not to claim that the child's words remain tied to specific situations and events: They obviously do not beyond the earliest phase. Rather what the child parses in terms of relations between words and the world are new ways of dividing experience to fit the language used. These bits can then be used in other situations and events that incorporate the same relations. But something else happens, as the analysis of discourse between adult and child reveals. In the course of learning to engage in conversation, and to construct sentences, the child amasses bits and pieces of language that are not mapped to the parsing of experience, but are used as elements of the language itself. At first, the claim is, these have no *meaning* in and of themselves, that is, no conceptualization is attached to them. At first they may be confined to particular discourse contexts, although they may be extended to other contexts to fit pragmatic functions. But these bits have importance in leading the child to a new level of language function, its function as a symbolic system that represents meanings in its own right.

Use without meaning or productivity without comprehension offers a clue to this process. This is a phenomenon that has been studied in a different guise for many years. For example, in the early 1970s many studies were reported in which words such as *before* and *after, because* and *so, these* and *those, more* and *less* were confused with one another by young children (E. V. Clark, 1971; Donaldson & Wales, 1970). Many of these terms—prepositions and adjectives—were seen to be paired in terms of positive and negative poles, with the positive form (e.g., *more, before*) being dominant and extended to the negative so that a request such as "show me the one with less" would typically elicit from a young child a point to the one with more. Theorists then concluded that "less means more" on the grounds that children used (or interpreted) both words to mean the same thing. Susan Carey (1982) carried out a study of *more* and *less*, however, in which she substituted the nonsense form *tiv* for *less*, and found that children responded to *tiv* in the same way, pointing to the tree with more apples on it. Children could not have attributed the meaning of more to tiv prior to the experiment, thus demonstrating that in at least some of these cases children had *no* meanings for the terms tested, although they responded to them readily and sometimes *used* them correctly.

Correct use in context by the words *before* and *after, because* and *so* were studied by Lucia French (French & Nelson, 1985). Children used these words correctly in appropriate contexts when reporting routine scripts at ages younger than the previous experimental work predicted. Subsequent experimental tests of comprehension in script contexts (Carni & French, 1984) showed that 3-year-olds actually understood the terms better when they were used in a script context than when they were used in a novel context. When presented with a series of 5 pictures illustrating a sequence of actions in a familiar routine or an unpredictable event (e.g., a trip to the park), they were able to identify what action came before or after the central action in the predictable routine context but not in the unpredictable context. Thus they seemed to have worked out the meaning of the terms, but only in specific familiar contexts.

Levy and Nelson (1994) studied the uses of temporal and causal terms over a 16-month period by a single child, showing that her first uses were neither context appropriate nor meaningful, but that she then began to model her uses on the contexts in which her father used the terms, gradually expanding the meaning contexts of causals to those demanding a psychological causal explanation. This study and others (see Levy, 1989; Nelson, 1995, 1996; Nelson et al., 1993) provided the basis for sketching out a general scheme for how meanings of words develop over time as a child experiences them in different contexts. The following is an abreviated outline from Levy and Nelson (1994) of this proposal for a theory of *learning meaning from discourse context*:

- New language *forms* are learned (recognized, produced) together with their distributional relations with other language forms, on the basis of the discourse context.
- Discourse patterns are interpreted first in terms of the child's event knowledge system.. Recognition of patterns and forms may be first restricted to the particular activity contexts in which they were originally experienced (where experienced means noticed by the child). The relevant event context may be different for the child from the immediate event observed by the adult; thus it is the child's "cognitive context" that determines relevance.
- On the basis of adult uses of the form the child may construct a discourse notion about how the form is used and subsequently use it herself in closely constrained "formats" and in the context of specific topics.
- Use of the form itself—especially in formally contrastive alternation with other forms—alerts the child to further uses by other speakers and leads to additional knowledge about the "meaning context" that it represents.
- Comparison of the uses of the form by self and others may lead to a period of resystematization of the form and other forms that are semantically or syntactically closely related.

- Subsequently the child's uses indicate at least partial control of the form in productive speech. However, comprehension tests may reveal gaps in the child's knowledge, and productive uses may remain confined to well-understood event contexts.
- Full control of some forms ("full meaning") may be delayed for years after the form is first acquired and readily used. Further reorganization of the meaning system may be required before adult-level understanding is achieved.

In its most general claims this description is expected to apply to the acquisition of all linguistic forms at all stages of development, but different types of forms may exhibit some of these developmental characteristics and not others. For example, the child may need to do very little refining of her use and understanding of names of common objects, whereas terms referring to abstract notions such as temporal perspective, quantification, or cognitive states may be used for many years before full meaning is achieved (see Levy & Nelson, 1994, for examples). This scheme incorporates the basic idea that Wittgenstein put forth, that meaning resides in use in discourse contexts and that different situations of language use incorporate different criteria for the use of particular terms.

System

Languages constitute systems of symbols conventionally used in constructions that convey meaning between people. The SSSS is not in anyone's head, but it is the basis for conversational exchange and for other discourse practices. Each person inhabits some part of it. For individuals it is a functional system composed of elements and construction patterns (Goldberg, 1995; Tomasello, 1998) that may be used informally, casually, or in more formal discourse contexts. The different codes and registers used in different discourse contexts (e.g., school talk and playground talk) suggest that people use, and children learn to use, varying systems for talking together in different settings and on different topics. Together these may draw on a set of grammatical principles, so that they are related through family resemblance, in a way similar to Wittgenstein's analysis of word uses and language games in terms of family resemblance. How a child acquires a *set of language systems* then may have much in common with how a child acquires the meaning of a category term like "game," which, again according to Wittgenstein, has no essential definition—no rules—but only overlapping criteria for how to use the term.

More specifically, a system of symbols relates them to each other, and not only to the concepts or real-world referents that they represent. Children begin relating words to each other very early in the language game, but they become more aware of these relations as their command of language forms (words and grammatical constructions) grows. Early in the process of language acquisition the symbols acquired are mapped directly onto the activity components (such as actors, objects, and actions) that are their referents; the system at this point is supplied by the activity, that is, by representations of connections between actions and related elements. Symbols are connected individually to activity components (acts, actors, and objects). When language is well under way, however, the symbolic forms are directly related to each other, in both grammatical and semantic relations and their relation to specific activity components is less direct and specific.

As one aspect of the sense system, words are organized into meaning domains that reflect both the enterprises of the humans who use the language and the constraints imposed by the grammatical structures of a particular language. How words fit together into phrases and sentence constructions (their syntagmatics) involves also how they fit together into paradigmatic structures that determine which words are alternatives within a structure. At the most general level these are word classes: nouns, verbs, adjectives. At the most specific level they are synonyms and antonyms. In between are those elusive "semantic fields" such as emotion words and taxonomic categories, ranging from everyday categories like animals, food, and clothes to esoteric categories like computer languages or galaxies.

When sense relations are established among words the correspondence relationship between symbol and signified can be extended as the system expands. One can state, for example, that Z symbolizes the proposition [a,b,c], or in less logical language that the word "animal," for example, means all creatures that move or breathe, or that it includes all animate creatures. Figure 2.4 illustrates that the super-triangle relation of concepts to words expands into one where sentences are related to symbols, and thus may connect the mental constructions, the conceptual representations of the recipients. Of course, it takes more than one statement of such a relation to establish it in the language-using community. It is this possibility of building a system of meanings that is significant as the language expands. It is this possibility that children must grasp as they grapple with the systemic interrelationships in the language or languages they use.

Concepts for intangible entities, categories, states, and qualities and their related symbols form the basis for some of the truly important social and cognitive advances that language use offers to human life. As Charles Taylor (1985) put it, language makes it possible for us to talk about ideas that would not exist without language. The profound implications of this assertion require us to ask how children go beyond talking about objects to talking about ideas. And the answer must lie in how they solve the *symbol system construction problem.*

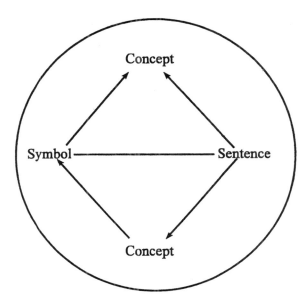

FIG. 2.4. The extended semiotic triangle showing that when a sense system is established the symbol can connect a sentence (or larger meaning unit) to the concepts of separate individuals.

How children build up and organize the system characteristics of language in use constitutes much of the traditional study of cognitive development. Taxonomies have attracted almost all the attention in developmental psychology (as grammar has in linguistics) and the unexamined assumption has been that somehow children will see the same relations in the world that are incorporated into a conventional language system. This assumption will not stand up to serious examination, however, as has been pointed out in studies of slot-filler categories (Lucariello & Nelson, 1985; Nelson, 1985, 1996). The assumption that it is an easy matter to map words to taxonomies ignores the great varieties of relationships that are reflected in the language in use, and that have been traditionally studied in general semantics. The different ways of organizing semantic concepts of the same domain (e.g., time, organized both linearly and cyclically) are many and varied across cultures and languages, and this fact forms the basis for claims by Whorf (1956) and others that language determines thought structures. We cannot evade these claims by assuming that language simply reflects thought structures without running into the problem that then thought structures must vary independently across cultures. The solution to this problem most likely lies in the recognition of different levels of cognitive structures and processes, with language as an overlay on basic dynamic levels of pattern mapping (A. Clark, 1997; Donald, 1991).

Language in this conception is, in Clark's words "the ultimate artifact," a public construction for communication, which has been adapted for use in private thought.

This conception is remarkably similar to Vygotsky's ideas, articulated in the 1920s and 1930s, as a developmental theory (Vygotsky, 1986). It is today a radical conception in the perspective of modern cognitive science, however. Cognitive science has been dedicated to the view of one architecture, either symbolic propositions or connectionism, and the arguments have been in terms of the weaknesses of each. A. Clark's (1997) view (similar to Donald, 1991) is to wed the two, essentially through the mechanism of the social artifactual construction of language, added onto the basic primate mind, with powerful cognitive results. When natural language is recognized as a developmental addition, as well as a phylogenetic addition, rather than as a basic characteristic of the "natural" human mind, it has far-reaching implications for views of cognitive development (Nelson, 1996). In particular, as A. Clark (1997) put it:

> Beware of mistaking the problem-solving profile of the embodied, socially and environmentally embedded mind for that of the basic brain. Just because humans can do logic and science, we should not assume that the brain contains a full-blown logic engine or that it encodes scientific theories in ways akin to their standard expression in words and sentences. Instead, both logic and science rely heavily on the use and manipulation of external media, especially the formalism of language and logic, and the capacities of storage, transmission, and refinement provided by cultural institutions and by the use of spoken and written text. (p. 220)

The implication for cognitive psychology is that studying normal adult functioning is not to study basic brain processes. The implication for developmental psychology is that the study of the acquisition of language and its uses should be a primary mode of investigation of cognitive development. One important aspect of this study is the investigation of the relation of the child's acquisition of words that are critical to the understanding of concepts in a domain of knowledge and the growth of conceptual understanding in that domain.

A cognitive development domain of great current interest is children's theory of mind, and the semantic domain corresponding to the purported theory is that of internal state words, especially mental states such as knowing and thinking. The development of mental state terms has been investigated by a number of researchers (Bartsch & Wellman, 1995; Bretherton & Beeghly, 1982; Shatz, Wellman, & Silber, 1983) for clues to children's understanding of the mind under the assumption that the use of such terms to refer to internal states reflects an organized theory of those states. Other investigators (Moore, Bryant, & Furrow, 1989) have related children's understanding of different terms to their performance on tests of theory of mind understanding. These studies implicitly reflect an assumption of expressions in public language as indexes of the attainment of a private theory.

Know *and* Think *from 2 to 4 by Children and Parents.* From the alternative perspective articulated here and consistent with Clark's statement quoted earlier, the initial use of the public language may serve as a scaffold for construction of an understanding (not a full-fledged theory) in this domain. This alternative requires an examination of the child's uses of the terms in question, with the recognition that these may be "uses without meaning," as well as the uses of the terms by adults with the child. Kessler Shaw (1999) has carried out such a study, examining the child's acquisition of meaning levels according to the Nelson and Lucariello (1985) scheme in relation to the Wittgensteinian conception of language games as contexts for use. For the purpose of analyzing abstract words like *know* and *think*, the first level is considered to be *embedded* in context (rather than referential as proposed for words in concrete domains). The highest level in the Nelson and Lucariello scheme it will be recalled is that of *sense*, or the system of related terms within a domain. The middle level is that of *denotation*, implying conceptual knowledge of the single term but without any necessary connection to related conceptual terms. This is the simple symbolic level as designated here. Words are used as symbols but are not organized in terms of sense relationships.

Previous studies have found that children often begin to use the terms *think* and *know* in the third year, but as Booth and Hall (1995) and their colleagues have shown, even at 10 or 12 years of age some aspects of the meaning of *know* remain unassimilated to children's uses. *Know* and *think* are closely related according to semantic analyses in linguistics and philosophy. A core meaning of *to know* is to have reliable evidence regarding some state of the world. In its related mental state sense *to think* is to conjecture on the basis of inference about some state of the world. Previous analyses have shown that mental state terms used in interpersonal discourse have many different functions, only some of which reflect these core semantic meanings. Moreover, there is a discrepancy between observations in natural conversational contexts and in experimental contexts, similar to that observed for other terms used without meaning (Levy & Nelson, 1994).

A question that has not been adequately addressed in previous work is how parents use the terms with young children, and how children begin to use them with parents. What has been noted is that children begin using the terms in routine or highly contextualized ways. This has led researchers to confine their analyses to those uses that can be attributed to reference to internal states. But if children are learning about concepts of internal states as they learn to use internal state terms, a process that seems indicated from the theoretical perspective of experiential semantics, then all uses of the terms by parents as well as children need to be examined for their clues to the criteria of use, and their relation to the mental conceptual domain.

Kessler Shaw (1999) undertook such a study of parent–child talk about thinking and knowing analyzed in terms of *language games*, following Wittgenstein's analysis of meaning in use (see also Montgomery, 1997). Two groups of children participated in this study, each visited four times over a 6-month period at roughly monthly intervals. The 12 younger children were 2½ to 3 years and the 11 older children were 3½ to 4 years. During each visit they engaged in four activities: free play with the child's toys, a hide and find game, a snack, and play with a doll house and doll house figures. This yielded approximately 75 hours of natural at-home interactions, from which all uses of the terms *know* and *think* were extracted in their conversational contexts of use.

What is of considerable interest is the fact that the two verbs, semantically closely related, were used in different situational contexts, and for different functions, referencing internal states, directing the interaction, or directing reflection (codes based on Furrow, Moore, Davidge, & Chaisson, 1992, and Shatz et al., 1983). Directing the interaction was the most frequent use for *think* by mothers, whereas the functions were more evenly distributed, and included a greater proportion of internal state uses for *know*. Similarly the children used *think* primarily to direct interaction at both ages, but used *know* more frequently for internal state reference, and increasingly so at 3½ years.

Table 2.2 shows that each verb occurred primarily in one of a small set of lexical frames. These frames did not overlap for the two verbs, each accounting for about 75% of all uses of the terms by mothers. The general picture indicates that *think* was used more for a planning function, for the mother to express what she herself thinks, as when she suggests ideas for the ongoing play activity. *Know* was used more by the mothers to talk of generalizations, and by the use of wh-questions, to ask about what the child, rather than the mother, knows.

Use by both members of the dyads was primarily for the here and now, or for fantasy references in play, underscoring the importance of shared understandings. In support of this point, 10 of the 12 younger children used *know* for reference to the here and now only or prior to more distanced uses. The data for *think* are less conclusive because of fewer overall uses and the fact that four of the younger children never used the term at all. The 3½- to 4-year-olds used both terms more frequently than younger children, and moved beyond the shared here and now to denotational (symbolic) uses for the past and future and to make generalizations.

TABLE 2.2
Lexical Frames Used by Mothers and Children for *Think* and *Know*

Think
I think (that) X
I don't think (that) X
(Do) you think X?
I/You (don't) think so
How/What/Where/Which/Who/Why do you think X? (wh-question)

Know
I don't know
I don't know (if) X
(Do) you know how/what/when/where/which/who/why X? (wh-question)
I know X or X, I know
X, you know or You know, X
(Do) you know X? or X, (do) you know?
I know
(Do) (you) know what?

For example, the following from a child of 43 months uses *think* to contrast thought and reality, indicating conceptual denotation:

M: So there was a ghost in the house?

A: Not you.

M: I wasn't a ghost, no.

A: There was a pre- there was a pretend um, ghost.

M: You were not afraid?

A: Nn-nn. I *thought* it was a real ghost, *but it wasn't*. It was a, a pretend ghost.

However, even by 4 years of age the mainstream children in this sample did not give evidence of having a *symbolic sense system* in this meaning domain. And whereas mothers were sometimes observed to provide presuppositions or sense contrasts these were not frequent in the talk recorded in this study.

Overall, reference to the here and now was the most frequent use by both mothers and children, with denotational uses (e.g., contrasting thinking and reality states) significantly more common than sense contrasts (e.g., of thinking and knowing). But although mothers did provide explicit meaning clues of this kind, only one child provided evidence of sense meanings, as in the following:

E: That block was my favorite.

M: And it's got teeth marks on it.

L: Why was that one your favorite?

E: I don't *know*. I *think* maybe it was my favorite color.

What then are these children learning about the use and meaning of these terms? First, different children seem to be acquiring different uses. One 2-year-old used *know* almost exclusively in the phrase "I don't know" whereas two others used it to assert competence or to provide new information, but rarely for "I don't know." Second, the children varied considerably in whether they used the term at all (three 2-year-olds did not), for here-and-now embedded use only (18 children) or also for conceptual/symbolic uses (past reference, contrast with reality states: 2 children). Only one child gave evidence for contrastive system use by the age of 4 years. Thus during these early preschool years they appear to be learning primarily *how* the terms are used in embedded discourse contexts rather than *what* the terms denote conceptually.

One of the disappointments of the study is that, although we expected on the basis of the prior literature, that we would find system-type (sense) meanings by 4 years, the evidence was primarily in terms of "reference" (that is, embedded uses) and denotation. These phases did produce the expected sequence; however, there was almost no evidence in this data set of any contrastive use of the terms, or use of the terms in the same discourse context, that would provide a case for the child's having a sense system that included both terms within a relational structure, even by children as old as 4 years.

An example of the limited understanding by the young children of the conceptual constraints on the meaning of *know* (here the important component of reliable and accessible source of knowing) is evident in the example shown in Table 2.3. As can be seen, this child commands the use of several mental state terms: *remember, know, think,* and her use of them grammatically and pragmatically is appropriate. But the dialogue tells us that her understanding of the mental concepts symbolized by these terms is underdeveloped, at best. She appears to be trying to access her mother's knowledge state or memory in the same way that she would access her own, by providing cues to an experience that she (the child) had, but that her mother did not have. It appears that she has not advanced beyond the socially shared understandings that are the beginnings of communicative exchanges to the point where self and other are recognized as having different knowledge of different reality states depending on their access to those states.

The complexities of this example (the child knows that the mother knows the person referred to but does not realize that the mother cannot

TABLE 2.3
Sharing the Meaning of *Know* (K, 42 months, Meal Context)

K:	You know something?
M:	What?
(Pause)	
K:	Let me think
(Pause)	
K:	What's her name again?
M:	What?
K:	What's her name again?
M:	Who?
K:	That girl
M:	Who?
K:	Don't you remember her?
K:	You've seen her before
M:	No
K:	Yes
M:	Where is she?
K:	I don't know
M:	Oh
K:	I don't know her name
K:	Somebody has a rocket
K:	That can turn into a big rocket
M:	Yeah?
K:	(nods)
M:	Who is this person?
K:	I don't know her
M:	Where'd you meet her?
K:	At our house!
M:	At our house?
M:	Somebody with a rocket came to our house?
K:	Uh huh
M:	Was I home for this?
K:	(shakes head)
M:	No
M:	So how would I know who this is?

****

M:	How do you know she had a rocket?
K:	Cause she told us
M:	Oh, okay
M:	Was this Katie?
K:	(nods)
M:	Oh, okay
M:	Well why didn't you say so?
K:	Cause

know who the child has "in mind") raise the question as to whether this is a matter of semantics of the verbs or of the child's "theory of mind." We would claim it is both. Knowing the denotation and sense of "know" must entail recognition of the difference in knowing states between people. This child seems to have grasped that *know* refers to one's accessible information ("I don't know her name") and she assumes that mother can help to access it (as she can help to solve many other kinds of problems). Her concept of knowing, however, is undifferentiated with respect to the difference between people's access to knowledge, the difference between shared and unshared knowledge, as well as lacking the pragmatic skills sufficient to provide clues to the information she is seeking. Obviously *know* for this child does not entail a causal relation between evidence and the mental state of knowing.

The point here is that mothers are using the mental state terms quite freely, that children are experiencing them in specific discourse contexts and syntactic frames, and that they in turn adopt uses of the terms in specific discourse contexts. These then provide clues as to the abstract components of their meaning, as well as the pragmatic uses. However, the children's uses primarily remain at the pragmatic/embedded level over these early years. Although we might call this "use without meaning" as we have done in previous work, it seems more reasonable to think that children are acquiring pragmatic meanings as a basis from which to launch semantic analyses. Their *experiential semantics* of the terms *know* and *think* is based in differential experiences with the terms and their discourse functions.

It is noteworthy that mothers did not correct children's uses, or try to amend children's understanding of the causal relation, although in the "rocket" example the mother seems to have been puzzled by the child's assertion. It is as though parents are looking through an invisible veil of words; they use the words unconsciously to express their own meaning. They are insensitive to the fact that the children are not privy to the meanings intended. This no doubt explains why the terms are not used by adults in a contrastive sense for the benefit of children, either to contrast thought and reality, or to contrast *think* and *know*.

This observation has implications for how we try to understand more generally the problems of learning word meanings as they are used in context. As Sternberg and Powell (1983), Miller (1990), Johnson-Laird (1987) and many others have written with regard to word learning in the grade school years and by adults, new words are not generally taught, nor are they learned in the explicit sense of the word; they are rather "gathered" or "picked up" in contexts of use and used by the "gatherer" in similar contexts. Later, in some reflective but not necessarily conscious process, the uses of the word become salient to the user, and the meanings emerge in a system of related uses. In Wittgenstein's terms, they fit into particular forms of discourse. In more cognitive terms, they fit into a system of meanings organized within domains of human enterprises.

To return to an earlier point, the child's using the "meaningless" terms in discourse with adults makes salient for the child distinctive other uses by other speakers. As found in one exchange between mother and child, the words "think" and "know" occurred in the same context but used by different speakers. Although not yet used contrastively and systematically by the same child speaker, the contrast could be extracted from such uses.

On the other hand, there is evidence, for example in the child's lack of understanding of the entailments of "know," that these terms may be used more or less as discourse fillers. This has important implications for how we interpret their use by children in experimental situations, such as some of the theory of mind tests, where children are asked "What did you *think* was in the box before we opened the box?" when for example a raisin box contains crayons inside. We have found (Plesa, Goldman, & Edmondson, 1995) that most 3-year-olds who respond incorrectly to this question by providing the "reality" answer (crayons) change their answers and respond correctly (raisins) if asked "What did you *say* was in the box before we opened it?" This bit of data has several plausible interpretations, but at least one of them is that children of this age (like those in the Kessler Shaw study) are not using "think" in a symbolic way, but as a pragmatic marker of some sort that indicates something about the state of the world. In this it is not different from the question "What was in the box?" Only a child who believed in magic (and one of the children in our study used this rationale) would respond that there were raisins in the box when it was closed and crayons when it was open.

The moral of the story is this: Even 4-year-olds may know a good deal about *the system of use* but little about the *system of meanings* for commonly used words, whose very meaning depends on their relations to other terms in a domain of knowledge and discourse.

CONCLUSION

How then is a shared symbolic system acquired on the individual level? It is developed as a *social practice*. The acquisition of a system of meanings adequate to the many different discourses (language games) that we all engage in is a social and cognitive process of considerable complexity. That children proceed as smoothly as they do is remarkable, but we should not overestimate what they are doing at any point in the process of development. When they learn to use object words symbolically (conceptually or denotationally) that is an achievement to be recognized as an important entry point into the larger symbolic system, a point beyond the social sharing and reference possible earlier. But as we trace their acquisition of words that have less correspondence to concrete material reality and more relevance to social, personal, and cultural meanings and relationships, we find, as I have indicated through the various studies noted here, that the system of meanings is complex, situated, and varied. The way that adults use the language facilely (without recognizing that children often do not understand what they say) no doubt entices the child to enter more fully into the discourses that swirl about her. And incredibly, they succeed more often than not.

However, our blindness to the problem of use without a grasp of the cultural conceptual meanings implied, and to the complexity of comprehension, can prevent us from addressing the real problems that face children in entering into our language games, and thus into our cultural knowledge systems. What seem to be cognitive failures in problem solving or conceptual understanding may instead be lapses in shared symbolic meaning systems. Reciprocally, closing such gaps may bring a child into a new level of cognitive functioning. This is not to say, of course, that knowledge acquisition is solely a reflection of word meanings, but certainly these are necessary to it, and indeed are keys to the child's construction of knowledge from experience with social-cultural discourse.

Many cognitive lacks of the preschool years may indeed be at base failures to understand how words work in particular cases, and how they relate in complex systems of knowledge. This is not to suggest that we can move children ahead cognitively by providing language drills. It is simply to draw attention to the importance of understanding the critical role of language in cognitive development, and the equally critical roles of cognition and conversation in language development.

REFERENCES

Bartsch, K., & Wellman, H. M. (1995). *Children talk about the mind*. New York: Oxford University Press.

Bates, E., Bretherton, I., & Snyder, L. (1988). *From first words to grammar: Individual differences and dissociable mechanisms*. New York: Cambridge University Press.

Bates, E., & Carnevale, G. F. (1993). New directions in research on language development. *Developmental Review, 13*, 436–470.

Benedict, H. (1979). Early lexical development: Comprehension and production. *Journal of Child Language, 6*, 183–200.

Bloom, L. (1973). *One word at a time*. The Hague, Netherlands: Mouton.

Bloom, L. (1993). *The transitions from infancy to language: Acquiring the power of expression*. New York: Cambridge University Press.

Booth, J. R., & Hall, W. S. (1995). Development of the understanding of the polysemous meanings of the mental state verb know. *Cognitive Development, 10*, 529–549.

Bretherton, I., & Beeghly, M. (1982). Talking about internal states: The acquisition of an explicit theory of mind. *Developmental Psychology, 18*, 906–921.

Bruner, J. S. (1983). *Child's talk: Learning to use language*. New York: Norton.

Carey, S. (1982). Semantic development: The state of the art. In E. Wanner & L. R. Gleitman (Eds.), *Language acquistion: The state of the art* (pp. 347–389). New York: Cambridge University Press.

Carni, E., & French, L. A. (1984). The acquisition of before and after reconsidered: What develops? *JECP, 37,* 394–403.

Chomsky, N. (1965). *Aspects of a theory of syntax.* Cambridge, MA: MIT Press.

Chomsky, N. (1988). *Language and problems of knowledge: The Managua lectures.* Cambridge, MA: MIT Press.

Clark, A. (1997). *Being there: Putting brain, body, and world together again.* Cambridge, MA: MIT Press.

Clark, E. V. (1971). On the acquisition of the meaning of before and after. *Journal of Verbal Learning and Verbal Behavior, 10,* 266–275.

Donald, M. (1991). *Origins of the modern mind.* Cambridge, MA: Harvard University Press.

Donaldson, M., & Wales, R. J. (1970). On the acquisition of some relational terms. In J. R. Hayes (Ed.), *Cognition and the development of language* (pp. 235–268). New York: Wiley.

Fenson, L., Dale, P., Reznick, J. S., Thal, D., Bates, E., Hartung, J., Pethick, S., & Reilly, J. (1993). *MacArthur Communicative Development Inventories: User's guide and technical manual.* San Diego: Singular.

Fischer, K. W., & Bidell, T. (1991). Constraining nativist inferences about cognitive capacities. In S. Carey & R. Gelman (Eds.), *The epigenesis of mind: Essays on biology and cognition* (pp. 199–236). Hillsdale, NJ: Lawrence Erlbaum Associates.

Frege, G. (1980). On sense and meaning. In P. Geach & M. Black (Eds.), *Translations from the philosophical writings of Gottlob Frege* (pp. 56–78). Oxford: Blackwell. (Original work published 1892)

French, L. A., & Nelson, K. (1985). *Young children's understanding of relational terms: Some ifs, ors and buts.* New York: Springer-Verlag.

Furrow, D., Moore, C., Davidge, J., & Chiasson, L. (1992). Mental terms in mothers' and children's speech: Similarities and relationships. *Journal of Child Language, 19,* 617–632.

Gentner, D. (1982). Why nouns are learned before verbs: Linguistic relativity versus natural partitioning. In S. A. I. Kuczaj (Ed.), *Language development: Vol. 2. Language, thought, and culture* (pp. 301–334). Hillsdale, NJ: Lawrence Erlbaum Associates.

Goldberg, A. (1995). *Constructions: A construction grammar approach to argument structure.* Chicago: University of Chicago Press.

Golinkoff, R., Mervis, C. B., & Hirsh-Pasek, K. (1994). Early object labels: The case for a developmental lexical principles framework. *Journal of Child Language, 21,* 125–156.

Gopnik, A., & Choi, S. (1990). Language and cognition. *First Language, 10,* 199–216.

Greenfield, P. M., & Smith, J. (1976). *The structure of communication in early language development.* New York: Academic Press.

Heath, S. B. (1983). *Ways with words.* Cambridge, England: Cambridge University Press.

Johnson-Laird, P. N. (1987). The mental representation of the meaning of words. *Cognition, 23,* 189–211.

Kessler Shaw, L. (1999). *The development of the meanings of "think" and "know" through conversation.* Unpublished doctoral dissertation, City University of New York.

Levy, E. (1989). Monologue as development of the text-forming function of language. In K. Nelson (Ed.), *Narratives from the crib* (pp. 123–170). Cambridge, MA: Harvard University Press.

Levy, E., & Nelson, K. (1994). Words in discourse: A dialectical approach to the acquisition of meaning and use. *Journal of Child Language, 21,* 367–390.

Lieven, E. M. (1978). Conversations between mothers and young children: Individual differences and their possible implications for the study of language learning. In N. Waterson & C. Snow (Eds.), *The development of communication: Social and pragmatic factors in language acquisition* (pp. 173–187). New York: Wiley.

Lieven, E. M., Pine, J. M., & Dresner Barnes, H. (1992). Individual differences in early vocabulary development: Redefining the referential-expressive distinction. *Journal of Child Language, 19*, 287–310.

Lucariello, J., & Nelson, K. (1985). Slot-filler categories as memory organizers for young children. *Developmental Psychology, 21*, 272–282.

Lyons, J. (1977). *Semantics* (Vol. 1). Cambridge, England: Cambridge University Press.

Macnamara, J. (1982). *Names for things*. Cambridge, MA: MIT Press.

Markman, E. M. (1987). How children constrain the possible meanings of words. In U. Neisser (Ed.), *Concepts and conceptual development: Ecological and intellectual factors in categorization* (pp. 255–287). New York: Cambridge University Press.

Markman, E. M. (1991). The whole-object, taxonomic, and mutual exclusivity assumptions as initial constraints on word meanings. In S. A. Gelman & J. P. Byrnes (Eds.), *Perspectives on language and thought: Interrelations in development* (pp. 72–106). New York: Cambridge University Press.

Markman, E. M., & Hutchinson, J. E. (1984). Children's sensitivity to constraints on word meaning: Taxonomic vs. thematic relations. *Cognitive Psychology, 16*, 1–27.

McCarthy, D. (1954). Language development in children. In L. Carmichael (Ed.), *Manual of child psychology* (2nd ed., pp. 492–630). New York: Wiley.

Miller, G. A. (1990). The place of language in a scientific psychology. *Psychological Science, 1*, 7–14.

Millikan, R. G. (1998). A common structure for concepts of individuals, stuffs, and real kinds: More Mama, more milk, and more mouse. *Behavioral and Brain Sciences, 21*, 55–100.

Montgomery, D. E. (1997). Wittgenstein's private language argument and children's understanding of the mind. *Developmental Review, 17*, 291–320.

Moore, C., Bryant, D., & Furrow, D. (1989). Mental terms and the development of certainty. *Child Development, 60*, 167–171.

Morgan, J. L., & Demuth, K. (Eds.). (1996). *Signal to syntax: Bootstrapping from speech to grammar in early acquisition*. Mahwah, NJ: Lawrence Erlbaum Associates.

Nelson, K. (1973). Structure and strategy in learning to talk. *Monographs of the Society for Research in Child Development, 38*(1–2, Serial No. 149).

Nelson, K. (1981). Individual differences in language development: Implications for development and language. *Developmental Psychology, 17*, 170–187.

Nelson, K. (1985). *Making sense: The acquisition of shared meaning*. New York: Academic Press.

Nelson, K. (1986). *Event knowledge: Structure and function in development*. Hillsdale, NJ: Lawrence Erlbaum Associates.

Nelson, K. (1988). Constraints on word learning? *Cognitive Development, 3*, 221–246.

Nelson, K. (1991). Concepts and meaning in language development. In N. A. Krasnegor, D. M. Rumbaugh, R. L. Schiefelbusch, & M. Studdert-Kennedy (Eds.), *Biological and behavioral determinants of language development* (pp. 89–116). Hillsdale, NJ: Lawrence Erlbaum Associates.

Nelson, K. (1995). The dual category problem in lexical acquisition. In W. Merriman & M. Tomasello (Eds.), *Beyond names for things* (pp. 223–250). Hillsdale, NJ: Lawrence Erlbaum Associates.

Nelson, K. (1996). *Language in cognitive development: The emergence of the mediated mind*. New York: Cambridge University Press.

Nelson, K., Hampson, J., & Kessler Shaw, L. (1993). Nouns in early lexicons: Evidence, explanations, and implications. *Journal of Child Language, 20*, 61–84.

Nelson, K., & Lucariello, J. (1985). The development of meaning in first words. In M. D. Barrett (Ed.), *Children's single word speech* (pp. 59–86). Chichester, England: Wiley.

Ochs, E., & Schieffelin, B. (1984). Language acquisition and socialization: Three developmental stories. In R. Schweder & R. LeVine (Eds.), *Culture theory: Essays on mind, self and emotion* (pp. 276–320). Cambridge, England: Cambridge University Press.

Ogden, C. K., & Richards, I. A. (1946). *The meaning of meaning*. London: Routledge & Kegan Paul. (Original work published 1923)

Olson, D. R. (1994). *The world on paper*. New York: Cambridge University Press.

Peirce, C. S. (1955). Logic as semiotic: The theory of signs. In J. Buchler (Ed.), *The philosophical writings of Peirce* (pp. 98–110). New York: Dover Books. (Original work published 1897)

Piaget, J. (1962). *Play, dreams, and imitation in childhood*. New York: Norton.

Pinker, S. (1994). *The language instinct: How the mind creates language*. New York: Morrow.

Plesa, D. N., Goldman, S., & Edmondson, D. (1995). *Negotiation of meaning in a false belief task*. Indianapolis, IN: Poster presentation at the Biennial Meeting of the Society for Research in Child Development.

Quine, W. V. O. (1960). *Word and object*. Cambridge, MA: MIT Press.

Saussure, F. d. (1959). *Course in general linguistics*. New York: The Philosophical Library. (Original work published 1915)

Schafer, G., & Plunkett, K. (1998). Rapid word learning by fifteen-month-olds under tightly controlled conditions. *Child Development, 69*, 309–320.

Shatz, M., Wellman, H. M., & Silber, S. (1983). The acquisition of mental verbs: A systematic investigation of first references to mental state. *Cognition, 14*, 301–321.

Snow, C. (1986). The social basis of language development. In P. Fletcher & M. Garman (Eds.), *Language acquisition* (2nd ed., pp. 69–89). Cambridge, England: Cambridge University Press.

Spelke, E. S., Breinlinger, K., Macomber, J., & Jacobson, K. (1992). Origins of knowledge. *Psychological Review, 99*, 605–632.

Stern, D. N. (1985). *The interpersonal world of the infant: A view from psychoanalysis and developmental psychology*. New York: Basic Books.

Sternberg, R. J., & Powell, J. S. (1983). Comprehending verbal comprehension. *American Psychologist, 39*, 878–891.

Sugarman, S. (1983). *Children's early thought*. New York: Cambridge University Press.

Tardif, T. (1996). Nouns are not always learned before verbs: Evidence from Mandarin speakers' early vocabularies. *Developmental Psychology, 32*, 492–504.

Taylor, C. (1985). *Philosophy and the human sciences: Philosophical papers* (Vol. 1). Cambridge, England: Cambridge University Press.

Tomasello, M. (1995). Understanding the self as social agent. In P. Rochat (Ed.), *The self in early infancy: Theory and research* (pp. 449–460). Amsterdam, Holland: Elsevier.

Tomasello, M. (1998). The return of constructions. *Journal of Child Language, 25*, 431–442.

Tomasello, M., & Kruger, A. C. (1992). Joint attention on actions: Acquiring words in ostensive and non-ostensive contexts. *Journal of Child Language, 19*, 313–333.

Tomasello, M., & Merriman, W. E. (Eds.). (1995). *Beyond names for things: Young children's acquisition of verbs*. Hillsdale, NJ: Lawrence Erlbaum Associates.

Trevarthen, C. (1980). The foundations of intersubjectivity: Development of interpersonal and cooperative understanding in infants. In D. R. Olson (Ed.), *The social foundations of language and thought* (pp. 316–342). New York: Norton.

Vygotsky, L. (1986). *Thought and language*. Cambridge, MA: MIT Press.

Werner, H., & Kaplan, B. (1963). *Symbol formation: An organismic-developmental approach to language and the expression of thought*. New York: Wiley.

Whorf, B. L. (1956). *Language, thought and reality: Selected writings of Benjamin Lee Whorf*. Cambridge, MA: MIT Press.

Wittgenstein, L. (1953). *Philosophical investigations*. New York: Macmillan.

Woodward, A. L., Markman, E. M., & Fitzsimmons, C. M. (1994). Rapid word-learning in 13- and 18-month-olds. *Developmental Psychology, 30*, 553–566.

Chapter 3

A Developmental-Functionalist Approach to Mental State Talk

Nancy Budwig
Clark University

An increasing amount of research has examined the interface between language and the development of a theory of mind. As noted by Astington and Jenkins (1999), several researchers have reported correlations between language and theory of mind development (see, e.g., Cutting & Dunn, 1999; Jenkins & Astington, 1996), but how to explain such correlations is poorly understood. One way to think about this interface has been to suggest that theory of mind development depends on language. Although several interesting proposals exist arguing for the role of language in theory of mind development, there has been surprisingly little discussion of the relationship between such proposals. In this chapter, I begin with a review of some critical differences in how language is understood and the methodological implications of adopting one or another perspective toward language. In clarifying such differences I also highlight some distinctions in the ways language is said to contribute to theory of mind development.

In comparing the various views adopted toward language, I claim that despite a number of differences among various researchers in the specifics of what aspect of language receives focus, they hold together as a group to the extent that all emphasize symbolic aspects of communication. In the second section of this chapter, I turn to consider an alternative way of viewing language, namely language as indexical, and consider how an indexical view of language differs in its methodological approach from other available approaches. In the final section of this chapter, I propose how adopting an indexical view contributes to an understanding of theory of mind development, illustrating this view from work that I have been conducting over the past few years.

HOW LANGUAGE INFLUENCES THE
DEVELOPMENT OF THEORY OF MIND

In thinking about how language influences mind we can begin by broadly considering how language is viewed and then examine how particular views of language contribute to the ways researchers study the theory of mind–language connection. That is, when one examines a variety of proposals supporting the claim that language plays a critical role in the development of a theory of mind, two main differences become clear. First, the different proposals distinguish themselves from one another in terms of how language is viewed, and second, they differ in terms of how such assumptions influence how one studies the connection between language, mind, and human development.

What Is Language?

At a broad level of analysis, language can be viewed in many different ways, three of which include: (a) language as symbolic, (b) language as iconic, (c) language as indexical (see Duranti, 1997, pp. 204–212). Most developmental psychologists have primarily made use of the first of these three views of language. In viewing language as symbolic the assumption is that these symbols have arbitrary relationships with what they represent (see Saussure, 1959). The association is dictated by convention (Peirce, 1940). Researchers, when adopting a symbolic view of language, have focused on one or another particular subdomain, often excluding other possibilities in their studies. For instance, researchers have focused on the role of the lexicon, or syntax, or pragmatics (see Astington & Jenkins, 1999, for further discussion).

Whereas clearly symbolic approaches to language have had much to contribute to the study of language, there are two other important ways language has been viewed. To some cognitive psychologists language has been viewed in terms of its iconic features. Here emphasis is placed on the relationship between the object and its referent. For instance, particular volume and lengthening of sounds has been associated with the expression of particular emotional states. Another example of focusing on iconic aspects of language is in the case of onomatopoeic words; that is, words that in their expression attempt to represent the object referred to.

Finally, we can turn to a third view of language that rarely has been discussed in psychology—namely, the view of language as indexical. As Duranti (1997) suggested: "An index is a sign that identifies an object not because of any similarity or analogy with it, but because of some relationship of contiguity with that object" (p. 209). Indexicals, or deictic terms (originally a Greek term meaning "pointing" or "indexing"), then, are linguistic forms that anchor conversation in relation to the act of speaking. Those adopting an indexical approach to language take a very different methodological stance toward language. Rather than studying one subdomain in isolation (i.e., the lexicon), an indexical approach necessarily examines language in terms of a simultaneous analysis of linguistic forms (either lexical items or grammatical constructions) and communicative functions.

In summary, to argue that language influences the development of mind leaves open many questions about how language is defined. Before turning to some specific proposals, first we consider a second related theme, namely the need to clarify the goals of studying language for various positions on the language–theory of mind connection.

Why Study Language?

Two main answers can be offered to the question: Why study language when examining the development of theory of mind? One reason to study language is that it presents the researcher with a remarkable tool for better understanding mind. A second reason, and one less commonly discussed in developmental psychology circles, is that language can be viewed as a tool for the child. That is, rather than simply viewing language as a tool in the research process, one can simultaneously argue that language provides the child with access to a powerful resource that allows the child new entry into the development of a theory of mind. For instance, as we note later, some have argued that language provides a cognitive resource for representing reality in fundamentally new ways, whereas others have argued that language provides a powerful mechanism in socializing cultural ways of being, feeling, and acting. Although both of these reasons provide important rationales for why researchers might examine language, it is the purpose of this chapter to focus primarily on the first of these. I have opted to do this because this is in keeping with much prior work that has gone on in the area of theory of mind that has examined language development (see, for instance, the discussion in Bartsch & Wellman, 1995, Chapter 2 for an illustration of this position). Although much of my own work has centered around the second way of viewing language, that is, language as mechanism for the child, I do not address this issue here (see Budwig, 1999, 2000a, 2000b, for such a discussion).

A Comparison of Some Approaches

The previous discussion highlights the point that the argument *that* language plays a role in theory of mind development can come in many varieties. We turn now to consider how these approaches differ with regard to the specifics of how they conceive of language and how this impacts on the way they methodologically approach the language–theory of mind interface. We will see that assumptions concerning what domain of language is investigated have significant impact on assumptions about methodological approach. It is hoped that teasing apart these assumptions will pave the way for a consideration of how to better understand the kind of evidence that currently exists and gaps in our understanding.

Semantic Approaches

There have been several studies that have examined a variety of mental-state terms and the path of their entry into the everyday speech of young children (see, for instance, Bartsch & Wellman, 1995; Bretherton & Beeghly, 1982; Dunn, Bretherton, & Munn, 1987; Shatz, Wellman, & Silber, 1983). Bartsch and Wellman's (1995) study is perhaps the most comprehensive to the extent that they examined a variety of English-speaking children and a large variety of lexical vocabulary items. Drawing on the CHILDES database (MacWhinney & Snow, 1985), they focused on the use and development of a range of words referring to both beliefs (*think, know, believe, expect, wonder, dream*) and desire (*want, hope, wish, care, afraid*). In addition to tracking the onset of usage, the authors also were interested in capturing a sense of semantic features associated with such usage. Such features included, for instance, whose beliefs and desires were referred to (*self, other*) and whether the use of such terms actually referred to "genuine references to psychological states" (Bartsch & Wellman, 1995, p. 31). Bartsch and Wellman are quite clear that they are not prepared to provide an answer to the question of the relationship between language and thought by suggesting: "We will make little progress in understanding how theory of mind is acquired unless we investigate more closely how development of theory of mind relates to development of language. Our investigation does not answer these questions, but it does show how language and concepts of mind can be investigated together" (p. 209). Bartsch and Wellman's analysis of language, consistent with several other researchers, involves examination of everyday talk in terms of assessing mental-state verbs in terms of what semantic aspects of their usage reveal about underlying conceptualizations. For them, the real benefit of language is that it provides the researcher with a better (though not perfect) understanding of underlying conceptualizations. "Even though language development does not map onto conceptual development in any strict sense, an analysis of discourse can nonetheless provide an important window onto conception" (p. 17). This view of language as a window is typical of those examining semantic aspects of mental state talk.

Syntactic Approaches

Quite a different view of language and reasons for studying language when considering the development of theory of mind can be found in research focusing on more formal aspects of language. Some researchers (see Astington & Jenkins, 1999; de Villiers, 1995; Tardif & Wellman, 2000) have claimed that growing syntactic ability in children promotes theory of mind development. De Villiers (1995) has argued that the development of complementation provides the mechanism for the child to acquire the representational format considered necessary for false-belief understandings. Similarly, Astington and Jenkins (1999) have argued that the development of syntax allows speakers to represent states other than those that are currently experienced. Astington and Jenkins were a bit more cautious given the observation that children can respond correctly when test sentences make use of complements with particular verbs (*pretend*), but not others (*thinks*). They suggested that although complementation is central, "something more than the acquisition of object complementation is required to explain why children can respond correctly in one case but not in the other" (p. 1318). Their own methodological approach has been to assess children's general language ability through a test that assesses both syntactic and semantic skills. Their findings indicate that children's receptive and expressive scores, based on the test requiring children to respond to questions and pictures, predict later theory of mind performance but not the reverse. In summary then, for Astington and Jenkins, certain syntactic abilities are a necessary but not sufficient component of language that accounts for theory of mind development.

Tardif and Wellman (2000) have highlighted the importance of addressing questions concerning the relationship of syntactic development and the development of theory of mind from a cross-linguistic perspective. They noted for instance that because the morphology and surface syntax of languages such as Mandarin and Cantonese are simpler than English, they can offer important information about whether such typological distinctions lead to different paths of development. Tardif and Wellman's approach is similar to others who study naturally occurring language between children and their caregivers. Examining, for instance, the English equivalent for "knowing that" in Mandarin and Cantonese, Tardif and Wellman reported these forms appear almost a full year earlier in the non-English samples. One possible explanation for this, they claimed, is that Mandarin and Cantonese have easier grammatical solutions to the expression of knowledge verbs given the lack of a complementizer after verbs of knowing. Put differently, English-speaking children's later appearance might be due, in part, to the specifics of English syntax, and not a general cognitive deficit per se.

Although I have noted some important differences in the specifics of the claims researchers examining syntactic aspects of language hold regarding the language–theory of mind interface, they come together in holding similar assumptions about why to study language. Rather than providing the researcher with a window to underlying conceptual categories (as was noted for researchers focusing on semantic aspects of language) the argument is that language plays a causal role in theory of mind development. In studying that causal role, researchers examining syntax have used quite distinct methodologies. Most use experimental paradigms or test assessments of general language abilities, though as we have noted in Tardif and Wellman's work, at times, examination also focuses on an analysis of natural language interactions.

Pragmatic Approaches

The idea that language plays a causal role in the development of theory of mind is not limited to those who focus on semantic or syntactic development. Others who have examined pragmatic aspects of language have also argued for the view that pragmatics is fundamentally linked to theory of mind development. Astington and Jenkins (1999), in summarizing prior work that provides evidence for the connection between pragmatics and theory of mind development, argued that by definition, pragmatics must be related to theory of mind development. They argued: "Pragmatic ability underlies the ability to use and interpret language appropriately in social situations, which depends on keeping track of listeners' and speakers' beliefs and intentions" (p. 1312). Astington and Jenkins cited evidence that general tests of pragmatic abilities have been noted to be related to false-belief task performance in autistic children (see Eisenmajer & Prior, 1991). They also noted evidence that specific pragmatic devices, such as the appropriate use of referential forms, are connected to false belief understanding (Charman & Shmueli-Goetz, 1998).

Along similar lines others have argued that pragmatic aspects of language are related to theory of mind development. Here, though, emphasis shifts from an examination of individual competencies to a view of language as embedded in ongoing interaction. This position is spelled out most clearly by Montgomery (1997), who suggested that an understanding of mind can best be understood in light of Wittgenstein's argument about private language. More specifically, the claim is made that in acquiring a theory of mind, children are learning language games. To this extent, in learning to talk, children are simultaneously learning about mind. Kessler Shaw (1998), in her doctoral dissertation, has empirically tested such a view, and similarly argued that children's initial uses of belief verbs (*think* and *know*) are linked to the initial language games in which they first appear (see Nelson & Kessler Shaw, chapter 2, this volume for further discussion). Methodologically, Kessler Shaw examined several semantic and pragmatic features associated with the uses of the particular mental-state lexical items as they occurred in the natural speech of caregivers and their children. The analyses revealed that the two mental-state verbs were initially distinguished by the children in terms of their conversational function. Although similar to the semantic work reviewed previously to the extent that focus is placed on children's actual language productions, Kessler Shaw (1998) and Nelson and Kessler Shaw (chapter 2, this volume) claimed that language is more than a window for the researcher to tap into underlying categories of mind. Rather, as several adopting a pragmatic approach to language have been noted to argue, it is within actual language practices that children come to collaborate in the construction of an understanding of mind (see Nelson, 1996; Nelson & Kessler Shaw, chapter 2, this volume; and Wootton, 1997).

INDEXICALITY

Language as Indexical

As noted earlier, these views of language, despite some fundamental differences, hold together in their view of language as symbolic. One characteristic of symbolic views is that they focus on one of many layers of language in developing claims about the role of language in theory of mind development. That is, symbolic views typically focus on either syntax, semantic, or pragmatic aspects of language. An alternative way of viewing language comes from indexical approaches. One main difference between symbolic and indexical views is that indexical views consider language in terms of multiple levels with a focus both on language forms and semantic and pragmatic functions. Like the already reviewed work by some who examine pragmatic aspects of language functioning, the idea that language is studied in terms of communicative practices is central. A distinction though is that in indexical approaches, language itself is not only acquired "in" practices, but also plays a fundamental role in the ongoing interpretation and construction of context. This sort of indexical approach to language draws on the work of several recent linguistic anthropologists who have been thinking about issues of language and thought (see, for instance, Duranti, 1997; Gumperz & Levinson, 1996; Hanks, 1996). Hanks (1996) summarized this position as follows:

> Our starting point is the three-way division of language as a semiformal system, communicative activities as semistructured processes, and actors' evaluations of these two (. . .). These evaluations could be called *ideological* in the sense of embodying broader values, beliefs, and (sometimes) self-legitimating attitudes. . . . The three elements come together in "practice," the moment of synthesis. . . . (pp. 230–231)

The point here is not only that language does more than refer to the world; it also suggests that there is a specific linkage between *various* language functions and linguistic forms. Put differently, language forms can be viewed as one way of grammaticalizing routine communicative practices. Ochs (1996) has referred to this as the *indexicality principle*:

> . . . to index is to point to the presence of some entity in the immediate situation at hand. In language, an index is considered to be a linguistic form that performs this function. . . . A linguistic index is usually a structure (e.g., sentential voice, emphatic stress, diminutive affix) that is used variably from one situation to another and becomes conventionally associated with particular situational dimensions such that when the structure is used, the form involves those situational dimensions. (p. 411)

The form–function relationship between indexicals and situational dimensions is not one-to-one but more complex: "It is important to distinguish the range of situational dimensions that a form (set of forms) *potentially* indexes from the range of situational dimensions that form (set of forms) *actually* indexes in a particular instance of use" (Ochs, 1996, p. 418). Indexicals, by providing ways to anchor conversation in relation to the act of speaking, play a pivotal role in constructing meaning. Forms such as personal pronouns (*I, You*), adverbials (*here, now*) and other spatial or temporal terms help in the co-construction of contextual meaning.

Language, according to a practice-based view, focuses both on language forms and functions, but even more so on the indexical power of language. As Duranti (1997) suggested:

> To say that words are indexically related to some "object" or aspect of the world out there means to recognize that words carry with them a power that goes beyond the description and identification of people, objects, properties, and events. It means to work at identifying how language becomes a tool through which our social and cultural world is constantly described, evaluated, and reproduced. (p. 19)

An Indexical Approach to Language Development

As one shifts from viewing language as symbolic and consequently focuses on its role as a linking process between word and object in the world, one simultaneously shifts in how language development is viewed. As many have noted, the examination of language in terms of form–function linkages described previously, opens up the possibility that development can be viewed as something more than the accumulation of new forms, meanings, or functions. An indexical approach views development also in terms of the changing relations between linguistic forms and language functions. To use a form need not imply that such usage is adult-like. Over ontogenetic time, there is a dynamic relationship between language forms and functions. In my prior work and that of others there has been an attempt to examine the changing ways particular linguistic forms (such as pronouns) change in the way they link up with situational meanings (see Budwig, 1995, for review). Borrowing from Werner and Kaplan's (1963/1984) discussion of the orthogenetic principle, one can argue that children are not only adding *new* and *more* vocabulary and syntax, but rather that old forms are given new functions and old functions are related to new forms (see also Bamberg, Budwig, & Kaplan, 1991; Berman & Slobin, 1994; Slobin, 1985, for further discussion).

The suggestion here regarding language is similar to one that has recently been made for theory of mind development (see, for instance, Gopnik, Slaughter, & Meltzoff, 1994), namely that such development is *protracted* (see also Nelson, 1996, Nelson & Kessler Shaw, chapter 2, this volume). One implication of this is the following: One cannot assume that early use of a form carries with it adult meaning. This implies the need to examine more than either the frequency or presence or absence of a form, and highlights the need to carefully examine the interrelationship between closely related forms and the functions they serve as parts of linguistic systems.

IMPLICATIONS FOR CONNECTION BETWEEN LANGUAGE AND THE STUDY OF THEORY OF MIND

Let me turn now to discuss the question: What are the implications of adopting an indexical approach to language for the study of theory of mind? I think there are multiple answers to this question but for now I focus on two. First, shifting to an indexical approach brings into relief the importance of looking not only at individual levels of language functioning (i.e., syntax, semantics, or pragmatics), but also at the consequences of examining the changing relationships between these distinct levels. One implication of this is methodological. Research examining the connection between language and theory of mind would focus on the examination of a wider range of forms including not only mental-state terms, but also potentially a variety of nonlexical forms such as deictic terms (pronouns) and voice alternations (active vs. passive construction usage). In addition, once one moves beyond the examination of forms, one includes examination of the semantic and pragmatic features co-occurring with such forms (see Budwig & Bamberg, 1996).

The second theme already raised has to do with a particular view of development. Here focus shifts away from age of onset of particular words to an examination of changes in the ways forms and functions are related over ontogenetic time. A second theme then involves the examination of the protracted nature of development that implies an emphasis on the changing relationship between forms and functions of the entire linguistic system. Children are not assumed to be passively adapting to an adult system.

We turn now to examine two illustrations of this indexical-developmental point of view, first by examining forms such as desire talk terms that have been studied by theory of mind researchers, and second by looking at some other places children seem to creatively mark similar notions with alternative linguistic devices.[1]

Mental State Terms From An Indexical-Developmental Perspective

I first turn to an analysis of how language is examined when it comes to the link between mental state desire terms such as *want* and theory of mind development. Data reported here stem from a study of 6 American children growing up in Northern California who ranged between the ages of 18 and 36 months and who were just beginning to combine multi-word utterances at the onset of the study. The children were videotaped for approximately 45 minutes twice a month (once with peers and once with mothers) for a 4-month period. The data were collected originally as part of a larger study of the early phases of children's grammatical development (see Budwig, 1989, 1995). Our analysis consisted of isolating all instances of desire talk forms—for now I only refer to the most frequently used form *want*—and coding these according to semantic, pragmatic, and discourse features. For the present purposes, I summarize here just a few

---

[1]I should note that my typical method of analysis makes use of crosslinguistic and culturally based comparisons but for our present purposes, I refer now to simply the English data patterns—though I am currently working with German and Hindi samples (see, for instance, Budwig, 2000b).

intriguing patterns found in our analyses of longitudinal differences and analyses focusing on differences in caregivers' and children's use of the mental state term *want* (see Budwig, Moissinac, & Smith, 2000; Moissinac & Budwig, 2000, for a more complete discussion).

General Characteristics of Children's and Caregivers' Desire Talk

The starting point of our analysis, as with any functional analysis, focuses on the relationship between forms, meanings and functions in the speech of the children and caregivers. After a brief description of some generalizations about children's and caregivers' systems, we turn to discuss some of the specific longitudinal findings (see Budwig, Moissinac, & Smith, 2000 for further details). Characteristic of indexical approaches, our analyses looked at the interface between particular desire forms, and how they linked up with particular semantic and pragmatic features of the utterances in which they were embedded. For instance, the use of desire talk verbs were examined in relationship to specific semantic characteristics such as who was the experiencer of the desire expressed (i.e., the child, the caregiver/others, or joint desire). In addition, desire talk verbs were examined in light of pragmatic aspects of how the utterance containing the desire term functioned (i.e., as an assertion, clarification, permission request, etc.). In examining caregiver and child discourse, emphasis was not on whether or not such talk occurred, but rather on the nature of the interface between language forms, meanings, and functions over developmental time.

In a preliminary analysis, an assessment was made of how frequently desire talk took place. Looking first at a comparison of the frequency of children's and caregivers' use of the term *want* we find that the two groups of speakers use them almost equally (caregivers had 236 uses across the study, whereas their children used the form 218 times). Both groups also used the term *want* similarly at the semantic level. When using *want* both children and their caregivers tended to use it in conjunction with a reference to the child's desire. That is, 90% of all children's uses were to their own desires, whereas 87% of all caregivers' uses involved references to their child's desires as well. Reference by both caregivers and their children to the caregivers' desires was quite infrequent, making up only 4% of all desire talk.

The real difference in how children and their caregivers used desire talk concerned the pragmatic functions of such talk. A complete listing of coding categories and their definitions can be found in the Appendix. For present purposes, it is primarily important to understand the most general levels of distinction. For instance, at the pragmatic level of analysis attention has been paid to whether desire talk is embedded within assertions, permission requests, clarification routines, and the like. Our analysis reveals that the majority of children's desire talk utterances functioned as action assertions. That is, children used desire talk in ongoing events in conjunction with actions that led to fulfillment of their desires. The next two most frequent functions of children's desire talk were permission requests and internal state assertions. Action assertions were distinguished from internal state assertions in that with action assertions the speaker immediately acts on the desire asserted, whereas with internal state assertions the child asserts the desire but no action on the part of the speaker follows. Permission requests involved using desire talk to seek permission to fulfill their own desire.

We also examined caregivers' desire talk in terms of communicative function. In contrast to the children, the caregivers rarely used assertions at all. In fact, active assertions and internal state assertions only made up a combined amount of 16% of all instances of desire talk. How then did caregivers' desire talk function? Two particularly frequent speech functions of caregivers' desire talk included inquiries (33%) and permission requests (22%), and clarifications made up 11% of all desire talk.

In summary, there was little overlap between the function of caregivers' and children's desire talk. Given the semantic characteristics noted for caregivers' and children's desire talk (i.e., the caregivers' desire talk focuses on the child, whereas the focus of the children's desire talk also focused on themselves) this should hardly seem surprising. Caregivers, with their focus on their children's desires, were more likely to inquire about them and clarify them. The children, more focused on expressing their own desires, were more likely to use assertions. Our general findings suggest that although both children and caregivers cluster the use of desire talk with particular semantic meanings and pragmatic functions, each group of speakers works with clusterings that meet their own communicative needs.

The following example illustrates the basic patterning of caregivers using *want* to refer to their children's desires in utterances functioning as inquiries, whereas the children used this term to refer to their own desires in assertions.

Example 1: Grice (20 months) and her mom are playing tea party.
a. Mom: mmm. It's very good.
b. Grice: chocolate.
c. Mom: It's chocolate tea?
d. Grice: yeah.
e. Grice: I (inaudible) some more.

f. Mom: You *want* me to pour some? → INQUIRY

g. Grice: Yeah (pause) in my cup.

h. Mom: mmm.

i. Grice: I *want* some. → ASSERTION

(pause)

j. Grice: Pour some in my cup.

k. Mom: (pretends to pour tea).

Note, for instance, how in this example in line 1e, the child makes a general request to her mother that her mother cannot quite understand. Her mother follows this up in in the next line by inquiring, which is then affirmed by the child. A few moments later, after both have been pretending to drink tea, the child again asserts her desire (see line 1i). Such uses are characteristic of the two speakers. When caregivers tended to talk about desires, not only was it the desire of their child, but also typically in sequences where they had trouble interpreting what the child wanted. Language was used in an attempt to clarify or inquire about the nature of the child's expressed desire. In contrast, the children's desire talk typically focused not only on their own desires, but also in the context of asserting something about them. Although these patterns describe the overall patterns of caregiver and children's desire talk, they say little about how individual caregivers' and children's systems change over developmental time. We turn now to examine some of the specific longitudinal findings concerning how the children's and caregivers' use changed over longitudinal time.

Longitudinal Characteristics of Children's and Caregivers' Desire Talk

Younger Versus Older Children. In examining the children's use of the desire term *want* we noted that the children underwent a shift in usage about the time they begin using multi-word utterances of over three morphological units (mean length of utterance greater than 3). Although there were some interesting differences in the frequency of the use of *want* (i.e., the frequency went down over time) the most interesting differences were in the changing set of semantic meaning and pragmatic function linkages children created.

Early on—roughly just before the children were 2 and before they moved to a stage of mean length of utterance (MLU in morphemes) over 3—the children used *want* to refer semantically to their own desire to obtain objects. In many of these cases it was a caregiver who acted instrumentally to fulfill the child's desires. In this sense, the dyad had worked out a routine in which the child asserted a state and the caregiver then worked to fulfill that desire. If the caregiver could not understand, which often was the case, then the caregiver would proceed to inquire about the child's desires until mutual understanding had been achieved. In this sense, many of the children's assertions about desire with *want* functioned pragmatically as requests:

> *Example 2:* Jeffrey (30 months, MLU 2.82) and Mom are playing with blocks.
> Jeffrey: My want something → ASSERTION
> Mom: Which — what would you like? . . . → INQUIRY
>   Would you like the red block? → INQUIRY

This usage contrasts with the later sessions when the children alter the patterning of form, meaning, and function. Although the children continue to primarily refer to their own desires, these desires now tend to be about *performing actions* and it actually is the child who goes ahead and fulfills the desire. As Example 3 illustrates, these utterances are not requests for the mother to act as an instrument to obtain goods for the child. Rather the child recognizes that she or he can act to realize her own desires, but instead the utterance functions to *seek permission.*

> *Example 3:* Jeffrey (33 months, MLU 3.68) and Mom.
> Jeffrey: What's this?
> Mom: That's a little microphone.
> Jeffrey: I wanna talk in it.   (Permission Request)
> Mom: Okay.
> Jeffrey: (talks into microphone)

The basic change that we found in the use of *want* in the usages that came later in the longitudinal study was not one of a form not being used to a phase of regular usage, as the form *want* was used by all children from the earliest video recordings. Rather the major changes concerned the semantic and pragmatic contexts in which this form occurred. Although across all sessions the children were primarily concerned with their own desires, over time there was a shift from the caregiver fulfilling the desire referred to, to the child at times acting to bring about change. In addition, there was a subtle shift in terms of what was being desired in the desire talk. Early on, the child desired objects that were unavailable or inaccessible to the child; over time there was a shift on the part of the child to also verbalize desires to perform actions. The significance of this transition becomes clarified when we simultaneously consider pragmatic changes that have taken place.

At the onset of the study, children's early uses of *want* coincided with assertions about desires, whereas later on *want* often functioned to seek permission. What is intriguing about this is that at the later point in development the children had the ability to act on their desires but first chose to verbalize those desires with their caregiver. That is, the child could have physically carried out the action desired but turned first to the caregiver to be sure this was sanctioned. What is most interesting about such cases is that they indicate that the children have a burgeoning awareness that desire alone is not enough to motivate human action. The children have come to recognize the social connectedness of action as well.

***Mothers' Versus Children's Use of* Want.** We can turn now to consider how the children's mothers used *want* and to discuss the connection between the children's and mothers' uses of this term. Mothers used *want* less frequently over time just like their children. And also like their children, across the timeframe of the study, caregivers also changed the ways desire verbs linked up with semantic and pragmatic notions. Nevertheless, although changes could be found, the linkages differed in important ways from those used by the children. Early on the moms tended, like their children, to focus exclusively on the child's *wants*. Their usage primarily functioned as *clarifications*:

Example 4: Jeffrey (31 months, MLU 3.52) and Mom.
Child: My build their house.
Mom: You *wanna* build their house?

Example 5: Megan (21 months, MLU 2.30) and Mom.
Child: My see the fireman.
Mom: You *wanna* what?
Child: My see the fireman.
Mom: You *wanna* see the fireman?
Child: Yeah.

Later on the mothers' role shifts from one of *providing clarification* to one of *suggesting* or *requesting permission* to act in particular ways. At the point of this shift the children have begun using conventional *want* statements rather than the sort of "*My* + action verb" statements of desire illustrated in Examples 4 and 5, which led the mother to query for clarification. That is, the shift away from mothers using *want* in clarification queries is in part motivated by the fact that the mothers are better able to interpret the children's expression of desire. Interestingly, at the later points in time, the mothers' use of *want* appears in scenes in which the children seem unfocused or are disengaged from playing with the toys. It is at these junctures that the mothers often provide suggests through the use of *want* queries:

> *Example 6:* Jeffrey (33 months MLU 3.68) and Mom.
> (Child has been adjusting blocks and muttering to himself)
> Child: wait wait I haft — no xx xx.
> Mom: You wanna build a little house to live in?
> Child: Yeah.
> (Mom and Child start to build house)
> Mom: You wanna live in this little house?
> Child: Yeah.

At times the mothers also use *want* in permission requests in which they not only seek permission but also are simultaneously making suggestions for how the child might proceed with the play:

> *Example 7:* Megan (23 months, MLU 2.58) and Mom playing with blocks.
> Mom: Do you want me to get you red triangles or . . .

These conversational uses often are not particularly tied to the children's desires at all. That is, there is no reason to believe that the mother's permission request in Example 7 is formulated in response to a sense that that is what the child desires. In this sense, the use of desire talk refocuses the dialogue, rather than being used to mirror some expressed desire on the part of the child.

Summary

To summarize, the findings reviewed here indicate that by the earliest transcripts (18 months) all children were able to use the mental state term *want*. As is noted in Examples 4 and 5, the children did not always use this terms in ways adults might have (see following discussion for an account of this). At the same time, it is important to note that the developmental changes found were not ones of the development of a new form, and in fact there is evidence that over the course of the longitudinal study the children's use of *want* actually decreased as they added new and related vocabulary items. What did change with development for the children was the range of pragmatic and semantic factors associated with the use of *want*.

Early on, the primary uses of *want* by the children were instrumental: Upon uttering a desire the caregiver acted to help the child gain access to objects or the caregiver provided a rationale to the child for why this was not possible. Later on, the children began using *want* with action verbs in utterances that functioned to gain permission to act in certain ways. As the children turned from the simple expression of *want* + object to include *want* + action utterances, a variation was found in form selection. *Want* was used with mention of objects and the variant *wanna* was used with utterances that talked about actions. This development suggests subtle changes in the recognition that desire alone often is not enough to motivate human action. That is, early on the child's statements of desire led others to act on their own behalf. As the children developed, they often had the physical capabilities to act on their desires, but came to realize that in some cases they needed to first obtain social permission.

The issue of what led the children to develop these systems cannot be fully answered. The caregivers early on could be said to help their children come to understand conventional ways of expressing desire through clarification routines. As is illustrated in Examples 4 and 5, the mothers' recasts highlight alternative ways for her child to make desires known. The later uses of *want* by the caregivers are more confusing to think about. The mothers typically appealed to the children's desires, but actually these could best be viewed as the caregivers' own desires disguised as those of their children's. The longitudinal data don't seem to provide any evidence that the children were confused by such usage. Indeed we see the children using desire verbs with permission requests themselves at around the same time the caregivers use them with permission requests as well.

In summary, research examining language from an indexical perspective strives to examine the ways children and caregivers link forms, meanings, and functions over developmental time. An argument has been made that from the start, children's usage is inextricably tied to ongoing dialogue, much like what was suggested earlier in our review of prior work on language games (see Montgomery, 1997; Nelson & Kessler Shaw, chapter 2, this volume; Wootton, 1997). But note that a subtle difference between the indexical approach and the research reviewed earlier on pragmatics, is the idea that all uses of desire talk, not just the children's, are what could be referred to as conversational. That is, rather than viewing development as moving from conversational uses of desire talk to desire talk that refers to genuine psychological reference, from an indexical perspective, all speakers—both caregivers and children alike—are quite tied to sense-making activities that are conversationally tied. Only with further crosslinguistic and cultural comparisons will we be in a better position to figure out the range of factors influencing the particular constellations of caregivers and their children (see Moissinac & Budwig, 2000; Tardif & Wellman, 2000).

Nonlexical Indexes of Desire Talk

I turn now to a second way to approach the connection between language and theory of mind from an indexical perspective. Although most theory of mind research has examined language in terms of words or lexical development, I have found that an examination of alternative linguistic means such as the early and creative use of pronominal forms and voice contrasts (such as shifting from active syntax to either the use of middle or passive constructions) also sheds light on theory of mind issues. Although such uses, at first glance, seem to be part of grammatical development and therefore not clearly linked to theory of mind development, the argument made here is that the use of such linguistic devices can be equally revealing about important milestones in children's development of an understanding of mind (see Wootton, 1997 for a similar discussion of request forms).

Pronominal Reference

In prior work (Budwig, 1989, 1995) I have extensively studied early errors in pronominal usage in the longitudinal sample already described based on the six children raised in Berkeley. The children were noted to creatively contrast between the use of a variety of pronominal forms in subject position. Briefly let me illustrate this difference between two forms: *I* versus *My*. Early on, between the ages of roughly 1½ and 2½ years of age the children alternated between these two forms to mark a distinction between self as experiencer (*I want nuts, I like peas*) and self as agent (*My build the tower, My cracked the eggs*). They also distinguished more refined notions of experience to the extent that both *I* and *My* could appear with mental state verbs such as *want*. Although the utterances *I want the nut* and *My want the nut* seem almost identical, a functionalist analysis revealed that they occurred at distinct conversational junctures. Instances like *I want the nut* were said as a child was en route to picking up a nut; it was a sort of informative statement made by one child to her interlocutor to provide a motive for her departure from the play table. That is, the utterance functioned to inform her partner that she was picking up a nut that had fallen. In contrast, *My want the nut* was uttered by the child as a request for action to her mother when she wanted to get an attractive nut out of a pill bottle with a safety cap top she could not operate. Children seemed to be distinguishing between asserting something about a desire (matching an ongoing state) and attempts to invoke desire to bring about change. Example 8 (as well as the children's productions in Examples 4 and 5) illustrate this contrast:

> *Example 8:* Megan (20 months, MLU 2.07) and Mom playing with manipulative toys.
> Child: *I* want that one (lifting childproof container with nut inside).
> Mom: Oh you want that one, okay.
> Child: (tries to open container, fails) *My* open that!
> Mom: What?
> Child: *My* open that, mommy (handing container to mom).
> Mom: Wanna open that?
> Child: Yeah.
> Mom: (opens container).

Note, for instance, that in her first utterance Megan appears to simply be stating her desire and goes ahead to try to obtain a nut that is inside a childproof container amidst some manipulative toys. After her attempts to open the container fail, she switches to the utterance "*My open that,*" and when her mother doesn't understand, Megan hands the container to her mother. Her mother's question of whether she wants her mom to open it (typical of the caregivers' early clarifying uses of *want* described previously) is responded to affirmatively and the mother complies.

Functional analyses revealed that at the time before the children regularly referred to others, they "borrowed" first person pronominal forms to situate themselves differently with regard to their perspective on their role in ongoing action frames. In addition to using *I* and *My*, the children also drew on a variety of other first person reference forms to mark other ways to situate self including affected agency through the use of *Me*, and use of their own name primarily in the context of referring to self in depictions without focus on intentional stance.

As I have noted in detail elsewhere, the children's systematic use of pronominal forms continued for several months and only gradually faded into a system more similar to adult-like usage (Budwig, 1995). Although there were some individual differences in the ways the children went about reconfiguring their pronominal systems, an overall pattern noticed was one of increasing differentiation and hierarchical integration. Two patterns are illustrated in Fig. 3.1 and Fig. 3.2.

Figure 3.1 depicts Megan's system across four months of longitudinal study. Megan's solution was quite straightforward. She began in Month I by differentiating between three different self-reference forms (two pronominal forms and one nominal form), each of which was used with a specific cluster of semantic and pragmatic notions. During Months II and III

Month I

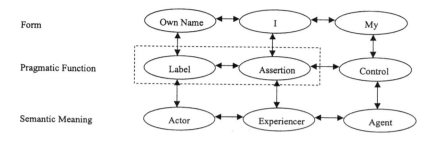

Month II & III

Month IV

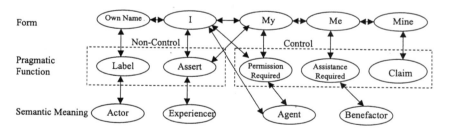

FIG. 3.1. Megan.

Megan referred to herself only in assertions about self as experiencer. She simply avoided the other forms and their corresponding functions. In Month IV several self-reference forms were used, but now with a variety of functions.

Jeffrey created a second type of solution. As is illustrated in Fig. 3.2, Jeffrey also began in Month I with a fairly clean system of one-to-one mapping between form and functions. But for Jeffrey, in contrast to Megan, the process by which *I* began being used multifunctionally involved a protracted set of interim solutions. In Month II, Jeffrey has arrived at a new functional contrast for *I* and *My*. *My* continues to be used in subject posi-

Month I

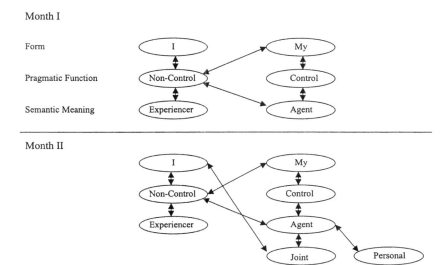

Month II

Month III

Identical to Month II except WE replaces the functions of MY and MY used as quasi-modal

Month IV

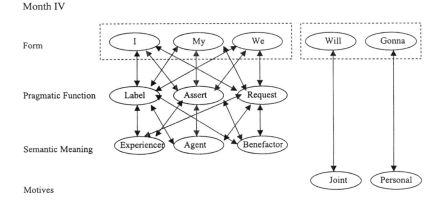

FIG. 3.2. Jeffrey.

tion in ways that deviate from adult usage, but the contrast now circles around the issue of motivation for action rather than control per se. If the motive for the action was personal desire, Jeffrey employed *My*, but if the motive was an interpersonal one based on a prior joint agreement, he switched to *I*. By Month III, Jeffrey viewed *My* as being more similar to modal forms. For instance, Jeffrey begins to say things like "I m'ant to build a tower." At this time, Jeffrey also includes new pronominal contrasts into the system replacing the *I/My* distinction found in Month II with the distinction between *I* and *We*. By Month IV, the distinction Jeffrey draws between personal and joint motivations is marked with modal forms, and *I*, *My*, and *We* are used multifunctionally (see also Budwig, 1990a). Thus we see for Jeffrey an extremely protracted period of adding new forms of self-reference, reorganizing the functional clusters associated with previously used forms, and adding new forms other than self-reference forms into the system to mark functions previously covered by pronominal forms.

Regardless of the particulars, all the children in the study shared some overlap in the ways they moved from the special use of pronominal forms to adult-like usage. They began with relatively global, contextually restricted uses of forms and moved toward solutions involving hierarchical integration and differentiation. Not only did all the children enter a wider range of communicative situations and need to express an increasingly varied set of communicative functions, but they also drew on a great variety of linguistic resources.

Voice Contrasts

In my most recent work I have been examining the development of voice shifts and the situational contexts in which they appear. What this involves is examining the difference between utterances like:

I spilled the juice	(Active)
The juice spilled	(Middle)
The juice got/was spilled (by x)	(Passive)

My crosslinguistic work reveals that around the age of 2½, just as children begin using *want* to seek permission, they also begin employing these sort of voice contrasts to index distinct stances on the ongoing context (see Budwig, 1990b; Budwig, Stein, & O'Brien, 2001). Whereas there is a clear preference (as in adult talk) for active voice, the shifts to passives and middles are intriguing. The American children use middles for several months in just one activity context, one that I have summarized as "resistance from the environment." That is, they appear in contexts when the child has announced particular desires (e.g. *I wanna build the tower*) and then the desire is somehow blocked. It is at these junctures of goal blocking that the middles appear. For instance, as the child attempts to clip on a microphone he wishes to wear and this fails he uses the middle: "*It came off again.*" As another child announces her desire to open the door of a toy helicopter and is unable to do this, she switches to the middle and utters "*The doors won't open.*" And when attempting to build a tall block tower which fails several children comment with a middle "*That fell over.*"

Whereas at first glance focus on voice contrasts may appear to have little to do with desire talk, I find them to be particularly relevant. Their onset of use is just around the time when these same children begin using *want* in permission requests and when they start using *We* as a marker that highlights actions that are not carried out due to personal desire per se (see Budwig, 1990a, for discussion). The middles mark action sequences that fail despite desires. Taken together, these findings provide converging evidence for intriguing developments in how children complexify the relation between desire and action. Such findings suggest that children recognize that desire is not sufficient to bring about change.

Summary

In the last section, I hope to have made the point that careful attention to aspects of language other than mental state terms can be productive for a better understanding of the connection between language and theory of mind development. What both the lexical analyses, as well as the analyses of pronominal and voice contrasts share, is simultaneous focus on multiple levels of language. In each instance, not only were particular words or constructions in focus, but also semantic and pragmatic aspects of such usage were considered.

Simultaneously, I have illustrated that language development itself undergoes subtle and important developmental shifts. This suggests the importance of going beyond measures of "earliest" usage or frequency and moving toward more fine-grained analyses of the relationships between forms and context over longitudinal time.

In particular, I have argued that once one begins to examine multiple layers of language simultaneously (i.e., forms, meanings, and functions), one recognizes some overall patternings best accounted for in terms of Werner and Kaplan's discussion of the orthogenetic principles and Slobin's crosslinguistic support for the idea that old forms replace new functions and new forms replace old functions. This complexifies any discussion of the mechanisms pushing understanding of mind, and in particular, the specific links between language, cognition, and development—a theme to which we return in the final section of this chapter.

CONCLUDING COMMENTS

In this chapter, I have outlined a developmental-functionalist approach suggesting the importance of looking at the use of linguistic forms embedded in social practices. I have attempted to illustrate that careful examination of the relation between linguistic forms and semantic and pragmatic features that co-occur with their usage can be a powerful analytic tool for the theory of mind researcher. The view of language that I have been forwarding here is somewhat different than that typically emphasized in developmental research. As I argued earlier, developmental psychologists have focused primarily on the symbolic aspect of language, that is language as representation means. Although representation is clearly an important function of language, I have emphasized the importance of looking at language in terms of indexicality (see also Budwig, Wertsch, & Užgiris, 2000). I have argued here that focusing on language as indexical provides the researcher with an important research tool including analysis of forms other than words "representing mind." I have made the argument elsewhere (Budwig, 1998, 1999) that indexicals not only provide an important tool for the researcher, but simultaneously provide the child a powerful means of socialization. I do not elaborate on this point here, however, my sense is that burgeoning work in the area of language socialization could well be integrated in intriguing ways into developmental work focusing on theory of mind.

A second point I have attempted to make in this chapter is that in examining the relationship between language and theory of mind, we must keep in mind that just as theory of mind has a protracted development, so too does language. Therefore, when examining language forms we must be careful not to assume that early use is equivalent to adult usage. At the same time, children's creative uses and developmental changes in the relationship between various forms and functions provide an excellent resource for better understanding the development of a theory of mind.

In concluding, I would like to return to the issue of the role of language in children's developing understanding of mind. I, like many others, have proposed that language can be viewed as more than a consequence of prior developed cognitive categories. Nevertheless, the particular view of language and the particular view of development lead to some alternative suggestions about how that relationship is best considered. Two that I consider here include (a) the grammaticalization of action, and (b) means–ends relations directing the organism toward increasing differentiation and hierarchical integration.

One central claim about the language–thought relationship is that it is a dynamic one. Following Humboldt's discussion of language as energia (energy, activity) that gives expression to thought emphasizes the idea that the relationship is bidirectional. On the one hand, language is a sort of map of how a speaker apprehends the world. It is one of many interpretations and to this extent plays a dynamic role in contributing to the development of worldview. Similarly, Wootton (1997) has argued that language, which he viewed as sequentially organized patterns of local understandings, plays a significant role in meaning-making:

> In these ways, for the child, the sequential context comes to be the bearer of a new order of information, information that permits more finely tuned forms of calibration with the views of her co-participant. The child's actions can now become contextualized along lines that are commensurate in precise ways, with the understandings which prevail in the local culture to which she is being exposed. (p. 9)

Both within and across utterances, language plays a dynamic role in the build-up of thought activity.

At the same time, I have noted that individuals bring to dialogue a propensity to use symbolic means for communicative ends. Here the bidirectional relation is more immediate. As noted earlier in discussing Werner and Kaplan's view of the orthogenetic principle, children from the start interpret their worlds in terms of certain "formula-like schemata" imposing certain action-models that guide the early development of symbol usage. The imposition of these schemata, which Slobin (1985) and others have shown to be a universal property of early language development (see Budwig, 1995, for review) remind us that any discussion of the role of language on thought must account for the inextricable linkage of conceptualization and language.

In summary, like others in this volume, I have argued that linguistic symbolization plays a fundamental role in concept development. Its role must be viewed, though, both as dynamic and bidirectional. Clearly, developments in language as a system provide important tools for thought. Likewise, development of language as a system of forms, meanings, and function pairings allows for developments in communicative interactions that themselves have been said to impact on conceptual development. Studying the intricate relations of language viewed in this way surely will provide a better view of the complex process involved in the ontogenetic development of an understanding of mind.

ACKNOWLEDGMENTS

I would like to thank Eric Amsel and Jim Byrnes for helpful feedback on an earlier draft of this manuscript. I have also benefited from ongoing discussions with members of the SCLD LIPS research group at Clark University. The chapter draws on studies that were conducted in collaboration with several undergraduate and graduate students, including Sara Curtin-Mosher, Melissa Smith, Luke Moissinac, and Martha Pinet. Joyce Lee provided valuable technical assistance for which I am most grateful.

APPENDIX

Pragmatic Coding

Active Assertion: Speaker asserts a desire and acts on it. This is not limited to actions that realize the desire, but also to actions that emphasize the speaker's desire or those that point in the direction of desire fulfillment.

Internal State Assertion: Speaker states desire without acting on it. This differs from an active assertion in that the speaker remains passive and waits for her interlocutor to act to fulfill the stated desire.

Clarification: Speaker reaffirms the desire or other.

Permission: Speaker seeks permission to fulfill her own or her interlocutor's desire.

Inquiry: Speaker acts on own desire to inquire about other's desire concerning an object or action in the form of a question, without seeking permission.

Invitation: Speaker invites other to co-participate in action.

Objection: Speaker protests/objects to other's desire/action.

Suggestion: Speaker suggests an action to her interlocutor. This is usually in statement form but occasionally takes the form of a question.

Other Directive: A directive that does not fit into above.

Multifunctional Act: Any combination of above.

Uncodable: Utterances that cannot be interpreted and pretend talk.

REFERENCES

Astington, J., & Jenkins, J. (1999). A longitudinal study of the relation between language and theory-of-mind development. *Developmental Psychology, 35*, 1131–1320.

Bamberg, M., Budwig, N., & Kaplan, B. (1991). A developmental approach to language acquisition: Two case studies. *First Language, 11*(31), 1–5.

Bartsch, K., & Wellman, H. (1995). *Children talk about the mind.* New York: Oxford University Press.

Berman, R., & Slobin, D. (Eds.). (1994). *Relating events in narrative: A crosslinguistic developmental study.* Hillsdale, NJ: Lawrence Erlbaum Associates.

Bretherton, I., & Beeghly, M. (1982). Talking about internal states: The acquisition of an explicit theory of mind. *Developmental Psychology, 6*, 906–921.

Budwig, N. (1989). The linguistic marking of agentivity and control in child language. *Journal of Child Language, 16*(2), 262–284.

Budwig, N. (1990a). A functional approach to the acquisition of personal pronouns. In G. Conti-Ramsden & C. Snow (Eds.), *Children's language, 7* (pp. 121–145). Hillsdale, NJ: Lawrence Erlbaum Associates.

Budwig, N. (1990b). The linguistic marking of non-prototypical agency: An exploration into children's use of passives. *Linguistics, 28*(6), 1221–1252.

Budwig, N. (1995). *A developmental-functionalist approach to child language.* Mahwah, NJ: Lawrence Erlbaum Associates.

Budwig, N. (1998). Buehler's legacy: Full circle and ahead. *From Past to Future, 1*, 35–64.

Budwig, N. (1999). The contribution of language to the study of mind: A tool for researchers and children. *Human Development, 42*, 362–368.

Budwig, N. (2000a). Language and the construction of self: Linking forms and functions across development. In N. Budwig, I. Č. Užgiris, & J. Wertsch (Eds.), *Communication: An arena of development* (pp. 195–214). Greenwich, CT: Ablex.

Budwig, N. (2000b). Language, practice, and the construction of personhood. *Theory & Psychology, 10*(6), 769–786.

Budwig, N., & Bamberg, M. (1996). Language and its role in understanding intentional relations: Research tool or mechanism of development? Commentary on: J. Barresi & C. Moore, Intentional relations and social understanding. *Behavior and Brain Sciences, 19*, 125–126.

Budwig, N., Moissinac, L., & Smith, M. (2000, June). *How literal is desire talk in two-year-olds interactions with their caregivers?: A comparative analysis of German and American dyads.* Paper presented at the Seventh International Pragmatics Conference, Budapest, Hungary.

Budwig, N., Stein, S., & O'Brien, C. (2001). Non-agent subjects in early child language: A crosslinguistic comparison. In K. Nelson, A. Aksu, & C. Johnson (Eds.), *Children's language, Vol. 11* (pp. 49–67). Mahwah, NJ: Lawrence Erlbaum Associates.

Budwig, N., Wertsch, J. V., & Užgiris, I. (2000). Communication, meaning and development: Inter-disciplinary perspectives. In N. Budwig, I. Užgiris, & J. Wertsch (Eds.), *Communication: An arena of development* (pp. 1–14). Greenwich, CT: Ablex.

Charman, T., & Shmueli-Goetz, Y. (1998). The relationship between theory of mind, language ability and narrative discourse: An experimental study. *Cahiers de Psychologie Cognitive [Current Psychology of Cognition], 17*, 245–271.

Cutting, A., & Dunn, J. (1999). Theory of mind, emotion understanding, language, and family background: Individual differences and interactions. *Child Development, 70*, 853–865.

de Villiers, J. (1995, April). *Steps in the mastery of sentence complements.* Paper presented at the biennial meeting of the Society for Research in Child Development, Indianapolis, IN.

Dunn, J., Bretherton, I., & Munn, P. (1987). Conversations about feeling states between mothers and their young children. *Developmental Psychology, 23*(1), 132–139.

Duranti, A. (1997). *Linguistic anthropology.* Cambridge, England: Cambridge University Press.

Eisenmajer, R., & Prior, M. (1991). Cognitive linguistic correlates of 'theory of mind' ability in autistic children. *British Journal of Developmental Psychology, 9*, 351–364.

Gopnik, A., Slaughter, V., & Meltzoff, A. (1994). Changing your views: How understanding visual perception can lead to a new theory of the mind. In C. Lewis & P. Mitchell (Eds.), *Children's early understanding of mind: Origins and development* (pp. 157–181). Hillsdale, NJ: Lawrence Erlbaum Associates.

Gumperz, J., & Levinson, S. (Eds.). (1996). *Rethinking linguistic relativity.* Cambridge, England: Cambridge University Press.

Hanks, W. (1996). *Language and communicative practices.* Boulder, CO: Westview Press.

Jenkins, J., & Astington, J. (1996). Cognitive factors and family structure associated with theory of mind development in young children. *Developmental Psychology, 32,* 70–78.

Kessler Shaw, F. (1998). *The development of the meanings of think and know through conversation.* Unpublished doctoral dissertation, City University of New York.

MacWhinney, B., & Snow, C. (1985). The child language data exchange system. *Journal of Child Language, 12,* 271–296.

Moissinac, L., & Budwig, N. (2000). The development of desire terms in early child German. *Psychology of Language and Communication, 4*(1), 5–25.

Montgomery, D. (1997). Wittgenstein's private language argument and children's understanding of mind. *Developmental Review, 17,* 291–320.

Nelson, K. (1996). *Language in cognitive development: Emergence of the mediated mind.* Cambridge, England: Cambridge University Press.

Ochs, E. (1996). Linguistic resources for socializing humanity. In J. Gumperz & S. Levinson (Eds.), *Rethinking linguistic relativity* (pp. 407–437). Cambridge, England: Cambridge University Press.

Peirce, C. (1940). Logic as semiotic: The theory of signs. In J. Buchler (Ed.), *Philosophical writings of Peirce: Selected writings.* London: Routledge & Kegan Paul.

Saussure, F. de (1959). *Course in general linguistics* (trans. W. Baskin). New York: McGraw-Hill.

Shatz, M., Wellman, H. M., & Silber, S. (1983). The acquisition of mental verbs: A systematic investigation of the first reference to mental state. *Cognition, 14,* 301–321.

Slobin, D. (1985). Crosslinguistic evidence for the language-making capacity. In D. I. Slobin (Ed.), *The crosslinguistic study of language acquisition* (Vol. 2, pp. 1157–1256). Hillsdale, NJ: Lawrence Erlbaum Associates.

Tardif, T., & Wellman, H. M. (2000). Acquisition of mental state language in Mandarin- and Cantonese-speaking children. *Developmental Psychology, 36*(1), 25–43.

Werner, H., & Kaplan, B. (1984). *Symbol formation.* Hillsdale, NJ: Lawrence Erlbaum Associates. (Original work published in 1963. New York: Wiley)

Wootton, A. (1997). *Interaction and the development of mind.* Cambridge, England: Cambridge University Press.

Chapter 4

Relational Language and Relational Thought

Dedre Gentner
Jeffrey Loewenstein
Northwestern University

Human cognitive abilities are remarkable. We easily go beyond what is perceptually available to reason about abstract systems. Our cognitive ability to adapt to a vast range of environments, and even to alter our environment to suit our desires, has given our species so great an advantage over other mammals that we are now poised to exterminate most of our former predators, and must use our ingenuity to preserve a few. Indeed, for many theorists, the sophistication of adult human reasoning defies any explanation based on learning.

How do we get so smart? Traditional theories of cognitive development can be grouped into four broad categories. Behaviorist accounts used mechanisms of association and stimulus generalization over perceptual gradients to explain learning, eschewing discussion of mental representations. Current descendants of this view rely on mechanisms such as statistical learning of transitive probabilities. Piagetian constructivism postulated increasingly complex mental representations learned through the child's interactions with the world and cognitive stages characterized by different representational formats and logical operations (Piaget, 1951, 1955). Another constructivist approach is Vygotsky's (1962) theory that abstract cognition develops through the child's interactions with cultural and linguistic systems. The fourth approach, of renewed interest of late, is a nativist approach that postulates that children possess nascent cognitive systems and theories that unfold through interaction with the world.

The theories of Piaget and Vygotsky offer a rich and appealing view of cognitive development. In particular, Piaget's claim that children can represent and reason over structured knowledge schemas and Vygotsky's claim that language and culture influence cognitive development have remained influential. However, Piagetian stage theory has been challenged by demonstrations of early learning. Further, both theories lack specificity in their accounts of *how* learning occurs.

The inadequacy of learning mechanisms powerful enough to explain the development of abstract cognition is all the more apparent in light of increasing evidence of the sophistication and generativity of early cognition and language (Mehler & Dupoux, 1994). The past two decades have seen many striking demonstrations of very early insight into number (Gelman, 1990; Gelman & Gallistel, 1978), the behavior of objects in space (Baillargeon, 1987, 1991; Spelke, 1988, 1990), and the composition of basic-level categories (Waxman, 1990; Waxman & Kosowski, 1990). Very young children have been found to categorize (Mandler & McDonough, 1993) and/or to differentiate between domains based on functional principles (Gelman, 1989; Hirschfeld & Gelman, 1994; Keil, 1994), and infants were seen to have remarkable early language proficiency (Gleitman & Wanner, 1982; Pinker, 1994). Children's early achievements vastly outstripped the predictions of the available accounts of learning. The inescapable conclusion, to many theorists, was that much of our knowledge is built in: There must be innate domain-specific principles or skeletal systems that frame our later knowledge.

But perhaps we have dismissed learning too quickly. True, purely behaviorist learning accounts, with minimal representational commitments and mechanisms of simple association and perceptual similarity generalization, cannot account for the acquisition of complex knowledge. And true, Piagetian and Vygotskian approaches have not met our current expectations for theoretical specificity. But we maintain that the richness of constructivist theorizing is compatible with current accounts of learning processes. Our proposal draws on insights from cognitive science models of learning. It is aimed at capturing the development of abstract relational thought—the *sine qua non* of human cognition.

Relational learning encompasses not only how children acquire abstract relational systems such as mathematics, but also how they learn the theory-like relational information that informs their understanding of ordinary concrete entities. For example, children come to know that both tigers and sharks are *carnivores*, whereas deer and hippopotamuses are *herbivores*, that tigers *prey on* deer, and so on; or, that a taxi is not defined as a yellow car but as a vehicle that can be *hired* (Keil & Batterman, 1984). Table 4.1 shows a sample of relational terms, chosen to suggest the range

TABLE 4.1
A Sampling of Relational Terms

Spatial Relational Terms		
in	bisector	approaching
on	symmetric	preceding
under	monotonic	increasing
between	equilateral	passing
across		
	the limit of	half
	y as x→0	quarter
More Relational Terms		
carnivore	cause	forget
parent	incite	expect
gift	prevent	remember
target	prohibit	intend
passenger	engender	persuade
weapon		deny
friend	inverse	
twin	converse	confiscate
	identical	borrow
		withdraw
		distribute

and utility of relational language. Many of these terms are acquired in childhood, although not necessarily with their full relational meanings.

To preview the approach, we suggest that much of children's learning prowess stems from carrying out comparisons that yield abstractions. Some of these comparisons are grounded in the child's own experience, as when infants repeat an interesting event over and over in the circular reactions noted by Piaget (1952). Other comparisons are culturally invited, either explicitly by the child's caretakers (e.g., "Look—see how the hawk looks like the eagle?") or implicitly by the fact that two situations have a common linguistic label (e.g., "These are both houses"). These early comparisons are typically based on close, concrete similarity. Later, comparisons among less obviously similar exemplars promote further inferences and abstractions. We suggest that comparison is not a low-level feature generalization mechanism, but a process of structural alignment and mapping that is powerful enough to acquire structured knowledge and rules (Gentner & Medina, 1998; Gentner & Wolff, 2000).

The plan of the chapter is as follows. We first discuss evidence that analogical learning processes can foster the acquisition of abstract relational knowledge. We then examine two ways to invite the comparison process: physical juxtaposition, that is, the direct observation of two comparable exemplars; and symbolic juxtaposition, that is, applying common language to two situations. The former is what we typically discuss in the course of studying analogical processing. Yet we think the latter is fundamentally important as well. We present evidence that language both invites specific comparisons and reifies the resulting abstractions. We begin by discussing structure-mapping as a learning process, and then turn to the role of relational language in furthering this process.

Comparison as Structural Alignment and Mapping

According to structure-mapping theory, the comparison process is one of alignment and mapping between structured conceptual representations (Falkenhainer, Forbus, & Gentner, 1989; Gentner, 1983, 1989; Gentner & Markman, 1994, 1997; Goldstone, 1994; Goldstone & Medin, 1994; Markman & Gentner, 1990, 1993, 1996; Medin, Goldstone, & Gentner, 1993). The commonalities and differences between two situations are found by determining the maximal structurally consistent alignment between their representations. A structurally consistent alignment is characterized by one-to-one mapping (i.e., an element in one representation can correspond to at most one element in the other representation) and parallel connectivity (i.e., if elements correspond across the two representations, then the elements they govern must correspond as well). When more than one structurally consistent match exists between two representations, contextual relevance and the relative systematicity of the competing interpretations are used. All else being equal, the richest and deepest relational match is preferred (the systematicity principle). An important psychological assumption—particularly if one hopes to model learning in children—is that achieving a deep structural alignment does not require advance knowledge of the point of the comparison. (If it did, it would be relatively useless as a developmental learning process.) Structural alignment can be accomplished with a process that begins blind and local.

We briefly describe a computer model of structure-mapping theory, the Structure-mapping Engine (SME), to give the flavor of this local-to-global alignment process (Falkenhainer, Forbus, & Gentner, 1989; Forbus, Gentner, & Law, 1995). When given two representations to align, SME begins blindly with a set of local, mutually inconsistent matches and gradually coalescences these into one or a few deep, structurally consistent alignments.

SME carries out its mapping in three stages. In the first stage, it proposes matches between all identical predicates at any level (attribute, function, relation, higher order relation, etc.) between the two representa-tions. At this stage, there are typically many mutually inconsistent (1→n) matches. In the second phase, these local matches are coalesced into small, structurally consistent connected clusters (called kernels). Finally, in the third stage these kernels are merged into one or a few maximal structurally consistent interpretations (i.e., mappings displaying one-to-one correspondences and parallel connectivity). SME then produces a structural evaluation of the interpretation(s), using a cascade-like algo-rithm in which evidence is passed down from predicates to their argu-ments. This method is used because it favors deep systems over shallow systems, even if they have equal numbers of matches (Forbus & Gentner, 1989). Finally, predicates connected to the common structure in the base, but not initially present in the target, are proposed as candidate infer-ences in the target. This means that structural completion can lead to spontaneous unplanned inferences. Thus, the process begins with local matches, allowing the interpretation to emerge from the commonalities. But the final interpretation of a comparison is a global match that pre-serves large-scale structures.

This process model has important implications for the process of com-parison in learning and development. First, because matches at all levels enter into the maximal alignment, the easiest and most inevitably noticed similarity comparisons should be those of rich overall (literal) similarity. Indeed, a concrete match like (1) and (2), in which both the objects and the relations match, is intuitively easier to process than an abstract match like (1) and (3), or yet more challenging, (1) and (4):

1. The mother Husky licks her puppies.
2. The mother wolf licks her cubs.
3. The mother falcon grooms her chicks.
4. Best Rubber Company nurtures its spinoffs.

For pairs like (1) and (2), the comparison process runs off easily, because the matches are mutually supporting, yielding one clear dominant inter-pretation. There is considerable evidence that novice learners and chil-dren can perceive overall similarity matches before they perceive purely analogical matches. There is also evidence that adults process concrete matches faster than purely relational matches (Kurtz & Gentner, 1998) and high-similarity matches faster than low-similarity matches (Wolff & Gentner, 2000). Further, there is evidence that rich concrete matches, such as two identical dachshunds, are perceived as more similar than sparse concrete matches, such as two identical circles (Gentner & Rattermann, 1991).

Comparison Can Promote Learning

On this account, there are at least four ways in which the process of comparison can further the acquisition of knowledge: (a) highlighting and schema abstraction—extracting common systems from representations, thereby promoting the disembedding of subtle and possibly important commonalities (including common relational systems); (b) projection of candidate inferences—inviting inferences from one item to the other; (c) re-representation—altering one or both representations so as to improve the match (and thereby, as an important side effect, promoting representational uniformity); and (d) re-structuring—altering the domain structure of one domain in terms of the other (Gentner & Wolff, 2000; Gentner, Brem, Ferguson, Markman, Levidow, Wolff, & Forbus, 1997). These processes enable the child to learn abstract commonalities and to make relational inferences.

Alignment and Abstraction. Highlighting commonalities may seem like a rather trivial learning process, but this is not true in the case of common relations. Here we present evidence to make the case for the importance of relational highlighting. SME's alignment process, taken as a model of human processing, suggests that the act of carrying out a comparison promotes structural alignment and renders the common structure more salient (Gentner & Wolff, 1997, 2000; Gick & Holyoak, 1983; Markman & Gentner, 1993; Wolff & Gentner, 2000). We have found considerable evidence that mutual alignment promotes learning and transfer. That is, when a learner is induced to compare two things—for whatever reason, be it common labels, perceptual similarity, or similar roles in pretend play—the alignment process renders the common relational structure more salient and prompts their re-representation at a more abstract level (Gentner, Rattermann, Markman, & Kotovsky, 1995; Gick & Holyoak, 1983; Kotovsky & Gentner, 1996; Loewenstein, Thompson, & Gentner, 1999; Thompson, Gentner, & Loewenstein, 2000).

In one set of experiments, we studied the effect of making comparisons on 3-year-olds' ability to perform mapping tasks (Loewenstein & Gentner, 2001). We used a version of the classic spatial mapping task developed by DeLoache and her colleagues (DeLoache, 1987, 1989, 1995; Uttal, Shreiber, & DeLoache, 1995). Children were tested on their ability to find a hidden toy in a model room after being shown the location of an identical toy in an analogous model room. The task was deliberately made fairly difficult. First, the "Hiding room" and the "Finding room" were perceptually different: That is, although the objects in the Hiding and Finding rooms belonged to the same categories, they were different in shape and color. Such perceptual differences between the corresponding objects make the mapping task more difficult for children (DeLoache, Kolstad, & Anderson, 1991; Gentner & Toupin, 1986). Second, the Hiding and Finding rooms each contained not only unique objects—a bed, a desk, and a rug—but also two identical "twin" stools (after Blades & Cooke, 1994). These twin objects made the task more challenging, because such mappings cannot be accomplished purely by matching objects: Children must also attend to spatial relational information to disambiguate the matches. This twin manipulation is particularly informative because it allows us to tell whether children can surpass the typical initial strategy of simply matching objects (Blades & Cooke, 1994; Gentner, 1988; Gentner & Rattermann, 1991; Halford, 1987). To succeed at this mapping task—particularly at mapping between the twin objects—children must note relational correspondences as well as object matches.

The basic procedure was similar to the DeLoache (1987, 1995) standard task. Children aged either 36 months or 42 months played a hiding and finding game in which the experimenter hid a toy in the Hiding room while the child watched. The experimenter explained that the child could find a similar toy in the same place in the Finding room. Before beginning this task, the children were divided into two groups that received different pre-task experiences. The *comparison* group received a brief introductory experience in which children saw the Hiding room, with another virtually identical room (the Hiding2 room) next to it. The only difference between these rooms was the color of the walls and furniture. The experimenter said "Do you see how these are the same? Let's see how these are the same." He then pointed to an object in the Hiding2 room, and asked the child to point to "the one in the very same place" in the Hiding room. The experimenter and the child went through all the objects in the room in this fashion.[1] The experimenter then removed the Hiding2 room and brought out the Finding room, and began the standard hide-and-find task just described.

The second group was the baseline control group, which was not given a pre-task comparison experience. However, to equate the amount of time children were given to study the Hiding room, we asked the control children to tell us the functions of all the objects in the Hiding room (or, in another study, the colors of all the objects).

Once the pre-task experience was completed, the experimenter brought out the Finding room. Both groups were then given the same search task. As predicted, comparing highly similar examples helped children in the subsequent mapping task. Children in the comparison condition (.77) performed better than children in the control condition

---

[1]The experimenter was careful not to say the names of any of the objects, because in other studies we have observed that this can improve performance.

(.56).[2] As already noted, a key test of whether mutual alignment via comparison processing promotes relational understanding is whether it improves performance on the twin items, which require matching both objects and spatial relations. Indeed, children in the comparison group (.69) performed better on the twin items than those in the control group (.44). We conclude that making a concrete comparison gave children insight into relational structure. Even though the two Hiding rooms compared were virtually identical, aligning their representations led children to a better grasp of their common spatial relational schema, which could then be applied to the Finding room.

The benefits of close concrete comparison found here are strikingly different from the traditional view of analogical insight, which centers on "far analogies" between cases that share relational content but not surface similarity. Yet we have repeatedly found benefits of close comparisons. In studies of word learning, Gentner and Namy (1999; Namy & Gentner, in press) found that 4-year-olds extended new words on the basis of perceptual commonalities if presented with a single standard. However, when children compared two highly similar standards, they were far more likely to extend according to taxonomic categories. In sum, comparing two items promotes noticing common causal and functional relational structure.

The Power of Comparison in Promoting Inductive Inferences.   So far we have discussed mutual alignment: learning by comparing two situations and abstracting their commonalities. Children also learn by mapping from well-understood systems to less understood systems, as shown, for example, in studies on children's understanding of biological properties. When young children are asked to make predictions about the behavior of animals and plants, they often invoke analogies with people (Carey, 1985b; Inagaki, 1989, 1990; Inagaki & Hatano, 1987, 1991; Inagaki & Sugiyama, 1988; see Rips, 1975, for findings with adults). For example, when asked if they could keep a baby rabbit small and cute forever, 5- to 6-year-olds often made explicit analogies to humans: for example, "We can't keep it [the rabbit] forever in the same size. Because, like me, if I were a rabbit, I would be 5 years old and become bigger and bigger." Inagaki and Hatano (1987) noted that this use of the human analogy was not mere "childhood animism" but a rather selective way of mapping from the known to the unknown. That children reason from the species they know best—humans—to other animals follows from the general phenomenology of analogy: A familiar base domain, whose causal structure is well understood, is used to make predictions about a less-well understood target

---

[2]Children's scores are the proportion of times their first finding attempt was correct over the four search trials (two on unique and two on twin items).

(Bowdle & Gentner, 1997; Gentner, 1983; Holyoak & Thagard, 1995). For example, knowledge about the solar system was used to make predictions about the atom in Rutherford's (1906) analogy (Gentner, 1983).

Based on what we have said about analogical processing, we might expect children's spontaneous comparisons to be initially constrained by perceptual similarity between base and target, but to become increasingly independent of surface features with increasing knowledge of the target domain. Indeed, examples from studies of biology seem to show this developmental progression. For example, children are more likely to use the analogy to humans the more similar the target entity is to humans (see also Carey, 1985b). There are two reasons to expect this similarity effect. First, high similarity promotes memory retrieval; children are likely to be reminded of creatures similar to the one they are reasoning about. Second, once both items are present, high similarity facilitates the process of alignment and mapping of inferences. In structure-mapping, because the alignment process occurs first and the projection of inferences second, the inferences that are drawn depend on the target as well as the base—specifically, on which system(s) of beliefs the target shares with the base (e.g., Clement & Gentner, 1991). Additionally, an inferential verification process acts to reject candidate inferences that are inconsistent with what is known about the target. Here the psychological advantages of high similarity go hand in hand with a reasoning advantage: Perceptual similarity is a fairly reliable indicator of biological proximity, such that perceptually similar species are likely to share structural features. Thus high similarity comparisons are more likely to yield valid inferences, that is, inferences that fit with the systematic causal structure of the target.

One alternative to the analogy-based account is the possibility that children's use of humans as their base for stems from a (possibly innate) category organization in which humans are the core members of their biological domain. Such an account might be consistent with theories that posit that children are innately endowed with an understanding of fundamental domains such as biology (e.g., Keil, 1994; Simon & Keil, 1995). However, Inagaki (1990) provided evidence for the analogy account in an ingenious study. She contrasted the inferential abilities of 5-year-olds who were raising goldfish with those who were not. On the analogy account, goldfish-raising children should be able to use their rich causal knowledge of goldfish as a source of analogical reasoning about other animals, even though no one would offer goldfish as the core animal species for our theory of biology. Inagaki's study revealed that goldfish-raising children drew inferences from goldfish to other unfamiliar animals, such as frogs. That is, they used goldfish as an analogical base for reasoning about less familiar animals. Further, goldfish-raising children not only used the *goldfish* analogy more often for frogs than the non-raisers, but also generated nearly twice as many uses of the *person* analogy for the frog as the non-raisers. Inagaki suggested that in the course of observing and tending goldfish, the goldfish-raisers derived some understanding of the underlying commonalities between goldfish and humans. This abstract perception paved the way for seeing commonalities between the humans and a frog, despite their surface dissimilarities. This is consistent with our earlier proposal of progressive alignment. An alignment and mapping between two kinds of animals promotes further alignments with still other animals.

As Piaget (1951) pointed out, young children often invoke personification analogies in their reasoning. Inagaki and Hatano's (1987, 1991) findings suggest that these analogies are not a sign of faulty logic, but rather are a means "to generate an educated guess about less familiar, nonhuman objects" (1987, p. 1020). Of course, animistic analogies (like other analogies) can lead to wrong conclusions, as when children believe a river flows because it wants to get to the sea (Piaget, 1951). But they stem from a highly sensible reasoning strategy, the same strategy used by adults in cases of incomplete knowledge. Inagaki argued that analogical reasoning is not restricted to special cases of inference concerning unfamiliar properties and situations, but, rather, that it is an integral part of the process of knowledge acquisition. Indeed, as the findings of Inagaki and Hatano suggest the process of analogical comparison and abstraction may itself drive the acquisition of abstract knowledge (Gentner & Medina, 1997, 1998). Analogy plays a formative role in acquisition of knowledge when a well-structured domain provides the scaffolding for the acquisition of a new domain.

The Career of Similarity

If, as we have argued, analogy and comparison in general are important in children's learning, then how does analogy develop? The progression found in biology mentioned earlier appears to be part of a general trend. Gentner and Rattermann (1991) reviewed a large set of studies and proposed the following account of the career of similarity. In the first stage, young infants respond to overall (literal) similarity and identity: For example, infants show memory for a prior experience with a mobile (by kicking in the same way to make it move) but only if there is a very close perceptual match with the original (Rovee-Collier & Fagan, 1981). The early stages appear governed by "global" or "holistic" similarity (Smith, 1989, 1993; see also Foard & Kemler-Nelson, 1984); infants can reliably make overall matches before they can reliably make partial matches. The earliest reliable partial matches are based on direct resemblances between objects, such as the similarity between a round red ball and a round red apple. With increasing knowledge, children come to make pure attribute matches (e.g., a red ball and a red barn) and relational similarity matches (e.g., a ball rolling on a table and a toy car rolling on the floor.) As an example of this developmental progression, when asked to interpret the metaphor *A tape recorder is like a camera*, 6-year-olds produced object-based interpretations (e.g., *Both are black*), whereas 9-year-olds and adults produced chiefly relational interpretations (e.g., *Both can record something for later*) (Gentner, 1988). Similarly, Billow (1975) reported that metaphors based on object similarity could be correctly interpreted by children of about 5 or 6 years of age, but that relational metaphors were not correctly interpreted until around 10 to 13 years of age.

The conservativeness of initial similarity processing shows up not only in direct interpretation of similarity statements but also in the way similarity is used in learning and transfer. Whereas older children are able to detect the underlying structure shared by analogous problems, younger children tend to need surface commonalities to transfer solution strategies across different problems (e.g. Chen & Daehler, 1989; Gentner & Toupin, 1986), or explicit hints about the usefulness of prior problems (Brown, 1989). For example, Baillargeon has found that even young infants can use comparison to perform a rudimentary kind of inferential mapping as a habituation task, however, at 4 months of age, they can do this only under conditions of near identity (Baillargeon, 1991; Baillargeon, Spelke, & Wasserman, 1985; see Gentner & Rattermann, 1991, for a summary). That is, they are more likely to (correctly) show surprise at an impossible "box crushing" event if another box of the same size and shape is placed next to the to-be-crushed box, but only if the "calibration" box (which remains visible throughout the event) is identical or highly similar to the box behind the screen. For example, given a visible box that was red with white dots, the 4-month-olds could successfully make the mapping (and thus show surprise) if the "crushed" box behind the screen was red with green dots, but not if it was yellow with green dots or yellow with a clown face. This finding suggests that the babies are doing a kind of similarity-based mapping, using the box that is visible to infer (or remember) the size of the occluded box as it disappears behind the crushing screen. What is striking is the conservativeness of the process. The babies appear to require a strong overall similarity match before they can make the match. Results like these bring home the magnitude of the human achievement in acquiring the kind of flexible, purely relational similarity capability that adults take for granted.

However, there is evidence that more abstract transfer can be induced during infancy for highly familiar relations such as containment (Kolstad & Baillargeon, 1991). For example, Chen, Sanchez, and Campbell (1997) found that 10-month-old infants could learn to pull on a cloth to reach a toy; but they failed to transfer to a new situation unless the new pulling situation was highly similar to the previously experienced situation. By 13 months, infants were able to transfer with less concrete similarity. Brown and her colleagues (Brown, 1989, 1990; Brown & Kane, 1988) have demonstrated that young children's success in analogical transfer tasks increases when the domains are familiar to them and they are given training in the relevant relations.

In addition to familiarity effects, an indirect argument for the claim that the relational shift is driven by gains in knowledge is that similar patterns are observed in the adult transition from novice to expert. Although people often rely on previously learned examples in problem-solving tasks (e.g., Pirolli & Anderson, 1985; Ross, 1987), novices often fail to retrieve relevant knowledge (e.g., Brown & Campione, 1985; Gentner, Rattermann, & Forbus, 1993; Gick & Holyoak, 1980, 1983; Novick, 1988; Ross, 1987, 1989; see Reeves & Weisberg, 1994, for a review). These transfer difficulties are manifested in what has been called the *inert knowledge* problem—that learners fail to be reminded of prior relevant cases; and the *surface similarity* problem—that learners are often reminded of prior cases with similar objects and entities but dissimilar relational principles.

With increasing expertise, learners shift from reliance on surface similarities to greater use of structural commonalities in problem solving and transfer (Chi, Feltovich, & Glaser, 1981). Novick (1988) showed that more advanced mathematics students were more likely to be reminded of structurally similar problems than were novices. Further, when the experts *were* initially reminded of a surface-similar problem, they were able to reject it quickly. In summation, novices appear to encode domains largely in terms of surface properties, whereas experts possess relationally rich knowledge representations. We speculate that experts tend to develop *uniform relational representations* (Forbus, Gentner, & Law, 1995; Gentner & Rattermann, 1991). On this account, expertise leads to a greater probability that two situations embodying the same principle will be encoded in like terms, and therefore will participate in mutual reminding.

The parallels between cognitive development and adult domain learning add support to the idea that the relational shift is at least partly a novice–expert shift, that is, that the shift is driven by changes in knowledge (Brown, 1989; Gentner & Rattermann, 1991; Gentner & Toupin, 1986; Goswami, 1992; Vosniadou, 1989). (However, the alternative explanation of a global and/or maturational change in processing capacity has also been defended [Halford, 1987, 1993].) Evidence for the knowledge-change view comes in three varieties: (a) the relational shift occurs at different ages for different domains and tasks; (b) in particular, even very young children can show considerable analogical ability in highly familiar domains; and (c) children's analogical performance can be improved substantially by providing them with additional relational knowledge.

Our focus on domain-specific advances in knowledge that drive advances in reasoning discards Piaget's global stage theory in favor of a domain-centered view of cognitive development (see also Carey, 1985a). This might seem to leave us with a piecemeal account, one that lacks any link between, for example, children's understanding of conservation of volume and their insight into conservation of weight. We speculate that analogy provides that link. The child who has caught on to conservation in prior domain is more likely to learn the principle in the next domain, and once two domains are grasped, the way is paved for the next (just as the child in Inagaki's studies who has drawn an analogy between goldfish and humans is more likely to see a further mapping to frogs). For example, Gelman (1969) taught 5-year-olds, who initially failed to conserve length, number, mass, and liquid, a discrimination learning task with length and number. Their subsequent conservation performance was near perfect on length and number. More importantly, the children also improved substantially on conservation of the two nontrained quantities, mass and liquid amount. In another study, Gelman (1982) taught children conservation of small numbers and found that they subsequently improved their performance on tasks involving conservation of large numbers. In a similar vein, Simon and Klahr (1995) suggested that an understanding of discrete numbers provides the basis for learning to reason about continuous quantities.

All these findings suggest the operation of analogical mapping within and between domains. Such a process could explain the décalage pattern found across domains in conservation studies. Having acquired conservation early in certain domains (perhaps because of their familiarity and transparency), children then come to perceive analogies to other domains.

We are suggesting that one way in which children and other novices improve their ability to detect powerful analogical matches is through comparison itself. In the next section, we provide evidence for the claim of progressive abstraction: Specifically, we show that experiencing concrete comparisons can promote noticing further more abstract analogies based on the same common structure. We suggest that there is a kind of mutual promotion cycle whereby analogy and similarity act to increase representational uniformity (through re-representation to increase alignment), and are in turn promoted by uniform representations (because the more alignable the representations, the more likely it is that the likeness will be noticed and the comparison made). This positive feedback cycle contributes to the systematization of knowledge, to the gradual replacement of the idiosyncratic perceptions of childhood by the sturdy, relatively uniform representations of the adult cultural world view[3] (Gentner & Medina, 1997, 1998; Gentner & Rattermann, 1991).

---

[3]One could view this evolution as the loss of the brilliant, richly embedded images of childhood in favor of the colorless regimentation of adulthood; uniform relational representation has its price.

What Prompts Learners to Engage in Comparison?

If comparison is so useful in development, then how does it come about? One simple way is via physical juxtaposition of similar items. A friendly mentor might increase the chances by asking questions that invite the child to compare the two things, as we did in the model-room task described earlier. But a second way to invite comparison is to give two things the same name—what Gentner and Medina (1998) referred to as *symbolic juxtaposition*. We turn to closely linked cases of physical and symbolic juxtaposition.

Juxtaposition of Similar Examples. Kotovsky and Gentner (1996) showed that experience with concrete similarity comparisons can improve children's ability to detect more abstract similarity. Specifically, 4-year-olds were given a similarity matching task using simple patterns, for example, small and large circles in a symmetric pattern (i.e., oOo). They had to choose which of two other triads this pattern was more similar to. Both alternatives had the same objects (xXx or xxX), but only one matched the original in terms of its relations among the objects. When the matches were across dimensions (e.g., small-large-small to light-dark-light), 4-year-olds performed at chance levels. However, children's ability to perceive cross-dimensional matches was markedly better when the cross-dimensional triads were presented after the within-dimension triads (blocks of size symmetry and blocks of color symmetry) than if the cross-dimension and same dimension triads were mixed together. The manipulation that led to this gain was extremely subtle. Both groups of children received the same triads, half within-dimension and half cross-dimension, and performed the same task of choosing the best match to the standard. No feedback was given to either group. Thus the results may be viewed as reflecting the effects of learning from concerted experience.

Why did the order of examples matter so much? Kotovsky and Gentner (1996) suggested a *progressive alignment* process that occurs when alignable exemplars of the same relational structure are presented together. The within-dimension comparisons, being strong overall matches, are easy to align—they align themselves, virtually without effort on the part of the child (as evidenced by children's high performance on these matches). Each time such an alignment occurs, the common structure is highlighted. This repeated experience on the within-dimension pairs acts to make the higher order relation of symmetry (or monotonicity, another pattern tested) more salient. Children who had received the blocked triads were therefore better able than children in the mixed condition to detect the common higher order structure in the cross-dimensional pairs. Making concrete comparisons improved children's ability to see relational similarities. In short, close alignments can potentiate far alignments.

These kinds of results are perhaps surprising. It might have been supposed that comparing highly similar examples would lead to the formation of a narrow understanding. Instead, comparison appears to have led to noticing relational commonalities that could then be used in a more abstract mapping. There are three points to be made here. First, what seems like close concrete similarity to an adult may function as an informative analogy to a child. High-similarity examples have the advantage for children that at least some of their correspondences are likely to be obvious, and these may invite more subtle correspondences. The second point is that similarity processing is inherently engaging. Children play matching games for fun, and at any age our attention can be captured when a spontaneous noticing of similarity leads to a flood of further commonalities. Third, because comparison processing tends to promote relational information, it can be revealing even for adults dealing with familiar topics, because relational information tends to be implicit and difficult to call forth within individual items (Gentner & Clement, 1988). In summation, comparison can provide a naturalistic experiential route by which children come to appreciate relational commonalities.

Symbolic Juxtaposition Through Common Language. If experiential juxtapositions were the sole source of analogical comparisons, learning would proceed very slowly. Even allowing for the fact that children seek out and enjoy repetition-with-variation, and for parents who artfully arrange for the child to encounter informative comparisons, the rate of purely experiential learning would fall well short of children's prodigious pace. Fortunately, we suggest, there is another way to promote comparison: symbolic juxtaposition through common language.

A further study by Kotovsky and Gentner (1996) provided some hints in this direction. Before engaging in the similarity task, 4-year-olds were given labels for higher order relations among the pictured objects (e.g., "even" for symmetry). They then received a categorization task (with feedback) in which they had to give the "picky walrus" only cards that showed "even." The same technique was used for "more and more" (for monotonic increase). After this training, children who succeeded in the labeling task scored well above chance in the cross-dimensional trials (72% relational responding), as opposed to the chance performance (about 50%) that children showed with no such training. As with the physical juxtaposition studies, the use of relational labels increased children's attention to common relational structure. This language effect provides the beginnings of a larger claim: The acquisition of relational language influences the development of relational thought.

Relational Language and Relational Thought

The suggestion that language might influence cognition is a contentious claim. The ideas of Vygotsky (1962), Sapir (1949), and Whorf (1956), once ardently embraced, have been even more ardently rejected. In recent times, a number of brilliant and influential thinkers have lined up against the position, some on empirical grounds (e.g., Li & Gleitman, 1999) and some on theoretical grounds (e.g., Fodor, 1975; Pinker, 1994). We return to these challenges later. For now, we briefly summarize the existing theories of how language might influence conceptual life[4] and then present our own account (see Devitt & Sterelny, 1987, pp. 172–221, Gumperz & Levinson, 1996, pp. 1–13, and Lucy, 1992, for useful discussions).

The Sapir–Whorf linguistic relativity hypothesis can be stated as follows:

> We dissect nature along lines laid down by our native language. The categories and types that we isolate from the world of phenomena we do not find there because they stare every observer in the face; on the contrary, the world is presented in a kaleidoscope flux of impressions which has to be organized by our minds - and this means largely by the linguistic systems of our minds. (Whorf, 1956, p. 213)

Three central claims constitute the Sapir–Whorf hypothesis as it has been construed in empirical psycholinguistics: (a) languages vary in their semantic partitioning of the world; (b) the structure of one's language influences the manner in which one perceives and understands the environment; (c) therefore, speakers of different languages should have at least partly incommensurable world views. Efforts to demonstrate the strong version of the Whorfian position mostly have failed to produce positive results (see Clark & Clark, 1977; and Pinker, 1994; however, see Hunt & Agnoli, 1991; Kay & Kempton, 1984; and Lucy & Schweder, 1979, for evidence on the positive side).

Vygotsky's (1962) theory also gives language a major role in cognition. However, his theory focuses chiefly on the general effects of learning a language, rather than on the specific conceptual construals invited by a given language. According to Vygotsky, with the advent of language children augment their pre-linguistic cognitive capabilities of reactive attention, associative learning, and sensorimotor intelligence with post-linguistic capabilities: focused attention, deliberate memory, and symbolic thought (see also Dennett, 1993). According to Vygotsky, acquiring a lan-

---

[4]This hypothesis has antecedents in the work of Wilhelm von Humboldt (1836, translated 1988), as well as in some aspects of French structuralism, such as the Saussurean idea that a linguistic term derives its value from its relations to all other terms, rather than directly from referential relations to the world.

guage gives the child control over his own mental processes: the ability to guide his thinking, to direct attention, and to formulate mental plans: "... learning to direct one's own mental processes with the aid of words or signs is an integral part of the process of concept formation" (Vygotsky, 1962, p. 59; quoted in Kuczaj, Borys, & Jones, 1989).

Thus the Sapir–Whorf view has it that the grammatical structure of a language shapes its speakers' perception of the world, and the Vygotskian view, that possessing a symbol system permits one to direct one's own mental processes. We are suggesting a third position: that learning specific relational terms and systems is important in the development of abstract thought (Gentner & Rattermann, 1991; Gentner, Rattermann, Markman, & Kotovsky, 1995; Kotovsky & Gentner, 1996).

We suggest that relational language provides tools for extracting and formulating abstractions. In particular, we focus on the role of relational labels in promoting the ability to perceive relations, to transfer relational patterns, and to reason about relations. Even within a single language, the acquisition of relational terms provides both an invitation and a means for the learner to modify her thought. When applied across a set of cases, relational labels prompt children to make comparisons and to store the relational meanings that result (Gentner, 1982; Gentner & Medina, 1997, 1998). In short, relational labels invite the child to notice, represent, and retain structural patterns of elements.

In seeking empirical evidence for this claim, we have focused on spatial relations like *on*, *in*, and *under* (Loewenstein & Gentner, 1998, in preparation) and *symmetry* and *monotonicity* (Kotovsky & Gentner, 1996; Rattermann & Gentner, 1998, submitted). These kinds of spatial terms satisfy three criteria for an arena in which to investigate possible effects of language on cognitive development: (a) they show substantial cross-linguistic variation; (b) they lend themselves to objective testing; and (c) they are accessible to children. The logic of these studies is first, to establish a challenging spatial relational task, and then to test whether language for spatial relations can improve children's performance.

Labeling Spatial Patterns Among Entities. Rattermann and Gentner (1998, submitted; Gentner & Rattermann, 1991) investigated the power of common relational labels to promote relational insight. First, Rattermann, Gentner, and DeLoache (1987) designed a simple mapping task to investigate whether preschool children could align a higher order perceptual relational structure. Children aged 3, 4, and 5 saw two triads of objects, the child's set and the experimenter's set, both arranged in monotonically increasing order according to size. As in DeLoache's model studies, noted earlier, the child watched as the experimenter hid a sticker under an object in the experimenter's triad; she was told that she could find her sticker by looking "in the same place" in her triad. The correct response was always based on relational similarity: that is, the child was meant to choose the object of the same relative size and relative position. (These two were always correlated.) Children were always shown the correct response after making their guess.

When the two sets were literally similar, as in Fig. 4.1, 3-year-old children readily learned the mapping. But when the objects were shifted to a cross-mapped pattern (in which the object matches were inconsistent with the best relational alignment) (Gentner & Toupin, 1986), the children had great difficulty, particularly when the objects were rich and detailed. Indeed, in the rich-object cross-mapped versions of the task, 3- and 4-year-old children performed at chance (32%) even though they were shown the correct response on every trial (14 trials total).

Having thus established a challenging relational task, Rattermann and Gentner (1998) then investigated whether providing relational language could help children perform this relational alignment. Before children carried out the cross-mapping task, they were provided with a brief training session in which we modeled using the labels *Daddy*, *Mommy*, and *Baby* (or in other studies, *big*, *little*, *tiny*) for both their own and the experimenter's triads. (These family labels are often used spontaneously by pre-

Cross-Mapping Task

Sparse

Rich

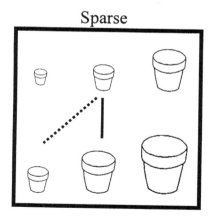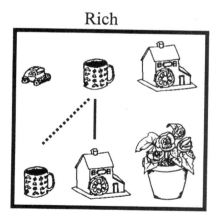

FIG. 4.1. Materials used in the Rattermann and Gentner (1998) cross-mapping studies, showing the sparse-object and rich-object conditions. E labels the experimenter's set; C labels the child's set. Assuming that the sticker is hidden under the experimenter's middle object, the correct relational alternative is the middle object in the child's set; the dashed line shows the (incorrect) object match.

school children to mark monotonic change [Smith, 1989].) The reasoning was that applying these labels to the three members of each triad would invite the child to highlight the higher order relational pattern of monotonic increase that forms the essential common system to align.

The results of the labeling manipulation were striking. The 3-year-olds performed well in the cross-mapping task on both the sparse (89% relational responding) and rich (79% relational responding) stimuli, as compared to performance rates of 54% and 32% without relational language correct, respectively. In fact, the 3-year-olds given relational language performed on par with 5-year-olds in the no-language condition. Further, children were fairly well able to transfer their learning to new triads with no further use of the labels by the experimenters. We suggest that the use of common relational labels invited attention to the common relation of monotonic increase and made it possible for the children to carry out a relational alignment. This interpretation is buttressed by the fact that other relational labels denoting monotonic size-change, for example, *big*, *little*, *tiny*, also improved performance, whereas neutral object labels, for example, *jiggy*, *gimli*, *fantan*, did not.

Labeling Spatial Relations Between Figure and Ground.   We have also investigated language effects in a spatial mapping task (Loewenstein & Gentner, 1998, 2001). We focused on a set of spatial terms that children learn early: the spatial prepositions *on*, *in*, and *under*. Children can comprehend and use these prepositions by the time they are 3 years old (Clark, 1974; Johnston, 1988). As in the Rattermann and Gentner studies, we first established a challenging spatial task and then tested whether labeling the relevant spatial relations would lead to successful task performance. We devised a spatial mapping task using two boxes, modeled after Wilcox and Palermo's (1980) neutral object. The box is designed to have three equally salient placement locations (on top, in the middle, and underneath the box in Fig. 4.2). Each box had three identical plastic cards, one in each position. One card had a star on its back, making it the "win-

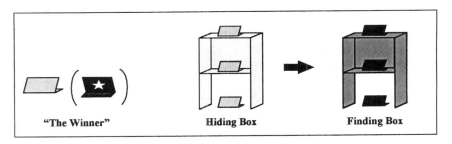

FIG. 4.2.   Materials used in the Loewenstein and Gentner (1998) spatial mapping test.

ner." Children were shown the location of the winner at the Hiding box, and had to find the winner in the corresponding location at the Finding box.

In some respects the task is a relatively easy version of the search task used in DeLoache's (1987, 1995) and our own model room studies. The Hiding and Finding models are nearly identical and they are placed close together so that they can be simultaneously viewed. However, in other fundamental respects, the task is more difficult than the standard search tasks. Our task uses only one reference object—the box—and all objects are placed with respect to it. Thus to solve the task the child must attend to the specific spatial relation between the hiding place and the box. Simple object correspondences are not enough.

The key manipulation was made during children's initial training. Children either placed toys as specified by spatial language (Language condition: "Can you put this *on* the box?"), or placed toys in locations the experimenter pointed to (Control condition: "Can you put this *here*?"). After performing one of these training exercises, all children performed the same mapping task between the two boxes. We found that 44-month-old Language group children performed better than Control group children on the mapping task, the latter performing at levels just better than chance. Thus, hearing relational language facilitated children's ability to map on the basis of spatial relations.

Summary of Empirical Results.   The research summarized here suggests several conclusions. First, it supports the career of similarity thesis: Children begin with highly concrete similarity matches and gradually become able to appreciate selective matches. Second, among partial matches there is a relational shift from early focus on object-based matches to a later ability to perceive purely relational commonalities. Third, this development is driven in large part by changes in domain knowledge. Fourth, one particular kind of knowledge that may be particularly important is the acquisition of relational language.

The findings reviewed are consistent with our claim that children's early representations are conservative and context-specific, relying on massive overlap of perceptual features, and that they gradually develop relationally articulated representations, which enable them to appreciate partial similarity and analogy. We considered two ways of fostering relational insight: first, the progressive alignment of a series of cases so as to reveal common relational structure; and second, the use of relational language to invite the perception of common relations. The first of these represents alignment through experiential juxtaposition; the second, alignment through symbolic juxtaposition.

DISCUSSION

We began this chapter by asking "Why are humans so smart?" That is, why is our cognition so much more adaptive and flexible than that of other creatures?[5] We focused on two contributors to our learning capacities. One of these, our penchant for analogizing and systematizing what we learn, is internal to our cognitive makeup, and one, the possession of a system that includes names for relational terms, arises from social communication systems. We reviewed evidence that comparison processes—not only abstract analogy but also mundane similarity—contribute importantly to children's experiential learning. In particular, we discussed three ways in which alignment and projection—analogical processing—contributes to learning: highlighting due to mutual alignment, inference projection, and re-representation.

We have argued for the career of similarity account of development, a progression from overall similarity to object similarity to higher level relational similarity, and from focusing on perceptual to focusing on conceptual properties. The course of similarity has wide ramifications. Virtually every cognitive process, from categorization to transfer, is influenced by explicit or implicit similarity comparisons. Thus, as similarity comparisons evolve from being initially perceptual and context-bound to becoming increasingly framed in terms of common higher order structure, children's general cognitive abilities show an increasing capacity to notice and reason about abstract situations.

The structural alignment and mapping process grades naturally from highly concrete literal similarity comparisons to purely abstract comparisons. Indeed, we speculate that some of children's learning prowess stems from a particular pattern of initial docile retention followed by comparison and analogical abstraction. Children originally acquire knowledge at a highly specific, conservative level; later, comparisons—initially concrete, but progressively more abstract—among exemplars promote abstraction and rule learning.

Similarity Reconsidered. Similarity is often treated rather slightingly in current theories of cognitive development. It is regarded as a deceiver,

---

[5]Many other species lead us in specific cognitive skills—the nuthatch in memory for multiple locations, the carrier pigeon and several others in navigational abilities, and so on. Nor are we the only generalists; formidable learning capabilities have been demonstrated by crows, parrots, dolphins, and chimpanzees, among others. But we clearly excel in our ability to learn and adapt to varying environments, and (for better or worse) to adapt the environment to ourselves.

a tempting fraud that lures children away from deeper understanding. This suspicion of similarity goes hand in hand with a suspicion of general learning mechanisms. Keil (1994) stated: ". . . the extraordinary ease with which all of us do learn about functional objects, such as tools, relative to other species that exhibit sophisticated learning in so many other areas . . . argues against reduction to general learning procedures" (p. 251). In contrast, we suggest that learning by analogy and similarity, even mundane within-dimension similarity, can act as a positive force in learning and development. We have argued that the simple process of carrying out similarity and analogy comparisons may play a fundamental role in the development of structured representations.

Further, although we have focused on children's analogical processing, there are other learning mechanisms that contribute to the development of abstract cognition. To name some examples, children learn via explanations (Callanan, 1990, 1991), via questions asked and answered, through dialogues with parents (e.g., Clark, 1993, 2001), by apprenticeship and scaffolded learning (Nunes, Schliemann, & Carraher, 1993; Rogoff, 1990); by observing successes and failures in goal-driven behavior (Tomasello, 1995), and by imitation (Meltzoff, 1988).

The Role of Language in Cognitive Development. There is abundant evidence for interactions between language and cognition in development (Nelson, 1995). First, children readily learn and extend new words (Markman & Hutchinson, 1984) and appear to assume that words refer to things of like kind. These patterns of extension may play a role in the development of taxonomic relationships (Byrnes & Gelman, 1991; Markman, 1989; Waxman & Gelman, 1986; Waxman & Hall, 1993: Waxman & Markow, 1995). Young children's willingness to make inductive inferences between entities is enhanced by the presence of a common label (Davidson & Gelman, 1990; Gelman, 1989; Gelman & Markman, 1987).

However, with a few exceptions (Gopnik & Choi, 1990; Shatz, 1991; Smith & Sera, 1992; Waxman & Markow, 1995) most of the previous empirical work on how labels influence categorization has focused on object concepts. Our research asks whether these benefits extend to relational concepts. The results reported here suggest that the answer is yes. Children who experienced the simple linguistic intervention of practicing with relational labels (e.g., *Daddy, Mommy, Baby*) showed substantially more relational responding than did baseline children. The interpretation is that the use of relational labels can highlight higher order relations (e.g., monotonic increase).

There is also intriguing cross-linguistic evidence that infants swiftly learn their language-specific semantic patterns (Bowerman 1989; Choi & Bowerman, 1991; Imai & Gentner, 1997). Although this in itself does not imply any influence of language on thought, it sets the stage for further investigations. For example, Gopnik and Choi (1990) have suggested that cross-linguistic semantic differences are associated with corresponding differences in the timing of cognitive achievements. As another example, Lucy (1994) has suggested that the linguistic pattern of numeral classifier languages such as Yucatec Mayan and Japanese, which focus relatively more on substance and less on shape than English, could lead to greater reliance on substance in nonlinguistic tasks. Consistent with this suggestion, adult similarity judgments in Yucatec (Lucy, 1996) and Japanese (Imai & Mazuka, 1997; see also Imai & Gentner, 1997, and Gentner & Boroditsky, 2001) show greater reliance on substance than similar tasks in English.

We conjecture that learning words for relations is crucial to the development of analogy. Throughout this chapter we have emphasized the role of language in inviting symbolic juxtapositions. By giving two things the same name, we invite children to compare them, whether or not they occur in experiential juxtaposition.

Why Relational Language Matters.   The prediction that relational language could contribute to higher order cognition is motivated by theoretical considerations about the relative saliency of objects and relations (Gentner, 1981, 1982). Objects are easy to notice; they are learned early, and even adults sometimes are swayed by object matches when relational matches would be more useful. The great value of analogy is in creating a focus on common relational systems—lifting an abstract pattern away from its object arguments. But such insights are often fleeting, and relational terms can preserve them. Relational language is cognitively useful both in promoting relational focus and in suppressing intrusions from objects and object matches. Learned systems of relations provide the child with the representational tools with which to structure knowledge.

To summarize, there are at least four ways in which relational language can foster the ability to retain and use relational patterns:

1. Naming a relational pattern helps to preserve it as a pattern, increasing the likelihood that the learner will perceive the pattern again across different circumstances. This is the effect obtained in our studies of mapping (Gentner & Rattermann, 1991; Loewenstein & Gentner, 1998, in preparation; Rattermann & Gentner, 1998, submitted) and in our similarity task (Kotovsky & Gentner, 1996).

2. Hearing a relational term used invites children to seek a relational meaning, even when none is initially obvious. Indirect evidence for this claim is the pattern whereby children initially interpret relational terms as object descriptors, and only later come to appreciate the relational mean-

ing. Similarly, kinship terms may be understood initially in terms of characteristics of individuals, and only later in terms of relational roles (Clark, 1993; Keil & Batterman, 1984). As another example, Hall and Waxman (1993) found that preschool children (even after being told that a certain doll was a *passenger* because he was riding on the train) tended to interpret *passenger* as an object-reference term, and apply it to a similar-looking doll rather than to another doll riding the train; only children who already knew an object-level name for the item were likely to take *passenger* as a relational term. In a related vein, the full relational meanings of terms such as *if* and *because* (Byrnes, 1991; Scholnick & Wing, 1982) or *mix* (Gentner, 1978) may be acquired gradually, and may not be fully present until 8 or 9 years of age. Admittedly, these findings demonstrate only that relational meanings are not immediately learned. Nevertheless, we conjecture that hearing relational terms invites the meanings.

3. Using a relational term helps to reify an entire pattern, so that new assertions can be stated about it. That is, a named relational schema can serve as an argument to a higher order proposition. For example, consider the economy made possible by terms like *betrayal, loss, revenge,* and *authority*. To express a relatively straightforward causal assertion like "The true cause of Clytemnestra's revenge was not the loss of her child but the betrayal of her authority," or the related counterfactual (e.g., No betrayal, no revenge) would be prohibitively awkward without such relational compaction. As another example of relational embedding, consider Wittgenstein's "Philosophy is a battle against the bewitchment of our intelligence by means of language" (itself, of course, a testimony to the power of language over thought).

4. Habitual use of a given set of relational terms promotes uniform relational encoding, thereby increasing the probability of transfer. As noted earlier, to the extent that a given domain is encoded in terms of a more or less standard set of relational terms, the likelihood of matching new examples with stored knowledge is increased. Relational language can increase the probability of appropriate principle-based transfer and mitigate the classic problems of inert knowledge and surface-based retrieval (Forbus, Gentner, & Law, 1995).

The fourth claim is perhaps the most speculative. Direct evidence is rather scant, but there are some promising leads. Clement, Mawby, and Giles (1994) gave adults passages to read and later gave them new passages that were structurally similar but differed on the surface, the classic situation in which poor retrieval abilities have been demonstrated (Gentner, Rattermann, & Forbus, 1993; Gick & Holyoak, 1980; Ross, 1989). For some learners, the parallel structure in the two matching passages was expressed using relational terms that had the same meanings: X *ate* Y and A *consumed* B. For others, the parallel structure was expressed using non-synonymous relational pairs: for example, X *munched on* Y and A *gobbled up* B. This was a fairly subtle manipulation; the differing relational pairs were partly overlapping in meaning, so that they could readily be aligned if both passages were seen together. However, even this minimal manipulation made a difference: People who received synonymous terms, such as *ate* and *consumed*, were more likely to retrieve the initial passage given the probe than those who received the differing pairs. Clement et al. (1994) concluded that the use of common relational labels can promote analogical retrieval in adults. Further afield, gestalt researchers found that a simple labeling manipulation could help subjects to overcome the "functional fixedness" effect (Glucksberg & Danks, 1968; Glucksberg & Weisberg, 1966).

In our own research, we have also found evidence that relational language promotes relational transfer. First, in the Rattermann and Gentner mapping task, children who were given relational terminology (e.g., *Daddy, Mommy, Baby*) performed better than a matched control group not only on the initial mapping task but also on both immediate and delayed transfer tasks without further mention of the labels. Loewenstein and Gentner have found a similar pattern: The benefits of using spatial relational terms appear to persist over time in the box mapping task (Loewenstein & Gentner, in preparation). We suggest that the relational labels invited an encoding of the higher order relational of monotonic increase, which not only helped the children accomplish the mapping task on the initial occasion, but was retained over time to provide a deeper structural encoding on subsequent occasions (Gentner & Rattermann, 1991; Kotovsky & Gentner, 1996; Rattermann & Gentner, 1998, in preparation).

Language and Thought. The position we are taking here is not identical to either the Sapir–Whorf hypothesis or Vygotsky's theory of language and thought. Without denying other kinds of linguistic influences, our purpose here is to argue that the learning of specific relational terms and relational systems fosters human ability to notice and reason about the corresponding abstractions.

We must be clear about some things we are not claiming. We do not claim (a) that all important concepts are relational; (b) that all abstract concepts are relational; (c) that all relational concepts are linguistically provided; or (d) that we can only reason and analogize about linguistically encapsulated relations. Counterexamples to (a) include important concepts like *tiger* and *banana*. Counterexamples to (b) include concepts like *mammal* and *plant*.[6] Counterexamples to (c) are best found by examining

---

[6]It could perhaps be maintained that mammal and plant are in some sense relational but the argument seems strained compared to the clear relationality of, say, *carnivore*.

cross-linguistic patterns that suggest that some relational concepts are formed prelinguistically, so that their corresponding linguistic terms are particularly easy to acquire (Choi & Bowerman, 1991). One counterargument to (d) is the existence of mechanisms such as metaphorical abstraction (Bowdle & Gentner, 1999, in preparation; Glucksberg & Keysar, 1990) that can allow concrete terms to be extended into abstract relational meanings. Another is the historical development in science, mathematics, or even the Internet, of progressively more higher order relational terms. Clearly, speakers constantly go beyond the current resources of their language to notice new relational commonalities. Our claim is that the set of currently lexicalized existing relations frames the set of new ideas that can be readily noticed and articulated.

Our position can be compared with other recent proposals aimed at achieving a psychologically defensible position on language and thought. Slobin's (1996) "thinking for speaking" view states that language may determine the construal of reality *during language use*, without necessarily pervading our entire worldview (see also Pinker, 1989, p. 360). Our proposal goes beyond thinking for speaking in that we argue for lasting benefits of language on thought. We have shown that children can retain the conceptual advantages of learning relational terms even when the terms are not overtly used. Our proposal is related to Carey's (1985b) notion of "tools of wide application" (see also Byrnes, 1991; Scholnick & Hall, 1991). We suggest that relational concepts serve as tools for thought of varying degrees of generality. Our proposal is also related to Gopnik and Meltzoff's (1987, 1997) proposal that there is a bidirectional relation between lexical and conceptual achievements. They provide evidence for the simultaneous emergence of lexical and conceptual insights. For example, they suggest an association between the rapid increase in object names during the second year and the onset of the ability to sort objects into basic-level categories, and between using means–ends planning and saying "uh-oh" for an error. Finally, our thesis is consistent with discussions by Nelson (1996) and Tomasello (1999) of language as a means by which culture influences the development of cognition.

Nonetheless, it could be argued that our position is so moderate as to be vacuous or trivial. Pinker refers to " 'weak' versions of the Whorfian hypothesis, namely that words can have some effect on memory or categorization" (Pinker, 1994, p. 65). Devitt and Sterelny (1987) put it more strongly: ". . . the argument for an important linguistic relativity evaporates under scrutiny. The only respect in which language clearly and obviously does influence thought turns out to be rather banal: language provides us with most of our concepts" (p. 178). These concessions hardly seem banal. If language influences categorization and memory—and if indeed language provides us with most of our concepts (a position considerably beyond what we have claimed)—then its centrality in cognition and cognitive development is beyond dispute.

In summation, we have suggested, first, that structure-mapping processes are a powerful engine of learning in children, and, focusing on relational learning, that a major influence on *what* to align is relational language. Symbolic comparison operates in tandem with experiential comparison to foster the development of abstract thought. It is fitting here to end with a prescient comment from Piaget (1954): ". . . after speech has been acquired the socialization of thought is revealed by the elaboration of concepts, of relations, and by the formation of rules, that is, there is a structural evolution" (p. 360).

ACKNOWLEDGMENTS

This research was supported by NSF grant SBR-9720313 and NSF-LIS grant SBR-9511757 to the first author. The development of the computer simulation was supported by ONR contract N-00014-92-J-1098. This chapter was partially prepared while the first author was a Fellow at the Center for Advanced Study in the Behavioral Sciences. We are grateful for the financial support provided by the William T. Grant Foundation, award #95167795. We thank Ken Forbus, Ken Kurtz, Art Markman, Jose Medina, Mary Jo Rattermann, Phillip Wolff, and the Analogy and Similarity group at Northwestern University for helpful discussions of these issues.

REFERENCES

Baillargeon, R. (1987). Object permanence in 3.5- and 4.5-month-old infants. *Developmental Psychology, 23*, 655–664.

Baillargeon, R. (1991). Reasoning about the height and location of a hidden object in 4.5- and 6.5-month-old infants. *Cognition, 38*, 13–42.

Baillargeon, R., Spelke, E. S., & Wasserman, S. (1985). Object permanence in five-month-old infants. *Cognition, 20*, 191–208.

Billow, R. M. (1975). A cognitive developmental study of metaphor comprehension. *Developmental Psychology, 11*, 415–423.

Blades, M., & Cooke, Z. (1994). Young children's ability to understand a model as a spatial representation. *Journal of Genetic Psychology, 155*, 201–218.

Bowdle, B., & Gentner, D. (1997). Informativity and asymmetry in comparisons. *Cognitive Psychology, 34*(3), 244–286.

Bowdle, B., & Gentner, D. (1999). Metaphor comprehension: From comparison to categorization. *Proceedings of the Twenty-first Annual Meeting of the Cognitive Science Society* (pp. 90–95). Vancouver, BC.

Bowdle, B., & Gentner, D. (submitted). *The career of metaphor.*

Bowerman, M. (1989). Learning a semantic system: What role do cognitive predispositions play? In M. L. Rice & R. L. Schiefelbusch (Eds.), *The teachability of language.* Baltimore: Brooks.

Brown, A. L. (1989). Analogical learning and transfer: What develops? In S. Vosniadou & A. Ortony (Eds.), *Similarity and analogical reasoning* (pp. 369–412). New York: Cambridge University Press.

Brown, A. L. (1990). Domain specific principles affect learning and transfer in children. *Cognitive Science, 14,* 107–134.

Brown, A. L., & Campione, J. C. (1985). Three faces of transfer: Implications for early competence, individual differences, and instruction. In M. Lamb, A. Brown, & B. Rogoff (Eds.), *Advances in developmental psychology* (Vol. 3, pp. 143–192). Hillsdale, NJ: Lawrence Erlbaum Associates.

Brown A. L., & Kane, M. J. (1988). Preschool children can learn to transfer: Learning to learn and learning from example. *Cognitive Psychology, 20,* 493–523.

Byrnes, J. P. (1991). Acquisition and development of *if* and *because*: Conceptual and linguistic aspects. In S. A. Gelman & J. P. Byrnes (Eds.), *Perspectives on language and thought: Interrelations in development* (pp. 3–27). London: Cambridge University Press.

Byrnes, J. P., & Gelman, S. A. (1991). Perspectives on thought and language: Traditional and contemporary views. In S. A. Gelman & J. P. Byrnes (Eds.), *Perspectives on language and thought: Interrelations in development* (pp. 3–27). London: Cambridge University Press.

Callanan, M. A. (1990). Parents' descriptions of objects: Potential for children's inferences about category principles. *Cognitive Development, 5,* 101–122.

Callanan, M. A. (1991). Parent-child collaboration in young children's understanding of category hierarchies. In S. A. Gelman & J. P. Byrnes (Eds.), *Perspectives on thought and language: Interrelations in development* (pp. 440–484). Cambridge, England: Cambridge University Press.

Carey, S. (1985a). *Conceptual change in childhood.* Cambridge, MA: MIT Press.

Carey, S. (1985b). Are children fundamentally different kinds of thinkers and learners than adults? In S. F. Chipman, J. W. Segal, & R. Glaser (Eds.), *Thinking and learning skills: Current research and open questions* (Vol. 2, pp. 485–517). Hillsdale, NJ: Lawrence Erlbaum Associates.

Chen, Z., & Daehler, M. W. (1989). Positive and negative transfer in analogical problem solving by 6-year-old children. *Cognitive Development, 4,* 327–344.

Chen, Z., Sanchez, R. P., & Campbell, T. (1997). From beyond to within their grasp: The rudiments of analogical problem solving in 10- and 13-month olds. *Developmental Psychology, 33*(5), 790–801.

Chi, M. T. H., Feltovich, P. J., & Glaser, R. (1981). Categorization and representation of physics problems by experts and novices. *Cognitive Science, 5,* 121–152.

Choi, S., & Bowerman, M. (1991). Learning to express motion events in English and Korean: The influence of language-specific lexicalization patterns. *Cognition, 41,* 83–121.

Clark, E. V. (1974). Non-linguistic strategies and the acquisition of word meanings. *Cognition, 2,* 161–182.

Clark, E. V. (1993). *The lexicon in acquisition.* Cambridge, England: Cambridge University Press.

Clark, E. V. (2001). Emergent categories in first language acquisition. In M. Bowerman & S. Levinson (Eds.), *Language acquisition and conceptual development.* Cambridge, England: Cambridge University Press.

Clark, H. H., & Clark, E. V. (1977). *Psychology and language: An introduction to psycholinguistics* (pp. 515–558). New York: Harcourt Brace Jovanovich.

Clement, C. A., & Gentner, D. (1991). Systematicity as a selection constraint in analogical mapping. *Cognitive Science, 15,* 89–132.

Clement, C. A., Mawby, R., & Giles, D. E. (1994). The effects of manifest relational similarity on analog retrieval. *Journal of Memory and Language, 33,* 396–420.

Davidson, N. S., & Gelman, S. A. (1990). Inductions from novel categories: The role of language and conceptual structure. *Cognitive Development, 5,* 151–176.

DeLoache, J. S. (1987). Rapid change in the symbolic functioning of very young children. *Science, 238,* 1556–1557.

DeLoache, J. S. (1989). Young children's understanding of the correspondence between a scale model and a larger space. *Cognitive Development, 4,* 121–139.

DeLoache, J. S. (1995). Early understanding and use of symbols—The model model. *Current Directions in Psychological Science, 4*(4), 109–113.

DeLoache, J. S., Kolstad, V., & Anderson, K. N. (1991). Physical similarity and young children's understanding of scale models. *Child Development, 62,* 111–126.

Dennett, D. C. (1993). Learning and labeling. *Mind and Language, 8*(4), 540–548.

Devitt, M., & Sterelny, K. (1987). *Language and reality: An introduction to the philosophy of language.* Oxford, England: Basil Blackwell.

Falkenhainer, B., Forbus, K. D., & Gentner, D. (1989). The structure-mapping engine: Algorithm and examples. *Artificial Intelligence, 41,* 1–63.

Foard, C. F., & Kemler-Nelson, D. G. (1984). Holistic and analytic modes of processing: The multiple determinants of perceptual analysis. *Journal of Experimental Psychology, 113*(1), 94–111.

Fodor, J. A. (1975). *The language of thought.* New York: Random House.

Forbus, K. D., & Gentner, D. (1989). Structural evaluation of analogies: What counts? *Proceedings of the Eleventh Annual Conference of the Cognitive Science Society,* 341–348. Hillsdale, NJ: Lawrence Erlbaum Associates.

Forbus, K. D., Gentner, D., & Law, K. (1995). MAC/FAC: A model of similarity-based retrieval. *Cognitive Science, 19,* 141–205.

Gelman, R. (1969). Conservation acquisition: A problem of learning to attend to relevant attributes. *Journal of Experimental Child Psychology, 7,* 167–187.

Gelman, R. (1982). Accessing one-to-one correspondence: Still another paper about conservation. *Journal of Psychology, 73,* 209–220.

Gelman, R. (1990). First principles organize attention to and learning about relevant data: Number and the animate-inanimate distinction as examples. *Cognitive Science, 14,* 79–106.

Gelman, R., & Gallistel, C. R. (1978). *The child's understanding of number.* Cambridge, MA: Harvard University Press.

Gelman, S. A. (1989). Children's use of categories to guide biological inferences. *Human Development, 32,* 65–71.

Gelman, S. A., & Markman, E. M. (1987). Young children's inductions from natural kinds: The role of categories and appearances. *Child Development, 58,* 1532–1541.

Gentner, D. (1978). On relational meaning: The acquisition of verb meaning. *Child Development, 49,* 988–998.

Gentner, D. (1982). Why nouns are learned before verbs: Relativity vs. natural partitioning. In S. A. Kuczaj (Ed.), *Language development: Syntax and semantics* (pp. 301–334). Hillsdale, NJ: Lawrence Erlbaum Associates.

Gentner, D. (1983). Structure-mapping: A theoretical framework for analogy. *Cognitive Science, 7,* 155–170.

Gentner, D. (1988). Metaphor as structure mapping: The relational shift. *Child Development, 59,* 47–59.

Gentner, D. (1989). Mechanisms of analogical learning. In S. Vosniadou & A. Ortony (Eds.), *Similarity and analogical reasoning* (pp. 199–241). London: Cambridge University Press.

Gentner, D., & Boroditsky, L. (2001). Individuation, relativity and early word learning. In M. Bowerman & S. Levinson (Eds.), *Language acquisition and conceptual development* (pp. 215–256). Cambridge, England: Cambridge University Press.

Gentner, D., Bowdle, B., Wolff, P., & Boronat, C. (2001). Metaphor is like analogy. In D. Gentner, K. J. Holyoak, & B. N. Kokinov (Eds.), *The analogical mind: Perspectives from cognitive science* (pp. 199–253). Cambridge, MA: MIT Press.

Gentner, D., Brem, S., Ferguson, R., Markman, A., Levidow, B. B., Wolff, P., & Forbus, K. D. (1997). Analogical reasoning and conceptual change: A case study of Johannes Kepler. *The Journal of Learning Sciences, 6*(1), 3–40.

Gentner, D., & Clement, C. (1988). Evidence for relational selectivity in the interpretation of analogy and metaphor. In G. H. Bower (Ed.), *The psychology of learning and motivation, advances in research and theory* (Vol. 22, pp. 307–358). New York: Academic Press.

Gentner, D., & Markman, A. B. (1994). Structural alignment in comparison: No difference without similarity. *Psychological Science, 5*(3), 152–158.

Gentner, D., & Markman, A. B. (1997). Structure mapping in analogy and similarity. *American Psychologist, 52,* 45–56.

Gentner, D., & Medina, J. (1997). Comparison and the development of cognition and language. *Cognitive Studies: Bulletin of the Japanese Cognitive Science Society, 4*(1), 112–149.

Gentner, D., & Medina, J. (1998). Similarity and the development of rules. *Cognition, 65,* 263–297.

Gentner, D., & Namy, L. L. (1999). Comparison in the development of categories. *Cognitive Development, 14,* 487–513.

Gentner, D., & Rattermann, M. J. (1991). Language and the career of similarity. In S. A. Gelman & J. P. Byrnes (Eds.), *Perspectives on language and thought: Interrelations in development* (pp. 225–277). London: Cambridge University Press.

Gentner, D., Rattermann, M. J., & Forbus, K. D. (1993). The roles of similarity in transfer: Separating retrievability and inferential soundness. *Cognitive Psychology, 25,* 524–575.

Gentner, D., Rattermann, M. J., Markman, A. B., & Kotovsky, L. (1995). Two forces in the development of relational similarity. In T. J. Simon & G. S. Halford (Eds.), *Developing cognitive competence: New approaches to process modeling* (pp. 263–313). Hillsdale, NJ: Lawrence Erlbaum Associates.

Gentner, D., & Toupin, C. (1986). Systematicity and surface similarity in the development of analogy. *Cognitive Science, 10,* 277–300.

Gentner, D., & Wolff, P. (1997). Alignment in the processing of metaphor. *Journal of Memory and Language, 37,* 331–355.

Gentner, D., & Wolff, P. (2000). Metaphor and knowledge change. In E. Dietrich & A. Markman (Eds.), *Cognitive dynamics: Conceptual change in humans and machines* (pp. 295–342). Mahwah, NJ: Lawrence Erlbaum Associates.

Gick, M. L., & Holyoak, K. J. (1983). Analogical problem solving. *Cognitive Psychology, 12,* 306–355.

Gick, M. L., & Holyoak, K. J. (1983). Schema induction and analogical transfer. *Cognitive Psychology, 15,* 1–38.

Gleitman, L. R., & Wanner, E. (1982). *Language acquisition: The state of the art.* Cambridge, England: Cambridge University Press.

Glucksberg, S., & Danks, J. H. (1968). Effects of discriminative labels and of nonsense labels upon the availability of novel function. *Journal of Verbal Learning and Verbal Behavior, 7,* 72–76.

Glucksberg, S., & Keysar, B. (1990). Understanding metaphorical comparisons: Beyond similarity. *Psychological Review, 97*(1), 3–18.

Glucksberg, S., & Weisberg, R. W. (1966). Verbal behavior and problem solving: Some effects of labeling in a functional fixedness problem. *Journal of Experimental Psychology, 71,* 659–664.

Goldstone, R. L. (1994). Similarity, interactive activation, and mapping. *Journal of Experimental Psychology: Learning, Memory, and Cognition, 20*(1), 3–28.

Goldstone, R. L., & Medin, D. L. (1994). Time course of comparison. *Journal of Experimental Psychology: Learning, Memory, and Cognition, 20*(1), 29–50.

Gopnik, A., & Choi, S. (1990). Do linguistic differences lead to cognitive differences? A crosslinguistic study of semantic and cognitive development. *First Language, 10,* 199–215.

Gopnik, A., & Meltzoff, A. N. (1987). The development of categorization in the second year and its relation to other cognitive and linguistic developments. *Child Development, 58,* 1523–1531.

Gopnik, A., & Meltzoff, A. N. (1997). *Words, thoughts, and theories.* Cambridge, MA: MIT Press.

Goswami, U. (1992). *Analogical reasoning in children.* Hillsdale, NJ: Lawrence Erlbaum Associates.

Gumperz, J. J., & Levinson, S. C. (1996). *Rethinking linguistic relativity.* Cambridge, England: Cambridge University Press.

Halford, G. S. (1987). A structure-mapping approach to cognitive development. *International Journal of Psychology, 22,* 609–642.

Halford, G. S. (1993). *Children's understanding: The development of mental models.* Hillsdale, NJ: Lawrence Erlbaum Associates.

Hall, D. G., & Waxman, S. R. (1993). Assumptions about word meaning: Individuation and basic-level kinds. *Child Development, 64*(5), 1550–1570.

Hirschfeld, L. A., & Gelman, S. A. (Eds.). (1994). *Mapping the mind: Domain specificity in cognition and culture.* New York: Cambridge University Press.

Holyoak, K. J., & Thagard, P. (1995). *Mental leaps: Analogy in creative thought.* Cambridge, MA: MIT Press.

Humboldt, W. von (1988). *On language: The diversity of human language-structure and its influence on the mental development of mankind* (Peter Heath, Trans.). Cambridge, England: Cambridge University Press. (Original work published 1836).

Hunt, E., & Agnoli, F. (1991). The Whorfian hypothesis: A cognitive psychology perspective. *Psychological Review, 98,* 377–389.

Imai, M., & Gentner, D. (1997). A crosslinguistic study of early word meaning: Universal ontology and linguistic influence. *Cognition, 62,* 169–200.

Imai, M., & Mazuka, R. (1997, April). *A crosslinguistic study on the construal of individuation in linguistic and non-linguistic contexts.* Poster session presented at the Society for Research in Child Development, Washington, DC.

Inagaki, K. (1989). Developmental shift in biological inference processes: From similarity-based to category-based attribution. *Human Development, 32,* 79–87.

Inagaki, K. (1990). The effects of raising animals on children's biological knowledge. *British Journal of Developmental Psychology, 8,* 119–129.

Inagaki, K., & Hatano, G. (1987). Young children's spontaneous personification as analogy. *Child Development, 58,* 1013–1020.

Inagaki, K., & Hatano, G. (1991). Constrained person analogy in young children's biological inference. *Cognitive Development, 6,* 219–231.

Inagaki, K., & Sugiyama, K. (1988). Attributing human characteristics: Developmental changes in over- and underattribution. *Cognitive Development, 3,* 55–70.

Johnston, J. R. (1988). Children's verbal representation of spatial location. In J. Stiles-Davis & M. Kritchevsky (Eds.), *Spatial cognition: Brain bases and development* (pp. 195–205). Hillsdale, NJ: Lawrence Erlbaum Associates.

Kay, P., & Kempton, W. (1984). What is the Sapir-Whorf hypothesis? *American Anthropologist, 86,* 65–79.

Keil, F. C. (1994). The birth and nurturance of concepts by domains: The origins of concepts of living things. In L. A. Hirschfeld & S. A. Gelman (Eds.), *Mapping the mind* (pp. 234–254). New York: Cambridge University Press.

Keil, F. C., & Batterman, N. (1984). A characteristic-to-defining shift in the development of word meaning. *Journal of Verbal Learning and Verbal Behavior, 23,* 221–236.

Kolstad, V., & Baillargeon, R. (1991). *Appearance and knowledge-based responses to containers in infants.* Unpublished manuscript.

Kotovsky, L., & Gentner, D. (1996). Comparison and categorization in the development of relational similarity. *Child Development, 67,* 2797–2822.

Kuczaj, S. A., Borys, R. H., & Jones, M. (1989). On the interaction of language and thought: Some thoughts and developmental data. In A. Gellatly, D. Rogers, & J. Slaboda (Eds.), *Cognition and social worlds.* Oxford, England: Oxford University Press.

Kurtz, K. J., & Gentner, D. (1998, November). *The mechanisms of mapping: Evidence from on-line judgments of analogy.* Poster session presented at the 39th Annual Psychonomic Society, Dallas, TX.

Li, P., & Gleitman, L. (1999). *Turning the tables: Language and spatial reasoning* (Tech. Rep.). University of Pennsylvania.

Loewenstein, J., & Gentner, D. (1998, August). Relational language facilitates analogy in children. *Proceedings of the Twentieth Annual Conference of the Cognitive Science Society* (pp. 615–620). Mahwah, NJ: Lawrence Erlbaum Associates.

Loewenstein, J., & Gentner, D. (2001). Spatial mapping in preschoolers: Close comparisons facilitate far mappings. *Journal of Cognition and Development, 2*(2), 189–219.

Loewenstein, J., Thompson, L., & Gentner, D. (1999). Analogical encoding facilitates knowledge transfer in negotiation. *Psychonomic Bulletin & Review, 6*(4), 586–597.

Lucy, J. A. (1992). *Language diversity and thought: A reformation of the linguistic relativity hypothesis.* Cambridge, England: Cambridge University Press.

Lucy, J. A. (1994). *Grammatical categories and cognition.* Cambridge: Cambridge University Press.

Lucy, J. A. (1996). The scope of linguistic relativity: An analysis and review of empirical research. In J. J. Gumperz & S. C. Levinson (Eds.), *Rethinking linguistic relativity* (pp. 37–69). Cambridge, England: Cambridge University Press.

Lucy, J. A., & Shweder, R. A. (1979). Whorf and his critics: Linguistic and nonlinguistic influences on color memory. *American Anthropologist, 81,* 581–618.

Mandler, J. M., & McDonough, L. (1993). Concept formation in infancy. *Cognitive Development, 8,* 291–318.

Markman, A. B., & Gentner, D. (1990). Analogical mapping during similarity judgments. *Proceedings of the Twelfth Annual Conference of the Cognitive Science Society,* 38–44.

Markman, A. B., & Gentner, D. (1993). Structural alignment during similarity comparisons. *Cognitive Psychology, 25,* 431–467.

Markman, A. B., & Gentner, D. (1996). Commonalities and differences in similarity comparisons. *Memory and Cognition, 24*(2), 235–249.

Markman, E. M. (1989). *Categorization and naming in children: Problems of induction.* Cambridge, MA: MIT Press.

Markman, E. M., & Hutchinson, J. E. (1984). Children's sensitivity to constraints on word meaning: Taxonomic versus thematic relations. *Cognitive Psychology, 16,* 1–27.

Medin, D. L., Goldstone, R. L., & Gentner, D. (1993). Respects for similarity. *Psychological Review, 100*(2), 254–278.

Mehler, J., & Dupoux, E. (1994). *What infants know.* Malden, MA: Blackwell.

Meltzoff, A. N. (1988). Infant imitation and memory: Nine-month-olds in immediate and deferred tests. *Child Development, 59,* 217–225.

Namy, L. L., & Gentner, D. (in press). Making a silk purse out of two sow's ears: Young children's use of comparison in category learning. *Journal of Experimental Psychology: General.*

Nelson, K. (1996). *Language in cognitive development: The emergence of the mediated mind.* Cambridge: Cambridge University Press.

Novick, L. R. (1988). Analogical transfer, problem similarity, and expertise. *Journal of Experimental Psychology: Learning, Memory, and Cognition, 14,* 510–520.

Nunes, T., Schliemann, A. D., & Carraher, D. W. (1993). *Street mathematics and school mathematics.* New York: Cambridge University Press.

Piaget, J. (1951). *The child's conception of physical causality.* London: Routledge & Kegan Paul.

Piaget, J. (1952). *The origins of intelligence in children*. New York: International Universities Press.

Piaget, J. (1954). *The construction of reality in the child*. New York: Basic Books.

Piaget, J. (1955). *The language and thought of the child*. New York: World Publishing.

Pinker, S. (1989). *Learnability and cognition: The acquisiton of argument structure*. Cambridge, MA: MIT Press.

Pinker, S. (1994) *The language instinct*. New York: Morrow.

Pirolli, P. L., & Anderson, J. R. (1985). The role of learning from examples in the acquisition of recursive programming skills. *Canadian Journal of Psychology, 39*, 240–272.

Rattermann, M. J., & Gentner, D. (1998). The effect of language on similarity: The use of relational labels improves young children's performance in a mapping task. In K. Holyoak, D. Gentner, & B. Kokinov (Eds.), *Advances in analogy research: Integration of theory & data from the cognitive, computational, and neural sciences* (pp. 274–282). Sofia: New Bulgarian University.

Rattermann, M. J., & Gentner, D. (submitted). *The effect of language on similarity: The use of relational labels improves young children's analogical mapping performance.*

Rattermann, M. J., Gentner, D., & DeLoache, J. (1987, April). *Young children's use of relational similarity in a transfer task.* Poster session presented at the biennial meeting of the Society for Research in Child Development, Baltimore, MD.

Reeves, L. M., & Weisberg, R. W. (1994). The role of content and abstract information in analogical transfer. *Psychological Bulletin, 115*(3), 381–400.

Rips, L. J. (1975). Inductive judgments about natural categories. *Journal of Verbal Learning and Verbal Behavior, 14*, 665–681.

Rogoff, B. (1990). *Apprenticeship in thinking: Cognitive development in social context*. New York: Oxford University Press.

Ross, B. H. (1987). This is like that: The use of earlier problems and the separation of similarity effects. *Journal of Experimental Psychology: Learning, Memory, and Cognition, 13*(4), 629–639.

Ross, B. H. (1989). Some psychological results on case-based reasoning. In *Proceedings: Case-based reasoning workshop* (pp. 144–147). San Mateo, CA: Morgan Kaufmann.

Rovee-Collier, C. K., & Fagen, J. W. (1981). The retrieval of memory in early infancy. In L. P. Lipsett (Ed.), *Advances in infancy research, 1* (pp. 225–254). Norwood, NJ: Ablex.

Rutherford, E. (1906). *Radioactive transformations*. New York: C. Scribner's Sons.

Sapir, E. (1949/1924). The grammarian and his language. In D. G. Mandelabum (Ed.), *The selected writings of Edward Sapir in language, culture, and personality*. Berkeley, CA: University of California Press.

Scholnick, E. K., & Hall, W. S. (1991). The language of thinking: Metacognitive and conditional words. In S. A. Gelman & J. P. Byrnes (Eds.), *Perspectives on language and thought: Interrelations in development* (pp. 225–277). London: Cambridge University Press.

Scholnick, E. K., & Wing, C. S. (1982). The pragmatics of subordinating conjunctions: A second look. *Journal of Child Language, 9*, 461–479.

Shatz, M. (1991). Using cross-cultural research to inform us about the role of language in development: Comparisons of Japanese, Korean, and English, and of German, American English, and British English. In M. H. Bornstein (Ed.), *Cultural approaches to parenting* (pp. 139–153). Hillsdale, NJ: Lawrence Erlbaum Associates.

Simon, D. J., & Keil, K. C. (1995). An abstract to concrete shift in the development of biological thought: The inside story. *Cognition, 56*, 129–163.

Simon, T. J., & Klahr, D. (1995). A computational theory of children's learning about number conservation. In T. J. Simon & G. S. Halford (Eds.), *Developing cognitive competence: New approaches to process modeling* (pp. 315–354). Hillsdale, NJ: Lawrence Erlbaum Associates.

Slobin, D. I. (1996). From "thought and language" to "thinking for speaking." In J. J. Gumperz & S. C. Levinson (Eds.), *Rethinking linguistic relativity* (pp. 70–96). Cambridge, England: Cambridge University Press.

Smith, L. B. (1989). From global similarities to kinds of similarities: The construction of dimensions in development. In S. Vosniadou & A. Ortony (Eds.), *Similarity and analogical reasoning* (pp. 146–178). New York: Cambridge University Press.

Smith, L. B. (1993). The concept of same. In H. W. Reese (Ed.), *Advances in child development and behavior* (Vol. 24, pp. 215–252). San Diego, CA: Academic Press.

Smith, L. B., & Sera, M. D. (1992). A developmental analysis of the polar structure of dimensions. *Cognitive Psychology, 24*(1), 99–142.

Spelke, E. S. (1988). Where perceiving ends and thinking begins: The apprehension of objects in infancy. In A. Yonas (Ed.), *Perceptual development in infancy: Minnesota Symposia on Child Psychology, 20* (pp. 197–234). Hillsdale, NJ: Lawrence Erlbaum Associates.

Spelke, E. S. (1990). Principles of object perception. *Cognitive Science, 14,* 29–56.

Thompson, L., Gentner, D., & Loewenstein, J. (2000). Avoiding missed opportunities in managerial life: Analogical learning improves case-based transfer. *Organization Behavior and Human Decision Processes, 82*(1), 60–75.

Tomasello, M. (1995). Pragmatic contexts for early verb learning. In M. Tomasello & W. E. Merriman (Eds.), *Beyond names for things: Young children's acquisition of verbs* (pp. 115–146). Hillsdale, NJ: Lawrence Erlbaum Associates.

Tomasello, M. (1999). *The cultural origins of human cognition.* Cambridge, MA: Harvard University Press.

Uttal, D. H., Schreiber, J. C., & DeLoache, J. S. (1995). Waiting to use a symbol: The effects of delay on children's use of models. *Child Development, 66,* 1875–1889.

Vosniadou, S. (1989). Analogical reasoning as a mechanism in knowledge acquisition: A developmental perspective. In S. Vosniadou & A. Ortony (Eds.), *Similarity and analogical reasoning* (pp. 413–437). New York: Cambridge University Press.

Vygotsky, L. (1962). *Thought and language.* Cambridge, MA: MIT Press. (Original work published 1934)

Waxman, S. R. (1990). Linguistic biases and the establishment of conceptual hierarchies: Evidence from preschool children. *Cognitive Development, 5,* 123–150.

Waxman, S. R., & Gelman, R. (1986). Preschoolers' use of superordinate relations in classification and language. *Cognitive Development, 1,* 139–156.

Waxman, S. R., & Hall, G. (1993). The development of a linkage between count nouns and object categories: Evidence from fifteen- to twenty-month-old infants. *Child Development, 64,* 1224–1241.

Waxman, S. R., & Kosowski, T. (1990). Nouns mark category relations: Toddlers' and preschoolers' word-learning biases. *Child Development, 61,* 1461–1473.

Waxman, S. R., & Markow, D. B. (1995). Words as invitations to form categories: Evidence from 12- to 13-month-old infants. *Cognitive Psychology, 29,* 257–302.

Whorf, B. L. (1956). Science and linguistics. In J. B. Carroll (Ed.), *Language, thought and reality: Selected writings of Benjamin Lee Whorf* (pp. 207–219). Cambridge, MA: MIT Press.

Wilcox, S., & Palermo, D. S. (1980). "In," "on," and "under" revisited. *Cognition, 3*(3), 245–254.

Wolff, P., & Gentner, D. (2000). Evidence for role-neutral initial processing of metaphors. *Journal of Experimental Psychology: Learning, Memory, and Cognition, 26*(2), 529–541.

Chapter 5

From Thought to Hand: Structured and Unstructured Communication Outside of Conventional Language

Susan Goldin-Meadow
University of Chicago

When we talk, we use the language that has been handed down to us. If we fail to do so, we end up talking to ourselves. Moreover, if we are speaking English (as opposed to Swahili, Georgian, or Chinook), we are forced to make certain distinctions that we might not otherwise choose to make. For example, as English speakers, we are obliged to note, and encode in our talk, the number of objects to which we are referring. When I ask you to "Look at the aardvark," I am asking you to consider a single aardvark. If I want you to examine several aardvarks, I must use the word "aardvarks." Even if I have no particular interest in whether you examine one versus several aardvarks, I must (if I'm speaking English) commit myself to one request or the other—either "aardvark" or "aardvarks."

As a second example, speakers of Turkish are required, when retelling an event, to indicate whether they themselves have actually witnessed the event (Aksu-Koc & Slobin, 1986). This, of course, is a fact that the speaker obviously knows. However, the speaker may not be interested in conveying this bit of information to the listener. Speakers of English have the option of leaving out whether they actually witnessed the event they are retelling; speakers of Turkish do not.

After many years of routinely marking plurals as an English speaker, or routinely marking whether you yourself have witnessed an event as a Turkish speaker, it is possible that speakers cannot fail to note these facts about the world, and that they will habitually attend to them even when *not* speaking. This hypothesis—that the language people use has an impact

121

on the way they perceive reality—is known as the Whorfian hypothesis (Whorf, 1956). The hypothesis has had a checkered history, having at one point been essentially dismissed for lack of supportive evidence (see Lucy, 1992a, for review), only to be revived in a current search to discover new ways of reframing and testing the hypothesis (e.g., Gumperz & Levinson, 1996; Hunt & Agnoli, 1991; Levinson & Bowerman, 1998; Lucy, 1992b).

Slobin (1996a) revitalized the Whorfian hypothesis by narrowing its claims. He explored the effect of language, not on thinking broadly construed, but only on the thinking that takes place within the act of communication itself. In other words, Slobin explored the influence language has on thought that has been mobilized for communication: thinking for speaking. During the communicative act, speakers must of course attend to the dimensions of experience that are encoded within the conventional linguistic frames available in their language. However, implicit within this claim is the assumption that, during the communicative act, speakers do *not* attend to dimensions of experience that are not easily encoded within the linguistic frames of their language; that thoughts communicated in speaking situations are entirely shaped by language.

My goal in this chapter is to push the limits of this assumption. I do so by focusing on two very different communication situations. In the first, thought is expressed by a language that is not learned from convention but is rather invented *de novo* to serve the needs of thought and communication, in gestural systems created in the absence of a conventional language model. Here there are *no* conventional language frames, and thus thought cannot be molded by such frames. In the second case, thought "creeps around" conventional language, in the spontaneous gestures that co-occur with conventional language. Here there *are* conventional language frames, but thought circumvents them. In both situations, the thoughts communicated in gesture are those that have *not* been molded by conventional linguistic frames: thought unconstrained by language.

I define gesture as hand movements used in the act of communication. Although the term *gesture* often includes a variety of body movements, including facial expressions, I restrict my focus to movements of the hand primarily because these are the motions that convey substantive information (cf. McNeill, 1992). We all know that nonverbal behavior such as smiles or frowns can reveal attitude or affective stance. What people do not instinctively realize, however, is that nonverbal behavior—hand gestures, in particular—can reveal thoughts as well as feelings, for example, a spiraling upward motion conveys the shape of the climbed staircase. I concentrate on hand gestures simply because they offer a window onto the thoughts (and not just the feelings) of the communicator.

I ask first what would happen to communication if a young child were forced to communicate *outside* of any conventional language. Does the child need the linguistic frames supplied by a conventional language to be able to communicate, and in a structured fashion, the wide range of thoughts encoded in language? This question is, of course, difficult to address simply because most children are exposed to a conventional language from birth, and begin to acquire the linguistic frames of that language from the earliest moments of language learning (e.g., Berman & Slobin, 1994; Choi & Bowerman, 1991; Slobin, 1987). There are, however, children who are unable to take advantage of the conventional language model to which they are exposed: deaf children whose profound hearing losses prevent them from making use of the oral linguistic input that surrounds them, and whose hearing parents have not yet exposed them to input from a conventional sign language. In this circumstance, children might be expected to refrain entirely from communicating in a symbolic fashion. It turns out, however, that they do not. The children communicate symbolically with those around them, and use gesture to do so. Moreover, the gestures they use to communicate are structured in language-like ways. Because these children lack a usable model of a conventional language, any communication that they produce with their hands is created without the benefit of the linguistic frames of a codified system. It therefore reflects thought that has not been filtered through those codified frames (cf. Goldin-Meadow & Zheng, 1998), and vividly illustrates the structured communication of thoughts unconstrained by conventional language.

The second question I ask concerns communication that takes place *within* the context of a conventional language. Speakers undoubtedly attend to what they are saying, that is, to the thoughts that are encoded in the linguistic structures of their conventional language. The question I ask is whether they also attend, while speaking, to dimensions of experience that are *not* easily encoded in their conventional language. To address this question, we must examine aspects of communication that are not dictated by linguistic convention. The spontaneous gesture that routinely accompanies speech is a salient example of a non-codified component of communication. Gesture is not part of a conventionally recognized symbolic system. Rarely is a speaker called on the carpet for gesturing inappropriately (unless, of course, the speaker produces a rude "emblem," cf. Ekman & Friesen, 1969, but emblems are not the type of gesture I am talking about here). However, gesture does convey substantive information to those who have their eyes open (Alibali, Flevares, & Goldin-Meadow, 1997; Goldin-Meadow, Kim, & Singer, 1999; Goldin-Meadow & Sandhofer, 1999; Kelly & Church, 1997, 1998; Kendon, 1994; McNeill, Cassell, & McCullough, 1994). Gesture therefore can communicate thoughts, but need not do so in the same way that speech does. It can, in principle, encode dimensions of experience that are not easily captured in conventional language. If so, gesture may reflect thoughts that creep around the edges of speech—the unstructured thoughts that will not be tamed by a conventional language model. Gesture then may provide insight into the unstructured communication of thoughts coexisting with conventional language.

In sum, I explore here two very different communicative situations and their implication for language, communication, and thought. In the first, children have not been exposed to conventional language; the thoughts they communicate have therefore not been shaped by the linguistic frames of a codified system. In the second, children use conventional language routinely but, along with their codified system, they also use an uncodified system of spontaneous gestures; the thoughts they communicate in those gestures have the potential to extend beyond the linguistic frames of their codified system. In both situations, gesture offers a tool for examining thought that is communicated outside of conventional language.

STRUCTURED COMMUNICATION WITHOUT CONVENTIONAL LANGUAGE

Deaf children, when exposed from birth to a conventional sign language by their deaf parents, acquire that language effortlessly and along the same developmental course as hearing children acquiring spoken language from their hearing parents (Newport & Meier, 1985). However, 90% of deaf children are born to hearing parents who are unlikely to know a conventional sign language (Hoffmeister & Wilbur, 1980). Although many hearing parents choose to send their deaf children to schools where they will be exposed to sign, some prefer to educate their children in oral schools—schools whose goal is to teach the deaf child to speak using kinesthetic and visual cues, along with whatever auditory signal the child can hear. Unfortunately, it is rare for profoundly deaf children to reach age-appropriate language levels in speech even with intensive oral instruction (Conrad, 1979; Mayberry, 1992), and the deaf children we have studied were no exception. At the time of our observations, the children in our studies could occasionally produce single, isolated words in speech, but never combined two spoken words within one utterance. In addition, at the time of our observations, none of the deaf children had been exposed to conventional sign language. They, like most deaf children in this situation (Fant, 1972; Lenneberg, 1964; Moores, 1974; Tervoort, 1961), used gesture to communicate with others in their world.

Our previous work has shown that the gestural systems the deaf children use to communicate are structured in language-like ways (Feldman, Goldin-Meadow, & Gleitman, 1978; Goldin-Meadow & Feldman, 1977; Goldin-Meadow & Mylander, 1984). The children use their gestures not only to get others to do things for them, but also to comment on both the here-and-now and the non-present (Butcher, Mylander, & Goldin-Meadow, 1991; Morford & Goldin-Meadow, 1997). Indeed, the gesture systems take on many of the *functions* of natural language, including gesturing to oneself and gesturing about the gestures themselves (i.e., a metalinguistic function; see Goldin-Meadow, 1993). In addition, the gesture systems take on many of the *forms* of natural language. I focus here on the kinds of categories or units that form the basis of these structured systems, for they reflect the type and level of information—the thoughts— that children are able to communicate to others without the benefit of a conventional language model. I begin by describing each of the three levels at which we find structure in the deaf child's gesture system, focusing on the type of category on which each structure depends: the lexicon of gestures, their syntax (across-gesture structure), and their morphology (within-gesture structure).

Levels of Structure in the Deaf Child's Gesture System

The Lexicon. The first important point to note is that there is *stability* in the lexical forms the deaf child uses. If the children were constructing gestures on-the-fly every time they needed to convey an idea, we might expect to find a certain amount of variability in the forms of those gestures. The child's gesture for jar, for example, might depend on the particular type of jar the child was describing and the particular situation the jar was in. However, in an analysis of all of the iconic gestures that a single deaf child, David, produced over a 2-year period, we found great consistency in the form each gesture assumed: 90% of the deaf child's gestures were stable in form over this period (Goldin-Meadow, Butcher, Mylander, & Dodge, 1994).

The second important point is that the child's lexicon was not undifferentiated. In the lexicons of all natural languages, we find different categories of words, the most common of which is a distinction between nouns and verbs (Sapir, 1921). The deaf child's gesture system was no exception. Moreover, we found a progression of techniques that the child developed to distinguish between nouns and verbs in his system (Goldin-Meadow et al., 1994).

When we first observed the child, he used different forms entirely to convey objects, people, and places (i.e., noun-like things) versus actions or activities (i.e., verb-like things). The child used pointing gestures to refer to objects that are typically conveyed by nouns (e.g., point at a jar to refer to the jar), and iconic gestures to refer to actions that are typically conveyed by verbs (e.g., a twisting gesture to refer to the act of opening a jar).

In the next observation sessions, in addition to using points to refer to objects, the child began using iconic gestures for this purpose as well. However, he continued to distinguish between noun and verb gestures by using one set of iconic gestures to refer exclusively to objects (e.g., a round gesture might be used to refer to the jar), and a different set of gestures to refer exclusively to actions (e.g., the twisting gesture was still used to refer to opening the jar). That is, his noun and verb lexicons did not overlap. Thus, the child avoided inventing words like "comb," which can be used as both a noun and a verb. Interestingly, during their earliest stages of word learning, children learning English either avoid using words like "comb" or use them in only one sense (i.e., as either a noun or a verb, but not both; Macnamara, 1982).

Finally, the deaf child began using the same iconic gesture in noun and verb roles, but he distinguished between the two uses by the gesture's position in a sentence and its markings. In English, the position of the word in a sentence frame, along with its morphological markings, reveals whether a word like "comb" is playing a noun or verb role (e.g., noun in "I cannot use a comb on her hair" vs. verb in "I combed her hair once already today"). To determine whether the deaf child developed devices of the same sort, we reviewed all of the child's iconic gestures over a 2-year period and classified them according to whether they were the focus of the discourse (potential nouns), or comments on the focus of discourse (potential verbs). In a separate pass through the data, we also noted the position of the gesture within its sentence frame, and its markings, in particular, whether it was *abbreviated* in form (i.e., fewer repeated motions, or one hand rather than two; e.g., the gesture was produced with one twisting motion rather than several) or *inflected* (i.e., produced not in neutral space at chest level, but near an object standing for an argument in the predicate; e.g., the gesture was produced, not in neutral space at chest level, but near the to-be-opened jar, the patient of the twisting motion).

The results are presented in Fig. 5.1, which displays the proportion of gestures classified as potential verbs, and the proportion of gestures classified as potential nouns, that were marked by inflection (top graph), marked by abbreviation (middle graph), or produced in second position of a two-gesture sentence (bottom graph). The child used gestures differently if they were serving noun versus verb roles. For example, if the child were using a twisting motion to refer to the act of opening the jar, the gesture would not be abbreviated (it would have several twisting motions), but it would tend to be inflected (it would be produced near, but not on, the jar to be twisted) and occur in second position of a gesture sentence (point at jar–TWIST,[1] used to request someone to open the jar). In contrast, if the child were using the twisting motion to refer to the jar itself, the gesture would not be inflected (it would be produced in neutral space), but it

---

[1]"Point at jar–TWIST" is a sentence consisting of two gestures. Deictic pointing gestures are displayed in lowercase letters, iconic gestures in capital letters. The boundary of a gesture sentence is determined by motoric criteria. If the hand is relaxed or returned to neutral position (chest level) prior to the onset of the next gesture, each of the two gestures is considered a separate unit. If there is no relaxation of the hand between the two gestures, the two are considered part of a single gesture sentence.

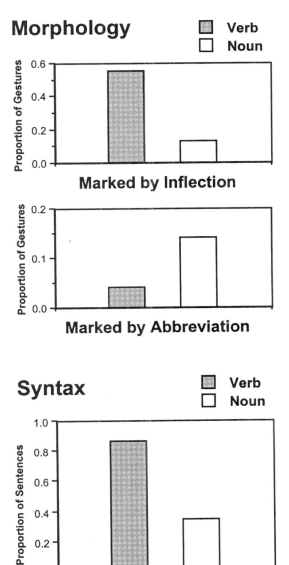

FIG. 5.1. The proportion of gestures categorized as playing a verb role (gray bar) or noun role (white bar) that were inflected (top graph) or abbreviated (middle graph). The bottom graph displays the proportion of two-gesture sentences in which gestures categorized as playing a verb versus a noun role occupied the second position of the sentence. Nouns were distinguished from verbs both in terms of morphologic (inflection and abbreviation) and syntactic marking devices.

127

would tend to be abbreviated (it would contain only one twisting motion) and occur in first position of a gesture sentence (TWIST–point at jar, used to identify the object as a jar).

Thus, even without the benefit of a conventional language model, a child can develop a stable lexicon, one that contains at least two different kinds of lexical items—nouns and verbs, the staple of all natural languages. Furthermore, over time, the child is able to introduce into the communication system more and more sophisticated techniques for maintaining the noun–verb distinction, providing good evidence that the system itself contains a set (albeit a small set) of grammatical categories.

Syntactic Structure Across Gestures.   I turn next to a syntactic analysis of the strings of gestures that the deaf children produce. The deaf children string their gestures into sentence-like units that convey propositional information. The idea conveyed in a sentence may be long, but the sentence itself tends to be short, usually containing no more than two gestures (Feldman et al., 1978). As a result, all of the elements of a proposition may not be able to be conveyed in a sentence. The question is whether there is a systematic basis for producing—or not producing—gestures for particular semantic elements.

It turns out that there is indeed systematicity underlying the child's productions. For example, when gesturing about a mouse eating cheese, the child is likely to produce a gesture for the cheese (the patient of the transitive action) but omit one for the mouse (the actor of the transitive action). Omitting gestures for actors, however, is not inevitable. When the actor participates in an action without an object (i.e., an intransitive action), it is likely to be gestured. For example, when gesturing about a mouse running to his hole, the child is very likely to produce a gesture for the mouse (the actor of the intransitive action). This pattern—that intransitive actors and patients are likely to be gestured, more likely than transitive actors—is shown in Fig. 5.2, which presents data from eight deaf children of hearing parents (four from America and four from Taiwan).

In addition to systematicity in whether or not a semantic element is produced (or omitted) in the deaf children's gesture system, there is a second device that distinguishes who does what to whom: the order of gestures in a sentence. Deaf children in both America and Taiwan (Goldin-Meadow & Mylander, 1998) tend to produce gestures for patients and intransitive actors in the first position of their two-gesture sentences (e.g., cheese–EAT; mouse–RUN). Moreover, the one deaf child who produced a sufficient number of gestures for transitive actors for us to examine a pattern (Goldin-Meadow & Mylander, 1984) tended to produce those gestures in the second position of his two-gesture sentences (e.g., EAT–mouse); that is, in a position distinctly different from the position typically occupied by patients and intransitive actors.

American Children　　Chinese Children

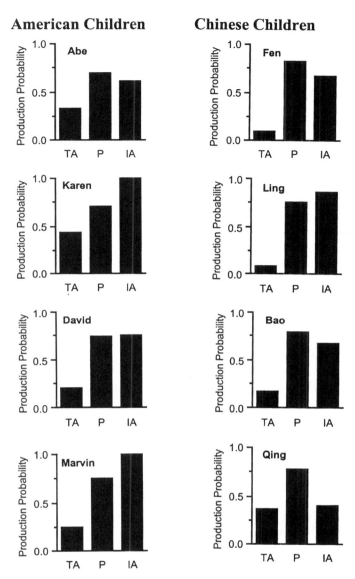

FIG. 5.2.   Probability that a gesture will be produced for Transitive Actors (TA), Patients (P), and Intransitive Actors (IA) in a two-element gesture sentence. Probabilities were calculated using sentences in which three semantic elements could be gestured but only two elements actually were gestured. As a group, the deaf children showed significant differences in production patterns across the three elements, $F(2, 7) = 22.52, p < .0001$. In seven of the eight children, gestures were produced more often for Patients and Intransitive Actors than for Transitive Actors—a structural analog of the Ergative pattern found in certain natural languages. The eighth child, Qing, exhibited an Accusative pattern—gestures were produced more often for Patients than for both Transitive and Intransitive Actors.

Thus, along with a lexicon that has grammatical categories, the deaf child has invented a simple syntax—rules of omission and rules of placement formulated in terms of semantic categories.

Morphological Structure Within Gestures.   I turn finally to morphological structure within the gesture itself. Words can often be parsed into smaller units. For example, even in English, which does not have a particularly rich morphological system, some words are built up of smaller morphemes: "dislike" is a combination of the prefix "dis" meaning 'not,' and the stem "like" meaning 'affection.' Does the deaf child's gesture system have structure at this level? We analyzed the iconic gestures produced by four deaf children and found evidence for three characteristics necessary for a morphological system (Goldin-Meadow, Mylander, & Butcher, 1995).

First, despite the fact that the manual modality provides the potential for an unlimited number of handshapes and motions, each deaf child used only a small set of handshapes and a small set of motions in his or her gesture system. Thus, each child had a discrete set of forms that could serve as the basis for a categorical system.

Second, each of the forms that the children used in their gestures was used for a particular meaning or set of meanings. Thus, for example, one child used a fist handshape to represent grasping a long (>5" in length) skinny (<2" in width) object, and a C-handshape to represent grasping a wide object (3–5" in width) of any length. The same child used a linear motion to represent change of location along a path, and a back-and-forth motion to represent bidirectional movement along an axis. Each handshape form was associated with a particular meaning, as was each motion form. In other words, the system was based on a categorical set of handshape and motion morphemes.

Finally, each of the children combined their handshape morphemes relatively freely with their motion morphemes. For example, the child could combine his fist handshape with a linear path motion to mean 'move a long, skinny object along a linear path' (e.g., move a drumstick to the table), or with a back-and-forth motion to mean 'move a long, skinny object bidirectionally' (e.g., wave a balloon string side-to-side). The system underlying the construction of gestures was not only categorical, but it was also combinatorial.

Categories and Alignments That Do Not Depend on Conventional Language

The Building Blocks.   What then have we learned from having surveyed the deaf child's gesture system? At the least, we have identified three types of categories that can be developed by children without the benefit of a con-

ventional language model: (a) morphological categories, based in this system on shapes and movement;[2] semantic categories, in this system patient
and actor; and (c) grammatical categories, in this system noun and verb.
These are basic units of communication found in all natural languages.
What the findings on the deaf children's gesture systems suggest is that
these basic units are universal to language not only because they are handed
down from one generation of speakers to the next, but because human communication—even when *not* guided by a conventional language model—
evokes categories of this sort.

The notion that thought can take place without language is no longer
controversial. The fact that these deaf children were able to develop their
gesture systems without a conventional language model offers further support for this claim (if further support were needed). However, we might
easily imagine that, without a language model, the children's thoughts
would be relatively uncategorized. That is, that language handed down by
others might be necessary in order to bundle thought into separable, discrete units. The data presented here make it clear that this is not so. A
child need not be exposed to a conventional language model to communicate using categories, and more strikingly, to communicate using these
particular sets of categories. It is impressive that deaf children can develop
categorical systems at each of the three levels surveyed here (lexical, syntactic, morphologic), and that those categories are grounded in the kinds
of notions that are typically conveyed in natural language (shapes, motions, actors, patients, nouns, verbs). The building blocks for their self-
generated systems appear to be no different from the building blocks in
languages that have existed for generations.

Alignments Among Semantic Categories.   I want to consider not only
the units on which the deaf children's gesture systems are based, but also
how those units are packaged within the system. To do so, I look at how
categories at a given level are aligned relative to one another. I turn first to
alignments among semantic categories and focus on how patients and actors are treated in the deaf child's gesture system.

All natural languages make a linguistic distinction between done-to's
(patients) and doers (actors), between eatens and eaters, for example. In
English, we typically put the actor of a transitive action before the verb,
and the patient after the verb ("the mouse eats the cheese") and, in cases
where morphologic markings are required (that is, in pronouns), we mark
the actor in one way, and the patient in another ("he hit him"). What hap-

---

[2]It is worth noting that in many morphologically rich languages (including American Sign
Language; Supalla, 1982), shape is frequently one of the dimensions that defines a set of
morphological categories, typically classifiers (cf. Allen, 1977).

pens, in this scheme, to actors that do not affect objects, that is, actors in intransitive actions, a runner, for example? A runner is, in one sense, comparable to an eater—both initiate the action. On the other hand, the runner is also comparable to an eaten—both are affected by the action. On conceptual grounds, a runner could be aligned with either the doer or the done-to.

Languages, it turns out, make different choices and align runners in different ways. In English, which adheres to an accusative pattern, the runner is aligned with the eater: It appears before the verb ("the mouse runs") and is marked morphologically like transitive actors ("he runs" rather than "him runs").

Other languages, called ergative languages (e.g., Chinook or Georgian), make the other choice, aligning the runner with the eaten (Dixon, 1979; Silverstein, 1976). If English were ergative, the intransitive actor would appear after the verb ("runs the mouse") and would be marked morphologically like the patient ("runs him").

Another look at Fig. 5.2 makes it clear that seven of the eight deaf children followed an ergative pattern with respect to production and omission; they produced gestures for the intransitive actor as often as they produced gestures for patients, and far more often than they produced gestures for transitive actors. The eighth child, Qing, followed an accusative pattern; she produced gestures for intransitive actors as infrequently as she produced gestures for transitive actors, far less than she produced gestures for patients. The deaf children did not have any particular model to adhere to, conventional or otherwise (the spontaneous gestures the children's hearing mothers produced followed no particular pattern at all; Goldin-Meadow & Mylander, 1998). They therefore were not compelled to show any consistency whatsoever. However, each child did exhibit consistency of production and omission within his or her gesture system. Moreover, the patterns the children displayed in their gesture systems are patterns found in natural language.

Most of the spoken languages in the world—including the two that surround the deaf children we have studied (i.e., English and Mandarin)—are accusative. Why then might the majority of the deaf children, across two very different cultures, exhibit an ergative pattern in their gesture systems? Du Bois (1987) has suggested that there is a discourse basis for ergative structure in spoken language. Indeed, he found that even in a language like English, which, at a syntactic level, is accusative, one can see evidence of an ergative pattern at the discourse level. It may be that ergative structure in the deaf children's gestures reflects these discourse pressures, although it is clear that the pressures make themselves felt through neither the hearing parents' words (which the deaf children cannot hear) nor their gestures (which are patterned very differently from their children's gestures; Goldin-Meadow & Mylander, 1983, 1998).

Alignments Among Grammatical Categories. I turn next to grammatical categories. In chapter 4 of this volume, Gentner proposes a continuum along which nouns and verbs can be aligned, with object-referring nouns at one end and relational-referring verbs at the other. One question, then, is where should adjectives be placed along this continuum? On one hand, adjectives are closely aligned with nouns, being their modifiers and therefore dependent on them for their existence; indeed, in many languages (like French) adjectives assume the markings of the noun they are modifying. On the other hand, adjectives are also relational and, in this sense, are more closely aligned with verbs.

In fact, adjectives tend to be a less robust category than either nouns or verbs in languages across the globe. Cross-linguistically, adjectives can form their own separate lexical category, or they can align themselves with, and assume the markings of, either nouns or verbs. However, there are also cases where adjectives share features with nouns as well as verbs in the language (Thompson, 1988). This is the pattern exhibited by the deaf child, David, described earlier.

Figure 5.3 presents data on this child's use of adjectives, gestures that were used to refer to properties (Goldin-Meadow et al., 1994). The adjective data are presented within the framework of the noun–verb data found in Fig. 5.1. Note that, in terms of morphologic markings, adjectives resembled *nouns* in this child's gesture system (the white bars in the top and middle graphs). For example, if the child were using the broken gesture (typically two fists held together side-by-side and then repeatedly broken apart) to describe the current state of a toy, that gesture would not be inflected (that is, it would be produced in neutral space at chest level) but it would tend to be abbreviated (that is, the breaking-apart movement would be produced only once). However, in terms of syntactic structure, adjectives resembled *verbs* in this child's gesture system (black bars in the bottom graph). The broken gesture would tend to be placed in the second position of a two-gesture sentence (point at toy–BROKEN).

Thus, the deaf child has invented an adjective category that fits the variable pattern found in natural languages. In this child's system, adjectives do not form a separate lexical category but rather align themselves, at times, with nouns and, at other times, with verbs and do so systematically, sharing morphologic features with nouns and syntactic features with verbs. There appears to be a robust noun–verb framework within which adjectives are located, not only in conventional languages, but also in unconventional systems developed by young children.

To summarize thus far, we have found that when gesture is used by deaf children as an alternative to conventional language, either signed or spoken, it assumes a language-like form. Language-like form is not inevitable in the manual modality; gesture can communicate information to others

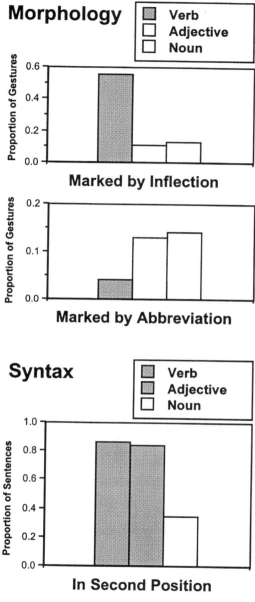

FIG. 5.3. The proportion of gestures categorized as playing an adjective role that were inflected (top graph) or abbreviated (middle graph). The bottom graph displays the proportion of two-gesture sentences in which gestures categorized as playing an adjective role occupied the second position of the sentence. Adjectives resembled nouns (white bars) in terms of morphological markings (inflection and abbreviation), but verbs (gray bars) in terms of syntactic position.

without taking on linguistic forms (McNeill, 1992). The fact then that gesture assumes the forms of language as well as many of its functions when a child attempts to communicate with others is noteworthy. Moreover, under these circumstances, gesture is structured at different levels, each based on its own type of category. These building blocks of the system—the morphological, semantic, and grammatical categories—are comparable to categories that form the foundation of conventional languages. Finally, the building blocks are packaged into frameworks. Those frameworks, and the alignments of categories within them, are comparable to those found in conventional languages.

It is clear that the properties gesture assumes when it is used as the deaf children's primary means of communication do not come from a conventional language model. They could, however, come from the spontaneous gestures that the children's hearing parents use as they attempt to communicate with them through talk. In previous work, we have found no evidence for this hypothesis. In terms of morphologic categories, the mothers' spontaneous gestures do not conform well at all to the handshape and motion morphemes that characterize their children's gestures (Goldin-Meadow et al., 1995). In terms of syntactic categories, the mothers' spontaneous gestures either assume no structure at all or a different structure from their children's gestures (Goldin-Meadow & Mylander, 1983, 1998). Finally, in terms of grammatical categories, the mothers' spontaneous gestures showed little stability of form over a 2-year period and no evidence for a systematic distinction between nouns, verbs, and adjectives (Goldin-Meadow et al., 1994). Thus, there is no evidence that the deaf children learned their gesture systems from observing the spontaneous gestures of their hearing mothers.

Nelson and Shaw (chapter 2, this volume) argue that there is a social aspect to language symbols in that the meanings incorporated in those symbols are shared between individuals. Note that the deaf child's gesture system is social, but in an unusual sense—the child produces gestures that, primarily because of their iconicity, can be understood by the child's hearing parents. But the hearing parents themselves produce gestures that are quite different in form from the deaf child's; the child is a producer, but not a receiver, of language-like gesture. The deaf child is therefore not required to do the "refining" to conform to societal norms that Nelson and Shaw describe in hearing children's acquisition of words.

One nagging question is, Why are the hearing parents' gestures so different from their deaf children's? One might have thought that, having to interact with one another day in and day out, the gesture systems of the two would begin to resemble one another, either the child's system assuming the properties of the mother's, or vice versa. We found no evidence of compromise on either participant's part, and the question is, Why? I sus-

pect that one reason may be that gesture is serving a very different function for the deaf children and for their hearing mothers (Goldin-Meadow,
McNeill, & Singleton, 1996). The deaf children use gesture as their primary means of communication. The hearing mothers do not use gesture
by itself but only as an accompaniment to speech (recall that the mothers'
educational goal for their children is to teach them oral language).
McNeill (1992) has proposed that the spontaneous gestures speakers produce along with their talk form a single, integrated system with that talk.
When the hearing mothers gesture as they speak, those gestures must conform to the gesture–speech system that underlies the communication. The
mothers' gestures are, in a sense, not free to assume the language-like
properties found in their deaf children's gestures. My goal in the next section of this chapter is to explore the gestures that routinely accompany
talk in hearing adults and children, focusing in particular on what gesture
can tell us about the thoughts that arise in communication when it accompanies, rather than replaces, speech.

To summarize thus far, Slobin (1996a) has suggested that conventional
language constrains thoughts communicated in a speaking situation. Each
conventional language nudges its speakers to notice, and communicate,
certain notions and not others. In order to appreciate just how much influence a language model may (or may not) have over the content and form
of communication, we need to know what communication can look like in
the absence of conventional language. The gesture systems invented by
the deaf children described here provide just this backdrop. The notions
that the deaf children express in their gesture systems are thoughts that
have *not* been molded by the linguistic frames of a conventional language.
By observing what happens to those thoughts once a conventional language such as English is learned, we can begin to see the impact that language may have on thoughts conveyed during speaking.

We turn now to the notions that children (and adults) express in the
gestures that accompany speech, for these, too, have the potential to be
thoughts that have *not* been molded by linguistic frames.

UNSTRUCTURED COMMUNICATION WITHIN
CONVENTIONAL LANGUAGE

Gesture Can Convey Information That Is Not Found
in the Conventional Talk It Accompanies

The first point to stress is that gesture is pervasive. When people talk, they
gesture. Across cultures (Feyereisen & de Lannoy, 1991), ages (McNeill,
1992), and many tasks (Iverson & Goldin-Meadow, 1998a), speakers spon-

taneously move their hands as they speak. Indeed, even congenitally blind children who have never seen others gesture move their hands as they talk (Iverson & Goldin-Meadow, 1997, 1998b).

We use gesture routinely when we speak and, crucially, it is not just hand waving. The spontaneous gestures that accompany talk can convey substantive and task-relevant information that is, at times, different from the information conveyed in the accompanying speech (Crowder, 1996; Goldin-Meadow, 1997; Goldin-Meadow, Alibali, & Church, 1993; Kendon, 1980; McNeill, 1992; Schwartz & Black, 1996). For example, consider a child participating in a Piagetian number conservation task. The child pronounces that the row of checkers spread out by the experimenter has a different number of checkers than the unspread-out row, and justifies his judgment by saying, "It's different because you moved them." At the same time, the child moves his pointing finger between the first checker in the spread-out row and the first checker in the unspread-out row, and then continues pairing the checkers in the two rows. In his speech, the child focuses on the fact that the experimenter spread the checkers out. In his gesture, however, the child demonstrates some understanding of the fact that the checkers in the two rows can be paired with one another, thus demonstrating an incipient understanding of one-to-one correspondence (Church & Goldin-Meadow, 1986).

What kinds of thoughts do children typically convey in the gesture that accompanies speech? Pointing, or deictic, gestures can indicate objects, places, people, and so on, in the surrounds. Indeed, at times, pointing gestures can be used to indicate objects that are not present. For example, when shown a tie that belongs to her father, a child might say, "It's dad's" while pointing, not at her father who is not present in the room, but at the dining room chair where her father typically sits (cf. Butcher, Mylander, & Goldin-Meadow, 1991). Iconic gestures can convey properties or actions. For example, in a conservation task, a child may say "It's short," while indicating the height of the container with a flat palm. Or the child might say, "All you did was pour it," while miming the pouring action with a hand shaped like a "C." When taken together, gestures produced in a string can also convey larger ideas. Consider the child who, with a string of pointing gestures, managed to convey one-to-one correspondence. Indeed, children are able to use strings of gestures to convey problem-solving strategies (Garber, Alibali, & Goldin-Meadow, 1998).

The thoughts hearing children convey in their gestures go beyond the thoughts they convey in their speech in two ways. First, because analog information is so easily captured by the manual modality, gesture is able to flesh out information that is conveyed, often only analytically, in speech (Goldin-Meadow & McNeill, 1999). For example, a child who says, "It's short" does not actually convey to the listener how short the container is.

However, if that speech were to be accompanied by a flat palm held two inches above the table, the listener would get a much richer sense of the height of the container.

The information hearing children convey in their gestures is not likely to be absolutely veridical; that is, their gestures are typically not exact replicas of the actions or objects they represent. However, the gestures that hearing children use along with speech come much closer to representing actual variations among objects and actions than the gestures that the deaf children use as their primary communication system. Recall that the deaf children's gestures are constructed out of a discrete and limited set of handshape and motion morphemes. The child uses a given handshape to represent a class of objects, not a particular object. For example, the deaf child whose fist handshape represents long, skinny objects would use the fist to describe grasping a kite string, a drumstick, or a banana. One could easily devise handshapes that could distinguish among these three objects, and a hearing child generating gestures to use along with speech is likely to do so. But the deaf child's gestures must adhere to the system of contrasts that dictates gesture formation (the morphological rules of the system). In addition to considering how well a handshape represents the object to which it refers (gesture-to-world relations), the deaf child must also consider how well that handshape fits with the other handshapes in the system (gesture-to-gesture relations; Singleton, Morford, & Goldin-Meadow, 1993). Thus, the deaf child's gestures are more constrained than the hearing child's. Hearing children are able to take fuller advantage of gesture's analog potential for representation, and use it to supplement the segmented information conveyed in their speech.

The second way in which the thoughts conveyed in hearing children's gestures can go beyond the thoughts conveyed in their speech is that gesture can focus on entirely different aspects of the situation than speech. Consider the example described at the beginning of this section. In his speech, the child focused on the experimenter's movements, but in his gestures, he focused on how the checkers in one row can be aligned with the checkers in the other. Examples of this sort make it clear that, with gesture, a speaker can transmit thoughts well beyond the bounds of what is being presented in the acknowledged and codified system.

We often find that when children convey information in gesture that is different from the information they convey in speech—that is, when they produce a gesture–speech mismatch (Church & Goldin-Meadow, 1986)—the information conveyed in gesture cannot be found anywhere in the children's speech and is therefore unique to gesture. As an example, we examined the entire repertoire of problem-solving strategies that children produced either in speech or in gesture on a series of mathematical equivalence problems, for example,

$$5 + 6 + 3 = \_\_ + 3$$

(Alibali & Goldin-Meadow, 1993). We determined which modality the child produced each strategy in across the set of six problems: (a) speech alone (the strategy was produced in speech but never in gesture), (b) gesture alone (the strategy was produced in gesture but never in speech), or (c) both speech and gesture (the strategy was produced in both modalities, perhaps on the same problem but not necessarily, i.e., the child could produce the strategy in speech on one problem and that same strategy in gesture on another). We found that, surprisingly, only 10% of the strategies the children produced appeared in speech alone—if children could convey a strategy in speech, they could also convey that strategy in gesture (Goldin-Meadow et al., 1993). Most of the children's strategies were either produced in both gesture and speech (45%) or in gesture alone (44%). Thus, a relatively large percentage of the problem-solving strategies in the children's repertoires were expressible *only* in gesture. To determine these children's understanding of mathematical equivalence, one must not only listen to them but also look at their hands.

Does Gesture Have Cognitive Significance?

The spontaneous gestures that speakers produce as they talk clearly convey thoughts that are not expressed in the talk itself. I next consider whether gesture has cognitive significance, that is, is it associated with learning, problem solving, or memory? Several lines of research suggest that it is (see Goldin-Meadow, 1999).

First, gesture, when considered in relation to the speech it accompanies, is an excellent predictor of readiness-to-learn. It turns out that, on certain tasks, some children frequently produce gestures that go beyond their speech—they frequently produce gesture–speech mismatches—whereas other children rarely do. When all of the children are given instruction in the task (none was successful on the task prior to instruction), the children who produce a relatively large number of gesture–speech mismatches are likely to make progress on the task—significantly more likely than children who produce a small number of gesture–speech mismatches. We have found this phenomenon on two tasks—conservation (Church & Goldin-Meadow, 1986) and mathematical equivalence (Perry, Church, & Goldin-Meadow, 1988)—and there is some evidence that the phenomenon may hold for adults learning a new task as well (Perry & Elder, 1996). Thus, learners who frequently convey information in gesture that is different from the information they convey in speech are ready to make effective use of instruction (although the instruction must help learners organize what they know about the task, and focus primarily on principles underlying the task rather than procedures for solving it; Perry, Church, & Goldin-Meadow, 1992). Gesture, in relation to speech, reflects the volatility of the learner's cognitive state.

Second, gesture when considered in relation to the speech it accompanies can predict how the speaker is going to solve a problem (Alibali, Bassok, Olseth, Syc, & Goldin-Meadow, 1995; Alibali, Bassok, Solomon, Syc, & Goldin-Meadow, 1999). This study was done with adults who were given a series of problems involving constant change (e.g., a bookcase has 6 shelves and the number of books on each successive shelf increases by a constant number; if there are 15 books on the top shelf and 45 on the bottom, how many books total are there?). We first asked the adult to describe the problem to a listener (a confederate), and later coded the speech and gesture in these descriptions according to whether gesture conveyed the same information as speech (reinforcing) or not (neutral or conflicting). We then asked the adult how he or she would solve the problem, and determined whether the problem-solving strategy the adult chose was compatible with that adult's description of the problem. We found that adults were very likely to use a problem-solving strategy that was compatible with their spoken description of a problem when their gestures reinforced that spoken description—significantly more likely than when their gestures either were neutral or conflicted with the spoken description of the problem. Gesture thus appears to reflect ideas that adults have, but do not say, about the problem. Those ideas deflect the adults from solving the problem with the strategy that one would have predicted from their talk; in other words, the ideas displayed in gesture have an impact on how the problems are solved.

Third, there is some evidence that the act of gesturing itself may affect memory. For example, Fisher and Brennan (personal communication, June 3, 1998) found that better recall was associated with gesture. Children observed a Red Cross lecture/demonstration that they were asked to recall after a week had passed. Although accuracy of recall was generally high (80%), it was much higher (99%) when the children gestured along with their recalled responses. Gesture was not a manipulated variable in Fisher and Brennan's study, it arose as a serendipitous finding. In contrast, Iverson (personal communication, June 1998) deliberately manipulated gesture to determine its effects on recall. Adults were shown a cartoon and asked to retell the story immediately after viewing it. During the immediate retelling, half of the adults were told to keep their hands still on the arms of the chair, and half were given no particular instructions. The second group gestured in retelling the cartoon, but the first obviously did not. There were no differences between the groups in the number of story details that were recalled during the immediate retelling. However, when asked to retell the cartoon again one week later (this time none of the adults was restricted in their movements), the group that was initially allowed to gesture recalled more details about the cartoon than the group that was initially prevented from gesturing. Gesturing during the first retelling thus made it more likely that the adult would retain and recall information during the second retelling. Although it is not yet clear what role gesture is playing in memory (e.g., at what point in the memory process does gesture make its contribution?), these studies do strongly suggest that gesture plays a beneficial role in recall.

Finally, we are currently conducting a study that explores whether gesture can serve as a "cognitive prop." Gesture externalizes ideas differently, and therefore may draw on different resources, than speech. Conveying an idea across two modalities may, in the end, require less effort than constraining the idea to speech alone. If so, using gesture may actually ease the processing burden (as does, e.g., a diagram), and thus free up cognitive effort that can then be used on other tasks. We asked children to explain their solutions to a mathematical equivalence problem and, at the same time, remember a list of words. We prevented the children from moving their hands on half of the math problems, but allowed free movement on the other half. When allowed to move their hands, children produced gestures conveying strategies for solving the problems. For example, to explain how she solved the problem

$$3 + 6 + 7 = \_\_ + 7,$$

one child said "I added the 3 and 6 and put 9 in the blank," while at the same time pointing at the 3 and 6 with her middle and index fingers forming a V-shape, and then pointing at the blank. Gesturing of this sort might be expected to increase the speaker's cognitive load simply because she must plan and execute communication in two modalities (speech and gesture). If, however, gesture and speech form a single, integrated system (McNeill, 1992), gesturing might make it easier for speakers to convey certain kinds of information and, as a result, reduce demands on their cognitive resources. We found that if the children gestured when explaining a math problem, they recalled significantly more words than if they did not gesture (Goldin-Meadow, 2001; Goldin-Meadow, Nusbaum, Kelly, & Wagner, in press). Thus, gesturing appeared to ease the burden imposed by the explanation task, releasing effort that could then be used on the word-recall task. Gesture may, therefore, function not only as a vehicle for thought, but also as a mechanism for effecting change in thought.

In sum, when gesture is used along with conventional spoken language, it conveys substantive information and does so in an analog fashion. Gesture therefore has the potential to "fill in" thoughts that are left unspecified in speech. Even more striking, gesture can at times convey information that focuses on very different aspects of a problem than the information conveyed in speech. Often this information is not found anywhere in the speaker's spoken repertoire, and made accessible only to the manual modality. Finally, gesture may have cognitive significance, playing a role in learning, problem solving, and recall.

THOUGHTS THAT ARE COMMUNICATED OUTSIDE OF CONVENTIONAL LANGUAGE

All natural languages, signed or spoken, are codified. That is, they contain grammatical and lexical devices dictating the form that notions can take in communication. The question I have addressed here is: How bound by our conventional language are the thoughts we convey when we communicate? I have explored this question by examining communication that is not codified, that is, communication that is not part of any conventional symbolic system. Gesture is a salient example of non-codified communication, and I have examined the spontaneous gestures that children produce in two very different situations: deaf children who use gesture as their *only* means of communication (gestural communication without a conventional language), and hearing children who use gesture as an accompaniment to speech (gestural communication within a conventional language).

Although gesture serves to convey the thoughts of the communicator in both situations, there are differences between the gestures that the deaf and the hearing children use. The deaf children's gestures are produced in order to communicate with those around them; indeed, one of the criteria we use for isolating gestures is that the children make eye contact with the listener as a measure of their intent to communicate (Goldin-Meadow & Mylander, 1984). Over time, it becomes clear that the children not only know they are using their gestures to communicate, but they also know the "correct" forms for those gestures; that is, they establish their own standards of form (Singleton et al., 1993). The gestures that the deaf children create are segmented and discrete, as are all natural languages. Although they are iconic, the gestures are not analog: They are composed of handshape and motion forms that represent *classes* of objects and actions. Moreover, these handshape and motion forms not only map systematically onto classes of objects and actions (gesture-to-world relations), they also conform to, and contrast with, the other handshape and motion forms in the child's repertoire (they adhere to gesture-to-gesture relations). Thus, the deaf child's gestures form a system and, in this sense, have the status of symbols (cf. Nelson & Shaw, chapter 2, this volume).

In contrast, the gestures that hearing individuals—both children and adults—spontaneously produce as they talk are idiosyncratic in form.

They adjust to the peculiarities of the communicative moment, and represent those peculiarities in an imagistic and analog form (McNeill, 1992). The communication that the gestures accompany is intentional; speakers know they are talking, but there is no evidence that they are aware of gesturing (Goldin-Meadow & Sandhofer, 1999). The gestures hearing individuals produce are thus not intentional in the same way that the deaf children's gestures are. In previous work, we have argued that the function gesture serves is important in determining its form. We argue that it is *only* when gesture serves as a primary communication system, as it does for the deaf child, that it assumes language-like forms (Goldin-Meadow et al., 1996). When gesture accompanies speech, it is speech that takes on the language-like form, leaving the imagistic and analog representation to gesture (Goldin-Meadow & McNeill, 1999). However, despite rather large differences in function, form, conventionality, and intentionality, it is important to note that the gestures of both the deaf children and hearing speakers convey substantive information about the gesturer's thoughts.

How does an examination of gesture in deaf and hearing children speak to the effects of language on thought? Although the findings I have reported here make it clear that children can think without language, we hardly needed additional confirmation of an idea so elegantly shown and in so many different ways by Piaget. What I have shown here is that our thoughts can go beyond the bounds of conventional language even when we are communicating; that is, that even our communicated thoughts are not completely dictated by the devices our conventional language provides for us. I have suggested that gesture can serve as a tool for discovering two types of thoughts that do not depend on having a conventional language.

Thoughts in Linguistic Packages

The fact that the deaf children can invent gesture systems characterized by language-like structure suggests that at least some linguistic categories and patterns can be developed without a conventional language model. The categories and alignments that the deaf children exhibit in their gestures are just those categories and alignments that do not depend for their development on the accumulated knowledge that resides in our conventional language systems. They are properties that can arise in a language developed *de novo* (albeit within a cultural world that has grown up with language at its core).

The building blocks found in the deaf children's gesture systems (actors, patients, nouns, verbs) are universally found in all natural languages. These then are *not* the places to search for Whorfian effects. Because conventional language is not necessary for these particular categories to surface in a communication system, it is reasonable to assume that children themselves bring these categories to the language-learning situation (whether they bring them as a result of internal predispositions to structure the world in this fashion, or as a result of pressures from the communicative situation itself is an open question, one that requires data of a different sort to discriminate between these two alternatives; cf. Goldin-Meadow et al., 1996; Goldin-Meadow, Yalabik, & Gershkoff-Stowe, 2000). Although it is possible that learning (and using) a conventional code for these categories will further strengthen their salience, it is not likely. These are the categories that children appear to expect to serve as the building blocks for symbolic communication.

What about the alignments of the building blocks? The particular alignments found in the deaf children's gesture systems are not universal across languages, nor even across all of the deaf children. Recall that whereas seven of the deaf children exhibited an ergative pattern in their gestures, one exhibited an accusative pattern (we have thus far explored the alignments of nouns, verbs, and adjectives in only one deaf child). However, the frameworks, or continua, on which the alignments are based are universal across languages, and have been found in the gesture systems of all of the deaf children studied thus far (a distinction between patients and actors in transitive actions; a distinction between nouns and verbs). Thus, we might expect to find Whorfian effects, not surrounding the continua themselves, but surrounding the idiosyncratic decisions about where to draw a dividing line along a particular continuum (whether to classify an intransitive actor as a patient or a transitive actor; whether to classify an adjective as a noun or a verb).

It may turn out that the alignments that predominate across the deaf children (e.g., ergativity) are basic states reflecting universal pressures on all communicators (cf. the Du Bois, 1987, argument regarding the discourse basis of ergativity). If so, some conventional languages (e.g., those that have accusative structure) will serve to reconfigure the speaker's alignment away from this basic pattern (note that once a speaker's alignments have been reconfigured away from ergativity, it may be hard to return; witness the difficulty most speakers of accusative languages have in making sense of an ergative configuration). Another scenario, however, is that the deaf children's alignments have been influenced by the idiosyncrasies of their own communication situation—the fact that their communication system is produced in the manual modality without a willing communication partner. Whatever the reasons for the particular alignments that we find in the deaf children's gesture systems, it is clear that they point the way to some of the best places to explore the interplay between the thoughts children bring to the communication situation and the effect that conventional language has on those thoughts.

Thoughts in Non-Linguistic Packages

The fact that hearing children express thoughts in gesture that they do not express in speech suggests that speakers can, and do, include in their communications non-categorical information that goes beyond the conventional code. Consider, for example, a speaker who is describing the coastline of the east coast of the United States. One well-formed gesture can do much more to convey the nuances of the coastline to a listener than even the best-chosen set of words (cf. Huttenlocher, 1976). Gesture thus allows speakers to convey thoughts that may not easily fit into the categorical system that their conventional language offers (Goldin-Meadow & McNeill, 1999).

In addition, gesture may allow speakers to convey unobtrusively thoughts that just do not fit into their acknowledged conceptual systems. Recall the child who expressed in gesture some insight into the notion of one-to-one correspondence, a fundamental idea at the heart of number conservation. In speech, this child was a relentless non-conserver, judging that the two rows had different numbers of checkers and explaining that judgment by pointing out that the experimenter had moved the checkers in one of the rows. The child had an incipient understanding of number conservation but was not yet able to integrate this insight into his system of articulated beliefs. Gesture provided him with an outlet for that budding belief. Gesture thus provides speakers with a vehicle for expressing thoughts that may be somewhat inchoate or untamed—thoughts that are not yet ready for prime time. The data I have described here illustrate this point on an individual level: A child who does not seem to be able to express a thought in speech is nevertheless able to express that thought in gesture. McNeill (1998) has evidence of a comparable effect at the cultural level.

According to Talmy (1985), each language has a characteristic way of packaging information about a motion event. Spanish bundles information about the path of motion into the verb itself, leaving information about the manner of motion to a gerund construction ("*y sale volando*" 'and exits flying'). Slobin (1996b) has found that Spanish speakers often omit explicit reference to manner of motion in their talk; for example, a speaker might indicate that a cat ascended a pipe without making it clear how he did so. However, although they may omit manner from their talk, Spanish speakers often convey this information in their gestures; a spoken reference to ascending the pipe may be accompanied by an upward movement in which the hand twists and wiggles left and right as it rises, thereby conveying the wiggling manner by which the ascent was accomplished (McNeill, 1998). In other words, gesture may convey information that is routinely omitted from the speaker's words.

As a final point, I note that, in addition to serving as a useful tool for conveying thought outside of conventional code, gesture may itself be a vehicle for thought. For example, the gesture that accompanies speech may not just be associated with, but may actually be involved in, processes of learning, problem solving, and remembering. We might also ask what the effect of routinely producing a thought in gesture and not in speech (e.g., manner for Spanish speakers) might have on the speaker. Would gesturing an idea, as opposed to talking it, affect the way that idea is remembered or acted on in the future? This is a Whorfian notion in the sense that gesture is a *symbolic* system that has the potential to affect thought. However, the notion departs from Whorf in that gesture is not a *codified* system and therefore not part of the conventional code shared across a culture. Even for the deaf children, it is precisely this function of language—to provide the child with access to cultural ways of being, feeling, and acting (Budwig, chapter 3, this volume)—that gesture does not really serve.

In sum, gesture, in many of the various conditions under which it is produced, can provide insight into those areas where conventional language does *not* dominate thought. The fact that language does not dominate all of the thoughts that we have, even while we speak, does not of course mean that language does not have any effect on thought. Indeed, I have suggested that gesture itself may affect thought, and, if so, we all may well want to pay closer attention to how we move our hands.

ACKNOWLEDGMENTS

This chapter is dedicated to the memory of Mimi Sinclair who started me thinking about language and its relation to thought many years ago when I spent my junior year abroad doing research under her tutelage at the Institut des Sciences de l'Education in Geneva. The experience made a lasting impression on me and essentially set the course of my future research. I thank as well all of my many collaborators who have contributed in countless ways to the research described here. Finally, I thank Terry Regier for insightful comments on the manuscript itself. This research was supported by BNS 8810769 from the National Science Foundation, RO1 DC00491 from the National Institute of Neurological and Communicative Disorders and Stroke, RO1 HD18617 from the National Institute of Child Health and Human Development, and a grant from the Spencer Foundation.

REFERENCES

Aksu-Koc, A., & Slobin, D. I. (1986). A psychological account of the development and use of evidentials in Turkish. In W. Chafe & J. Nichols (Eds.), *Evidentiality: The linguistic coding of epistemology* (pp. 185–201). Norwood, NJ: Ablex.

Alibali, M. W., Bassok, M., Olseth, K. L., Syc, S. E., & Goldin-Meadow, S. (1995). Gestures reveal mental models of discrete and continuous change. In J. D. Moore & J. F. Lehman (Eds.), *Proceedings of the Seventeenth Annual Conference of the Cognitive Science Society* (pp. 391–396). Hillsdale, NJ: Lawrence Erlbaum Associates.

Alibali, M. W., Bassok, M., Solomon, K. O., Syc, S. E., & Goldin-Meadow, S. (1999). Illuminating mental representations through speech and gesture. *Psychological Science, 10,* 327–333.

Alibali, M. W., Flevares, L., & Goldin-Meadow, S. (1997). Assessing knowledge conveyed in gesture: Do teachers have the upper hand? *Journal of Educational Psychology, 89,* 183–193.

Alibali, M. W., & Goldin-Meadow, S. (1993). Gesture-speech mismatch and mechanisms of learning: What the hands reveal about a child's state of mind. *Cognitive Psychology, 25,* 468–523.

Allen, K. (1977). Classifiers. *Language, 53,* 285–311.

Berman, R. A., & Slobin, D. I. (1994). *Relating events in narrative: A crosslinguistic developmental study.* Hillsdale, NJ: Lawrence Erlbaum Associates.

Butcher, C., Mylander, C., & Goldin-Meadow, S. (1991). Displaced communication in a self-styled gesture system: Pointing at the non-present. *Cognitive Development, 6,* 315–342.

Choi, S., & Bowerman, M. (1991). Learning to express motion events in English and Korean: The influence of language-specific lexicalization patterns. *Cognition, 43,* 83–121.

Church, R. B., & Goldin-Meadow, S. (1986). The mismatch between gesture and speech as an index of transitional knowledge. *Cognition, 23,* 43–71.

Conrad, R. (1979). *The deaf child.* London: Harper & Row.

Crowder, E. M. (1996). Gestures at work in sense-making science talk. *Journal of the Learning Sciences, 5,* 173–208.

Dixon, R. M. W. (1979). Ergativity. *Language, 55,* 59–138.

Du Bois, J. W. (1987). The discourse basis of ergativity. *Language, 63,* 805–855.

Ekman, P., & Friesen, W. V. (1969). The repertoire of non-verbal behavior: Categories, origins, usage, and coding. *Semiotica, 1,* 49–98.

Fant, L. J. (1972). *Ameslan: An introduction to American Sign Language.* Silver Springs, MD: National Association of the Deaf.

Feldman, H., Goldin-Meadow, S., & Gleitman, L. (1978). Beyond Herodotus: The creation of language by linguistically deprived deaf children. In A. Lock (Ed.), *Action, symbol, and gesture: The emergence of language* (pp. 351–414). New York: Academic Press.

Feyereisen, P., & de Lannoy, J.-D. (1991). *Gestures and speech: Psychological investigations.* Cambridge, England: Cambridge University Press.

Garber, P., Alibali, M. W., & Goldin-Meadow, S. (1998). Knowledge conveyed in gesture is not tied to the hands. *Child Development, 69,* 75–84.

Goldin-Meadow, S. (1993). When does gesture become language? A study of gesture used as a primary communication system by deaf children of hearing parents. In K. R. Gibson & T. Ingold (Eds.), *Tools, language, and cognition in human evolution* (pp. 63–85). New York: Cambridge University Press.

Goldin-Meadow, S. (1997). When gesture and words speak differently. *Current Directions in Psychological Science, 6,* 138–143.

Goldin-Meadow, S. (1999). The role of gesture in communication and thinking. *Trends in Cognitive Science, 3,* 419–429.

Goldin-Meadow, S. (2001). Giving the mind a hand: The role of gesture in cognitive change. In J. McClelland & R. Siegler (Eds.), *Mechanisms of cognitive development: Behavioral and neural perspectives* (pp. 5–31). Mahwah, NJ: Lawrence Erlbaum Associates.

Goldin-Meadow, S., Alibali, M. W., & Church, R. B. (1993). Transitions in concept acquisition: Using the hand to read the mind. *Psychological Review,* 279–297.

Goldin-Meadow, S., Butcher, C., Mylander, C., & Dodge, M. (1994). Nouns and verbs in a self-styled gesture system: What's in a name? *Cognitive Psychology, 27,* 259–319.

Goldin-Meadow, S., & Feldman, H. (1977). The development of language-like communication without a language model. *Science, 197,* 401–403.

Goldin-Meadow, S., Kim, S., & Singer, M. (1999). What the teacher's hands tell the student's mind about math. *Journal of Educational Psychology, 91,* 720–730.

Goldin-Meadow, S., & McNeill, D. (1999). The role of gesture and mimetic representation in making language the province of speech. In M. C. Corballis & S. Lea (Eds.), *The descent of mind* (pp. 155–172). Oxford: Oxford University Press.

Goldin-Meadow, S., McNeill, D., & Singleton, J. (1996). Silence is liberating: Removing the handcuffs on grammatical expression in the manual modality. *Psychological Review, 103,* 34–55.

Goldin-Meadow, S., & Mylander, C. (1983). Gestural communication in deaf children: The non-effects of parental input on language development. *Science, 221,* 372–374.

Goldin-Meadow, S., & Mylander, C. (1984). Gestural communication in deaf children: The effects and non-effects of parental input on early language development. *Monographs of the Society for Research in Child Development, 49,* 1–121.

Goldin-Meadow, S., & Mylander, C. (1998). Spontaneous sign systems created by deaf children in two cultures. *Nature, 391,* 279–281.

Goldin-Meadow, S., Mylander, C., & Butcher, C. (1995). The resilience of combinatorial structure at the word level: Morphology in self-styled gesture systems. *Cognition, 56,* 195–262.

Goldin-Meadow, S., Nusbaum, H., Kelly, S., & Wagner, S. (in press). Explaining math: Gesturing lightens the load. *Psychological Sciences.*

Goldin-Meadow, S., & Sandhofer, C. M. (1999). Gesture conveys substantive information about a child's thoughts to ordinary listeners. *Developmental Science, 2,* 67–74.

Goldin-Meadow, S., Yalabik, E., & Gershkoff-Stowe, L. (2000). The resilience of ergative structure in language created by children and by adults. In S. C. Howell, S. A. Fish, & T. Keith-Lucas (Eds.), *Proceedings of the 24th Annual Boston University Conference on Language Development* (Vol. 1, pp. 343–353). Somerville, MA: Cascadilla Press.

Goldin-Meadow, S., & Zheng, M.-Y. (1998). Thought before language: The expression of motion events prior to the impact of a conventional language model. In P. Carruthers & J. Boucher (Eds.), *Language and thought: Interdisciplinary essays* (pp. 26–54). New York: Cambridge University Press.

Gumperz, J. J., & Levinson, S. C. (Eds.). (1996). *Rethinking linguistic relativity.* New York: Cambridge University Press.

Hoffmeister, R., & Wilbur, R. (1980). Developmental: The acquisition of sign language. In H. Lane & F. Grosjean (Eds.), *Recent perspectives on American Sign Language* (pp. 61–78). Hillsdale, NJ: Lawrence Erlbaum Associates.

Hunt, E., & Agnoli, F. (1991). The Whorfian hypothesis: A cognitive psychology perspective. *Psychological Review, 98,* 377–389.

Huttenlocher, J. (1976). Language and intelligence. In L. B. Resnick (Ed.), *The nature of intelligence* (pp. 261–281). Hillsdale, NJ: Lawrence Erlbaum Associates.

Iverson, J., & Goldin-Meadow, S. (1997). What's communication got to do with it: Gesture in blind children. *Developmental Psychology, 33,* 453–467.

Iverson, J. M., & Goldin-Meadow, S. (Eds.). (1998a). The nature and functions of gesture in children's communications, in the *New Directions for Child Development* series, No. 79. San Francisco: Jossey-Bass.

Iverson, J. M., & Goldin-Meadow, S. (1998b). Why people gesture when they speak. *Nature, 396,* 228.

Kelly, S., & Church, R. B. (1997). Can children detect conceptual information conveyed through other children's non-verbal behaviors? *Cognition and Instruction, 15,* 107–134.

Kelly, S., & Church, R. B. (1998). A comparison between children's and adults' ability to detect conceptual information conveyed through nonverbal behaviors. *Child Development, 69,* 85–93.

Kendon, A. (1980). Gesticulation and speech: Two aspects of the process of utterance. In M. R. Key (Ed.), *Relationship of verbal and nonverbal communication* (pp. 207–228). The Hague, Netherlands: Mouton.

Kendon, A. (1994). Do gestures communicate?: A review. *Research on Language and Social Interaction, 27,* 175–200.

Lenneberg, E. H. (1964). Capacity for language acquisition. In J. A. Fodor & J. J. Katz (Eds.), *The structure of language: Readings in the philosophy of language* (pp. 579–603). Englewood Cliffs, NJ: Prentice-Hall.

Levinson, S. C., & Bowerman, M. (Eds.). (1998). *Language acquisition and conceptual development.* New York: Cambridge University Press.

Lucy, J. A. (1992a). *Language diversity and thought: A reformulation of the linguistic relativity hypothesis.* New York: Cambridge University Press.

Lucy, J. A. (1992b). *Grammatical categories and cognition: A case study of the linguistic relativity hypothesis.* New York: Cambridge University Press.

Macnamara, J. (1982). *Names for things.* Cambridge, MA: MIT Press.

Mayberry, R. I. (1992). The cognitive development of deaf children: Recent insights. In S. Segalowitz & I. Rapin (Eds.), *Child Neuropsychology, Vol. 7. Handbook of Neuropsychology* (pp. 51–68). Amsterdam: Elsevier.

McNeill, D. (1992). *Hand and mind.* Chicago: University of Chicago Press.

McNeill, D. (1998). Speech and gesture integration. In J. M. Iverson & S. Goldin-Meadow (Eds.), *The nature and functions of gesture in children's communications,* in the *New Directions for Child Development* series (No. 79, pp. 11–27). San Francisco: Jossey-Bass.

McNeill, D., Cassell, J., & McCullough, K.-E. (1994). Communicative effects of speech-mismatched gestures. *Research on Language and Social Interaction, 27,* 223–237.

Moores, D. F. (1974). Nonvocal systems of verbal behavior. In R. L. Schiefelbusch & L. L. Lloyd (Eds.), *Language perspectives: Acquisition, retardation, and intervention.* Baltimore: University Park Press.

Morford, J. P., & Goldin-Meadow, S. (1997). From here to there and now to then: The development of displaced reference in homesign and English. *Child Development, 68,* 420–435.

Newport, E. L., & Meier, R. P. (1985). The acquisition of American Sign Language. In D. I. Slobin (Ed.), *The cross-linguistic study of language acquisition: Vol. 1. The data* (pp. 881–938). Hillsdale, NJ: Lawrence Erlbaum Associates.

Perry, M., & Elder, A. D. (1996). Knowledge in transition: Adults' developing understanding of a principle of physical causality. *Cognitive Development, 12,* 131–157.

Perry, M., Church, R. B., & Goldin-Meadow, S. (1988). Transitional knowledge in the acquisition of concepts. *Cognitive Development, 3,* 359–400.

Perry, M., Church, R. B., & Goldin-Meadow, S. (1992). Is gesture-speech mismatch a general index of transitional knowledge? *Cognitive Development, 7,* 109–122.

Sapir, E. (1921). *Language: An introduction to the study of speech.* New York: Harcourt Brace Jovanovich.

Schwartz, D. L., & Black, J. B. (1996). Shuttling between depictive models and abstract rules: Induction and fallback. *Cognitive Science, 20,* 457–497.

Silverstein, M. (1976). Hierarchy of features and ergativity. In R. M. W. Dixon (Ed.), *Grammatical categories in Australian languages* (pp. 112–171). Canberra: Australian Institute of Aboriginal Studies.

Singleton, J. L., Morford, J. P., & Goldin-Meadow, S. (1993). Once is not enough: Standards of well-formedness in manual communication created over three different timespans. *Language, 69,* 683–715.

Slobin, D. I. (1987). Thinking for speaking. *Proceedings of the Thirteenth Annual Meeting of the Berkeley Linguistic Society, 13,* 435–444.

Slobin, D. I. (1996a). From "thought and language" to "thinking for speaking." In J. J. Gumperz & S. C. Levinson (Eds.), *Rethinking linguistic relativity* (pp. 70–96). New York: Cambridge University Press.

Slobin, D. I. (1996b). Two ways to travel: Verbs of motion in English and Spanish. In M. Shibatani & S. A. Thompson (Eds.), *Grammatical constructions: Their form and meaning* (pp. 195–217). Oxford, England: Oxford University Press.

Supalla, T. (1982). *Structure and acquisition of verbs of motion and location in American Sign Language.* Unpublished doctoral dissertation, University of California at San Diego.

Talmy, L. (1985). Lexicalization patterns: Semantic structure in lexical forms. In T. Shopen (Ed.), *Language typology and syntactic description. III. Grammatical categories and the lexicon* (pp. 57–149). Cambridge, England: Cambridge University Press.

Tervoort, B. T. (1961). Esoteric symbolism in the communication behavior of young deaf children. *American Annals of the Deaf, 106,* 436–480.

Thompson, S. A. (1988). A discourse approach to the cross-linguistic category "adjective." In J. A. Hawkins (Ed.), *Explaining language universals* (pp. 167–185). Cambridge, MA: Basil Blackwell.

Whorf, B. L. (1956). *Language, thought, and reality: Selected writings of Bejamin Lee Whorf.* Cambridge, MA: MIT Press.

Part III

NOTATIONAL SYSTEMS AND COGNITIVE DEVELOPMENT

Chapter 6

What Writing Does
to the Mind

David R. Olson
OISE/UT, Toronto

My concern in this chapter is with the role of artifacts in human cognition. The mind/brain of humans is a product of evolution and the growth of mind can be studied as the gradual development and recruitment of those biological resources, a tradition which owes much to Jean Piaget. This tradition treats artifacts just as it would treat other objects in the natural world, that is, as a part of reality that the cognizer can progressively accommodate to in the course of development. Thus there are assumed to be stages in the development of understanding of manmade artifacts such as alphabetic writing just as there are stages of understanding motion or living things.

But just as the brain has evolved to better serve a variety of functions, so too have artifacts. Artifacts are cultural-historical products of mind that develop and evolve but do so outside of the evolutionary-biological loop. Unlike biological evolution in which adaptive change occurs over millennia, artifacts acquired in one generation could be passed on to the next and serve as the basis for yet another evolutionary level. Thus, for the case I consider here, namely writing, one can trace the evolution of writing systems through three millennia noting the major shifts thats have occurred quite independently of any parallel changes in biological resources of the mind. And yet the products of this evolution can be acquired by children in a brief period of schooling; what took perhaps a millennium to evolve is acquired in a year or two. Durkheim and Vygotsky are famous for their view that, through social collective representations, knowledge can grow in a society rather than within the mind of any particular individual. Individual minds "inherit," take over, or appropriate these accumulating historical artifacts (Whartofsky, 1979). On this view, the evolution and subsequent internalization of a certain class of artifacts, those serving representational and communicative purposes, are responsible for the reflective properties of our mental lives.

Now I take it as true, without further argument, that we think differently because of our writing systems, number systems, and information technologies and it is important to figure out just how this is so. As a number of writers have suggested, such notational artifacts serve as "tools of the intellect" (Goody, 2000). Certainly this premise is acceptable to both Piagetians and Vygotskians as well as to all of us who are interested in higher levels of cognition. Beyond the "tool" metaphor, three hypotheses as to how these artifacts play a role in cognition may be distinguished.

One important and widely held view is that artifacts are extensions of memory, that is, they are devices for storing information outside of memory, tagging that information by means of an appropriate notational cue, and then using that cue to retrieve that information when needed (Donald, 1991). The string on the finger is a simple case; signs and labels on boxes, cans, and buildings are more complex examples in that they allow a greater diversity of mnemonics. This view of artifacts treats them as a handy alternative to working memory but as having no particular role in altering cognitive processes. One consequence of this assumption is that psychologists are tempted to treat notations as "transparent" substitutes for psychological content, treating written expressions, for example, as if they were equivalent to spoken ones.

The second view of the role of notational artifacts, including writing, in cognition is the computational view. Artifacts are seen as not merely devices for reminding but as having a computational function. Here such things as finger counting as well as mathematical notations come into play. A slide rule, calculator, or computer allows one to compute functions that would be difficult or impossible without those technologies and notations (Hutchins, 1995). Their importance comes from the fact that they permit part of a complex cognitive function to be off-loaded on to a technical routine with the product of that technology to be reinserted in the execution of a higher order cognitive problem. Here we should think not only of instruments but also of marks for counting with and for writing with. Consider, for example, the invention of a notation for zero. Here one value of the notation or artifact is that it serves as a place holder, thereby aiding computation. Thus the written zero in the number 201, by explicitly indicating that there are no tens, allows one to mechanically compute its multiplication by another number, say five (five times zero is zero). Here again, however, no conceptual change is involved; before the zero was invented, people presumably knew there were no tens. Computation was difficult but not impossible. Invention, on this view, served to facilitate the use of knowledge but not to offer up new thoughts, new cognitions.

It is the third view that I attempt to spell out and defend in this chapter. It is that the invention of certain notational artifacts involves the creation of new concepts and new knowledge, indeed, a new consciousness. The invention of a notational system, it may be argued, involves the creation of a new conceptual scheme with new possibilities for thinking. Similarly, children's learning to use an existing artifact requires them to acquire new knowledge and new possibilities for thinking. On this view, inventing or learning the zero is not just learning a computational device but learning a concept that allows for a new way of conceptualizing absence; the zero in 201 explicitly represents the fact that there are no tens. And more generally, inventing a writing system and learning to deal with a writing system is not just a matter of improved storage and communication of information but a new form of representation, thought, and consciousness. I address how this could be the case by discussing the implications of writing, specifically, of notations for letters, words, sentences, and number.

There is, of course, an extensive literature on how notational systems, and artifacts more generally, are passed from generation to generation. Learning to read, for example, is the biggest psychological and educational topic in psychology. Yet assumptions and theories about learning derive from the conception of notations mentioned previously. If notations are seen as mnemonic or computational devices, learning is primarily a matter of learning signs for the already known. This is the assumption underlying much of learning and reading theory. If, however, artifacts and notations are seen as having important new cognitive functions, learning is seen as primarily a matter of "internalizing" or "appropriating" or otherwise taking on the cultural treasures embodied in those notational systems; notational schemes can serve as new modes of thought. Thus, musical scores may allow one to think about musical structure in a new way (Bamberger, 1979) and mathematical notations are at the foundation of mathematics (Chemla, in press). This perspective is perhaps more familiar in the Vygotskian than in the Piagetian tradition and is developed with some lucidity in Katherine Nelson's recent book, *Language in Cognitive Development* (1996) in which she postulated that language is the intermediary between the external world of artifacts (including adult knowledge) and the internal world of the child's mind. This is close to my own view and, like Nelson, I am enough of a Piagetian to hold that the outside-to-inside view of "internalization" is flawed; rather the child has to construct his or her own knowledge *even if that knowledge is already present in some sense in the culture.* So, let us consider in more detail what is involved in learning a script, that is, a notation for speech.

Inventing and Learning Letters

There is an enormous literature on children's learning to read, much of it premised on the faulty assumption that "writing is mere transcription." This assumption can be traced to Saussure (1916/1983) who claimed, falsely, I believe, that writing was not language, but merely a means of recording language (see also Bloomfield, 1933, p. 21). The mistake is in the assumption that writing is the transcription of the already known. On the contrary, the "big" discovery about reading, made only in the recent past, is that the requisite knowledge about speech needed for reading, does not pre-exist learning to read. As Shankweiler and Liberman (1972) claimed, "In reading an alphabetic language like English, the child must be able to segment the words he knows into the phonemic elements that the alphabetic shapes represent . . . His competence in speech production and speech perception is of no direct use to him here" (p. 309). That is, learning to read is to an important extent a matter of learning how to analyze one's speech in a new way, a way compatible with the properties of the writing system. Thus, the child has to learn to hear the sounds represented by letters in their own and others' speech, to hear the b represented by the letter /b/ in "baby," "bath," and "bottle," and so on. This is to think about an aspect of language in a new way, a way dictated by the alphabetic script. In addition, alphabetic order, critical for dictionaries and indexes, becomes possible; the "cart" comes before the "horse" at least in the dictionary.

However, Shankweiler and Liberman did not go far enough. They noted, correctly, in my view, that the child has to segment words into phonemic segments in order to learn to read an alphabetic script. But they assume that the child already knows about words in a way compatible with learning to segment them. This is just what is in question. To segment words, the child has first to learn that an utterance can be segmented into words and that knowledge, too, may be acquired in the process of becoming literate.

Inventing and Learning Words as Words

A landmark in children's development is when they, as we say, learn their first word. They go on, again, as we say, to the "two-word stage" and so on. So if they already know words, what is there to reading other than recognizing their written forms? On the writing as mnemonic view, nothing more is required. But, it is important to note that it is we, literate adults, who describe children's learning as learning words. To the rest of the world, children are learning to talk (not learning words). To the child, they may be learning what things are called or, perhaps, names for things, or more generally, how to share ideas with others. Only to us, literate adults, are they learning words. So our question is, How do children come to see utterances as composed of lexical constituents we think of as words? My suggestion is that, like phonemes, words were inadvertent discoveries in the history of writing and they are learned, that is, come into consciousness of the learner, when they learn to read a word-segmented, alphabetic script.

There is a complex relation here between linguistic ability, the ability to use words and sentences, and metalinguistic ability, the concepts of words and sentences. It is plausible to suggest that to learn a notational system requires the metarepresentational concepts to understand how such symbols work. That is, to read (as opposed to speak) a word, one must have a concept of what a word is. The concept of "word" is, of course, a metalinguistic concept.

We can get a glimpse of the problem of discovering/inventing words by looking at children's learning to read. Here the work of Emilia Ferreiro (1985), Ferreiro and Teberosky (1982), and their colleagues is particularly relevant. Their primary concern was with what children make of written signs. Their research program applies a Piagetian perspective to the acquisition of an alphabetic writing system. In doing so they have made, and continue to make, a number of important discoveries: Children learn that pictures are categorically different from words, that words require arbitrary signs, that a certain number of these signs must be combined to make a readable object, that different signs are required for different objects. But children also come up with some incorrect hypotheses such as that a duplication of signs is required for the duplication of objects. Furthermore, Ferreiro (1994) has suggested that "language, as a cognitive object, needs to be reconstructed at the same time that the representation of it is being constructed" (p. 119). Such a claim is indicative of the fact that Ferreiro adopted the third view of notations mentioned at the outset. Notations, for her, do not merely transcribe the known, that is, they are not simply mnemonic or computational devices, but instruments of consciousness and thought. Karmiloff-Smith (1992) and her colleagues (Karmiloff-Smith, Grant, Sims, Jones, & Cuckle, 1996) too, explored children's understanding of notational systems, and like Ferreiro, were concerned with notational systems as "problem spaces" for learners, but unlike her, have suggested that, developmentally, words as psychological objects may precede writing. Karmiloff-Smith (1992) proposed that development of concepts such as the concept of word, proceeds by "representational redescription," an endogenous process, as opposed to "internalization," a more exogenous process. But that position, in my view, underestimates the importance of cultural forms such as written words in fostering development. Yet it must be acknowledged that in learning what a word is, the child cannot simply take on this cultural knowledge but must rather construct the concept out of his or her own implicit knowledge, a kind of "representational redescription." Again, to know what a word is it is not enough to recognize visible printed forms but also to realize that their own speech may be seen as composed of lexical units corresponding to those printed words.

Our own research program, conducted by Nancy Torrance, Bruce Homer, Deepthi Kamawar, Jens Brockmeier, and myself, comes from a somewhat different perspective; namely, What can we infer about children's understanding of speech and language from their learning of scripts? Whereas Ferreiro has emphasized concepts of print, we have emphasized concepts of speech and language. Nonetheless, the two lines of work converge in that children's hypotheses about writing tend to reflect their knowledge about their own speech and language. For pre-reading children, a word is something to read, not something to speak (Francis, 1975). Discovering that written words can be seen as representing constituents of speech is one of their most important discoveries. More precisely, the claim is that children's important discovery is that their own and others' more or less continuous speech may be thought of as a sequence of lexical items or "words."

Four types of evidence sustain this view. First, in both their reading of signs and their writing of signs, pre-reading children first assume that written signs represent events and meanings rather than words or sentences about those events. For example, Ferreiro (1986) observed that a young subject, Martin, used three letters to represent the name "duck"; when shown a picture of three ducks, he repeated the original string three times "duck, duck, duck" but then read it back as "ducks." Why did the child not simply add the plural marker to the word duck? Presumably because he was trying to represent the ducks and not the word "ducks." In our laboratory, Bruce Homer has asked pre-reading children to both "pretend to write" and in a separate study to read back simple sentences that had previously been read to the child. As the child has to invent a response there is considerable diversity, but the patterns are similar to that reported by Ferreiro. Figure 6.1 shows a typical transcript obtained from one such pre-reading 4-year-old.

When asked to write "cat," this child produced a scribbled mark (Ferreiro frequently observed a letter string); when asked to write "two cats," this child, like Ferreiro's subjects, repeated the first string; when asked to write "three cats" this child produced three scribbles, volunteering the comment "I did three scribbles because there are three cats." Note that this was in response to a dictated utterance and yet the writing reflected the events described rather than the linguistic expression. (As an aside we may recall that in Ferreiro's study, children were responding to a picture of three cats, which may induce a simple naming of the entities in the picture as has been observed, for example, in the Binet "Picture Description" task. Yet, in our studies, a dictated expression produced the same type of

Adult: Can you write "cat"?

Child

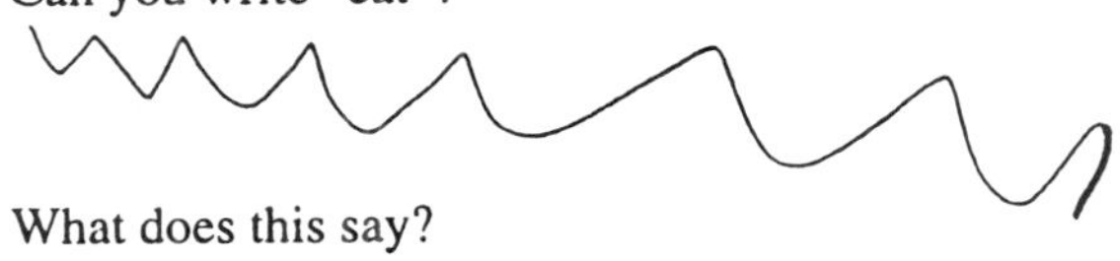

Adult: What does this say?

Child: "cat"   "one cat"

Adult: Can you write "two cats"?

Child:

Adult: What does this say?

Child: "One cat" (pointing to the longer line)

         "Two cats" (pointing to the shorter line)

Adult: Can you write "three cats"?

Child:

Child: I did three scribbles because there's three cats.

Adult: Can you write "no cats"?

Child: (waves pencil in the air)

Child: There's no cats so I didn't write anything.

FIG. 6.1.   A 4-year-old's representation of number and negation.

response.) The inference we draw is that the child knows something about writing—hence the scribbles—but does not know that writing maps on to utterances not on to events or objects.

A second line of evidence comes from the corresponding reading task, in which children are presented with simple sentences that are then read to the child and the child is then asked what each part of the written text says. Thus, the child may be shown a card bearing the text "Three little pigs," which is read to the child and then part of the text covered and the child asked "What do you think this now says?" Children frequently say "Two little pigs." Such observations suggest that pre-readers assume a link not between an utterance and a written text, but between a meaning or message and a written text. They do not realize that writing represents not events, but language about events. Language appears to be transparent to them. The aspects of language that are to be brought into consciousness are those that are dictated by the script, in this case the concept of "word."

A third piece of evidence comes from the representation of absence. A major limitation of object or event-based scripts is their inability to represent oral expressions of negation. If one uses three marks to represent three cats, one for each cat, how do you write "No cats?" Ferreiro (1985) had observed that 50% of her prereaders when asked to write "No birds fly" said it could not be done. She attributed the difficulty to the "apparent contradiction between presence (the letters) to refer to an absence ('no birds')." However, Ferreiro's study fails to distinguish between children's attempts at writing a falsehood and writing a true negation. When asked to write a true statement containing a negation, Homer and I found that pre-reading children still said it could not be written "because there are no cats" (see Fig. 6.1).

A final piece of evidence supporting this view is from the historical and anthropological sources. Writing systems in the West derive from Cuneiform writing. Prior to the invention of cuneiform, the ancient Sumerians used a tokening system largely for inventorying goods. In this script a vat of oil was represented by a triangle; two vats of oil were represented by two triangles, three for three, and so on, one for each object.[1] My suggestion is that young children think of written symbols as tokens for objects rather than as representations for words. Other writing systems based on things and events rather than language about those events are found in some Amerindian scripts, those of the pre-Columbian Mixtex (Boone & Mignolo, 1994), and in the relatively recent scripts of the Blackfoot of Southern Alberta (see Figs. 6.2 and 6.3).

How are we to know that the confusions children make are not simply developmental? I have already mentioned the historical evidence that indicated that adults, too, discovered words only at a certain stage in the history of writing. In a study currently underway, Alice Moro from the Uni-

---

[1]Why did not the inventors of writing simply design signs for words? Presumably because they had no concept of a word. Cultural historians such as Illich (1994), who have studied the development of literate cultures, have noticed that in the 12th century, prior to the invention of writing in the Vernacular, consciousness of linguistic constituents of the Vernacular was limited. Illich wrote, "The alphabet did not yet throw a shadow on labels or words. There was no way of analyzing the vernacular in syllables or words. The time for the concept of language as a generic term, allowing a comparison of two kinds—Vernacular and Latin—had not yet arrived" (p. 67).

For whatever reasons, designing signs to represent words was a relatively late invention, tied to the invention of a syntax for writing (see Olson, 1994).

FIG. 6.2. Codex Nuttall Facsimile 43: Lord 8 Deer "Jaguar Claw," who conquers the location Eagle Hill in the Year 7 Reed, on the day 10 Vulture. Peabody Museum.

 When many horses drowned

 When berries stayed on the trees all winter

 When the bear came into the camp

 When many horses died of starvation

FIG. 6.3. Blackfoot "Winter Count."

161

versity of Calgary has observed that young adults who had had little or no exposure to written materials responded in much the same way to written texts as do pre-reading children. Shown a text that was read to them as saying "Three wild horses," when one word was covered, 5 of the 10 subjects thought the remaining text said "Two wild horses." Hence, the pattern is not only an expression of childhood limitations but a consequence of dealing with a particular kind of language-based writing system.

That is not to say that segmentation of an oral text into word units is impossible without writing. It can be taught orally quite easily, as Karmiloff-Smith et al. (1996) have shown. But as Homer and Olson (1999) have discovered, that learning is associated with the comparable understanding of the segmentation of writing.

Conceptual Uses of Writing

What does this tell us about children's knowledge about speech and language? First, it suggests that children frame their hypotheses about writing on the basis of what is most conspicuous to them, namely, the objects or events themselves and not the linguistic form by means of which those objects and events are represented. When they learn to read and write, whether as children or adults, they must begin to think about the linguistic properties of speech. This is not a natural development; it is a consequence of learning to deal with a particular writing system. But once writing brings the lexical properties of language into consciousness, learners are in a position to go on to the analysis of words into phonological constituents represented by letters of the alphabet, the step emphasized by Shankweiler and Liberman and others as so important to learning to read an alphabetic script.

But thinking about words not only provides a handy access to a particular kind of script; writing serves as a model for thinking about our speaking. We all have notions of grammatical standards even if we violate them in speaking. This is the much maligned notion of a "prescriptive grammar," the grammar we were taught (if we were lucky) in school. And we use this grammar to correct ourselves and, even more pleasurably, others. We cringe when we hear kids say "John and me went fishing" or "He bought it for you and I." What makes them "ungrammatical" is that they violate the norms of the written standard that educated people attempt to honor. With writing, editing becomes inevitable (Urban, 1996).

Writing also serves as a model for meaning. Both the concepts of word meaning as opposed to speaker meaning (the insight that makes dictionaries possible) and the concepts of literal meaning as opposed to indirect meaning (which makes literary and textual criticism possible) presuppose that words and sentences are fixed objects in the world, that fixing being produced by writing. Geoffrey Lloyd (1996) has noted that only Aristotelean cultures draw a firm distinction between literal meaning and metaphor (see also Kennedy, 1998, p. 229). All cultures use language in essentially all ways; they do not think about their uses in similar ways. Writing affects the way they, and we, think about our language.

Finally, words have become the centerpiece of the Western intellectual tradition. They show up in dictionaries and grammars, in spelling lists, and on IQ tests. Written words, decontextualized, serve as objects of philosophical reflection: "What is justice?" "What is truth?" Who could imagine a philosophy of "nothingness" if there was no written sign for negation? Furthermore, the writing, editing, reading, and rewriting of documents aids in the formulation of ideas and invites attention to the problems of interpretation, analysis, and reflection. The accumulation of written documents allows the formation of disciplined knowledge stored in archival form that makes up our sciences. In these ways, writing contributes to both our intellectual history and to the development of literate societies.

So writing has certain intellectual advantages produced by turning aspects of language into objects of reflection. Such learning is not merely the discovery or bringing to consciousness of the already known. Rather, it involves the invention or learning of a new set of categories with new possibilities for thought. This is why writing is not merely a mnemonic or computational tool. The invention of a script, just like the learning of a script, creates new knowledge, a new set of concepts for thinking with, in this case, concepts built around the concept of the word. Interestingly, Vygotsky (1986) took word meaning to be central to the most advanced levels of conceptual thinking but he seemed not to have noticed that the concept of word is associated with the effects of writing and literacy. According to Downing (1987), Luria, a colleague of Vygotsky, emphasized writing, advancing the metaphor that to a child a word is "like a glass window through which the child looks at the surrounding world without making the word itself an object of his consciousness" (p. 36). Presumably, for Luria, literacy instruction was seen as instrumental in making the word an object of consciousness but that was not, to my knowledge, put to empirical test. The studies I summarized earlier indicate how writing brings words into consciousness. Even the great Piaget assumed that in learning to speak one was learning words. He showed that children's conceptions of names (not words) change with development but he did not, to my knowledge, notice that words themselves are in part created by writing and, for learners, come to be seen as words because of writing.

Words are in a sense lexicographers' artifacts; lexicographers are the ones who decide what shall be considered a word. Consequently, words are not simply natural objects existing in speech awaiting their discovery by the dictionary maker.[2] I do not wish to encourage the opposite fallacy, namely, that words are simply social constructions with no basis in reality. Linguistic structure is composed of lexical structure that can be meta-represented as "words." Words are, moreover, natural objects of modern alphabetic scripts. That is why our young children think that words are written things. But once learned, the child is in a position to see that all speech may be thought of as isolatable constituents called words. This allows the learner to see that a word is not the same thing as a name and that "not" is a word too, and that it, too, may be represented by a mark.

For too long we have left unexamined the Saussurean legend that writing is not language but only a means of recording language. Writing is what introduces our speech to us, revealing our speech as having a particular structure. Children do not know that they speak words, that is, that the flow of speech can be thought of as a string of lexical items. But children in an alphabetic society do come to think about language, mind, and world in terms of the category systems employed in writing. To paraphrase Whorf (1956), we dissect language along lines laid down by our scripts.

REFERENCES

Bamberger, J. S. (1979). *The art of listening: Developing musical perception*. New York: Harper & Row.

Bloomfield, L. (1933). *Language*. New York: Holt, Rinehart & Winston.

Boone, E. H., & Mignolo, W. D. (Eds.). (1994). *Writing without words: Alternative literacies in Mesoamerica and the Andes*. Durham, NC: Duke University Press.

Chemla, K. (in press). What is the content of this book? A plea for developing history of science and history of text conjointly. *Philosophy and the History of Science*.

Donald, M. (1991). *Origins of the modern mind*. Cambridge, MA: Harvard.

Downing, J. (1987). Comparative perspectives on world literacy. In D. Wagner (Ed.), *The future of literacy in a changing world* (pp. 25–47). Oxford: Pergamon Press.

Ferreiro, E. (1985). Literacy development: A psychogenetic perspective. In D. R. Olson, N. Torrance, & A. Hildyard (Eds.), *Literacy, language, and learning: The nature and consequences of reading and writing* (pp. 217–228). New York: Cambridge University Press.

Ferreiro, E. (1986). *Proceso de alfabetizacion: La alfabetizacion en proceso* [The process of alphabetization: Alphabetization in process]. Buenos Aires: Bibliotecas Universitarias.

---

[2]Nor do I endorse the extreme constructivist view that words are purely the inventions of the lexicographer. There is structure to speech and some aspects of that structure can be captured in the concept of a word. But "word" is an abstract category including not only names but also verbs, copulas, prepositions. What falls in that category is not always obvious and that is where the lexicographer comes in. Children's conceptions of words, like that of most adults, are based on the notion of a name. But whereas names are words, the converse is not true.

165

Ferreiro, E. (1994). Written representations of language. In K. Keller-Cohen (Ed.), *Literacy: Interdisciplinary conversations*. Cresskill, NJ: Hampton Press.

Ferreiro, E., & Teberosky, A. (1982). *Literacy before schooling*. Exeter, NH: Heinemann. (Original work published 1979)

Francis, H. (1975). *Language in childhood: Form and function in language learning*. London: Paul Elek.

Goody, J. (2000). *The power of the written tradition*. Washington, DC: Smithsonian Institution.

Homer, B., & Olson, D. (1999). Literacy and children's conception of words. *Written Language and Literacy, 2*, 113–137.

Hutchins, E. (1995). *Cognition in the wild*. Cambridge, MA: MIT Press.

Illich, I. (1993). *In the vineyard of the text*. Chicago: University of Chicago Press.

Karmiloff-Smith, A. (1992). *Beyond modularity: A developmental perspective on cognitive science*. Cambridge, MA: Bradford Books/MIT Press.

Karmiloff-Smith, A., Grant, J., Sims, K., Jones, M., & Cuckle, P. (1996). Rethinking metalinguistic awareness: Representing and accessing knowledge about what counts as a "word." *Cognition, 58*(2), 197–219.

Kennedy, G. A. (1998). *Comparative rhetoric*. Oxford, England: Oxford University Press.

Lloyd, G. (1996). The Greek and Chinese cases and their relevance to the problems of culture and cognition. In D. R. Olson & N. Torrance (Eds.), *Modes of thought* (pp. 15–33). New York: Cambridge University Press.

Nelson, K. (1996). *Language in cognitive development: The emergence of the mediated mind*. New York: Cambridge University Press.

Olson, D. R. (1994). *The world on paper: The conceptual and cognitive implications of writing and reading*. Cambridge, England: Cambridge University Press.

Saussure, F. de (1983). *Course in general linguistics*. London: Duckworth. (Original work published 1916)

Shankweiler, D., & Liberman, I. (1972). Misreading: A search for causes. In J. Kavanaugh & I. Mattingly (Eds.), *Language by ear and language by eye: The relationships between speech and reading* (pp. 293–317). Cambridge, MA: MIT Press.

Urban, G. (1996). Entextualized, replication and power. In M. Silverstein & G. Urban (Eds.), *Natural histories of discourse* (pp. 21–44). Chicago: Chicago University Press.

Vygotsky, L. (1986). *Thought and language* (A. Kozulin, Trans.). Cambridge, MA: MIT Press.

Whartofsky, M. W. (1979). *Models: Representation and the scientific understanding*. Boston: Reider.

Whorf, B. L. (1956). Science and linguistics. In *Selected writings of Benjamin Lee Whorf* (pp. 207–219). Cambridge, MA: MIT Press.

Chapter 7

Symbolic Communication in Mathematics and Science: Co-Constituting Inscription and Thought

Richard Lehrer
Leona Schauble
University of Wisconsin-Madison

> *The major feature of literate thought is that it is about representations such as explicit statements, equations, maps, and diagrams rather than about the world.*
>
> —Olson (1994, p. 277)

In this chapter we describe a coordinated program of intervention and research with elementary school children and their teachers. The focus of this work is on the long-term development of literacy in model-based reasoning, a form of symbolic communication that is particular to mathematics and science. Our emphasis on models follows from the observation that, regardless of their domain or specialization, scientists' work involves building and refining models (Giere 1992; Stewart & Golubitsky, 1992).

However, because we are educators who work with school students, we are primarily interested in the development of modeling, not just its mature expression as exemplified in the work of practicing scientists. Therefore, we begin by identifying forms of modeling that are well aligned with children's development and then proceed to generating and testing conjectures about best ways to support the evolution of modeling practices. We do so by working intensively with collaborating teachers who are our partners in the enterprise of learning about the development of students' thinking.

INSCRIBING AND MATHEMATIZING

Our research to date suggests that there are two kinds of foundational resources that are particularly important underpinnings for student modeling, and therefore, we and our collaborators have oriented teaching and learning toward the development of these resources (see Lehrer & Schauble, 2000). The first is children's inscriptions. "Inscription" is a term that we borrow from Latour (1990) to refer to drawings, diagrams, maps, physical models, read-outs of instruments, and mathematical expressions—in short, the range of symbolic tools that can be used for representing aspects of the world that are theoretically important. As many (e.g., Olson, 1994; Grosslight, Unger, & Smith, 1991) have emphasized, representing is not a matter of simply copying what one sees. Instead, it involves inventing or adapting conventions of a representational system for the purpose at hand: for example, to select, magnify, fix, compose, or transport information and to recruit it in the service of disciplinary argument (Latour, 1990). We argue in this chapter that the evolution of inscriptions and the evolution of conceptions are mutually supportive and occur hand in hand (Lehrer, Schauble, Carpenter, & Penner, 2000), so that thought and inscription are reciprocally bootstrapped.

The second major resource for developing modeling in school classrooms is mathematics. The historical trajectory of Western science is one in which scientific description and argument have become increasingly mathematical (Kline, 1980). For example, mathematization of geographic space made the European "voyages of discovery" feasible, because the world could be viewed not just as round, but "as a sphere with the mathematical properties of a sphere" (Olson, 1994, p. 207). Research reports and other professional texts have also pressed toward increasing mathematization, an approach to argument that, with Newton, came to be universally accepted as the most compelling (Bazerman, 1988). In this chapter, we provide evidence of a similar kind of evolution—although occurring over a much shorter time span—in the inscriptions of school students. When teachers push for increasing clarity, precision, power, and accountability to evidence, in response, children's initial attempts to represent the world through inscriptions become increasingly mathematical as they conduct repeated cycles of representation, evaluation, and revision. For example, children's initial "maps" of their school's playground are often drawings of items in the space. However, with emphasis on using these maps for navigation, drawings are transformed into mathematical objects that employ coordinate geometry to fix position and direction (Lehrer, Jacobson, Kemeny, & Strom, 1999; Lehrer & Pritchard, 2000).

We most often begin our efforts to help students develop models, like the maps of the playground, by expanding on children's senses of similarity and resemblance. Thus, initial maps of the playground are drawings of the visible and serve to present what children consider self-evident. With explicit attention to communication of position and direction, mathematization of the space comes to dominate discourse. However, we find that this process (and other processes like it that we describe later) becomes truncated if students' mathematical resources are limited to the usual emphasis in elementary school on arithmetic as the predominant (or even the only) form of mathematics. Arithmetic is not sufficient to support the development of modeling. Therefore, a major objective of our work is to develop a wider base of mathematics. Geometry and space, measure, data, and uncertainty can be included in youngsters' mathematics education from the earliest grades (consistent with standards developed by the National Council of Teachers of Mathematics, 1991). As we show later, these forms of mathematics are critical for supporting the development of children's model-based reasoning.

We have been working for the past several years with teachers in four elementary schools within a school district near Madison. In these schools, teachers in Grades 1 through 5 are collaborating with researchers to reorient mathematics and science instruction to emphasize modeling approaches. As instruction changes, we are conducting collective study of the student thinking that emerges. This approach, in which intervention and research are closely intertwined, reflects our belief that the development of these forms of reasoning cannot be adequately understood without considering their history and the classroom contexts (including cultural tools, classroom norms, and teaching) that generate them (these issues are discussed in detail in Lehrer & Schauble, 2000). The opportunity to track student thinking over years of instruction is critical, given that mathematical and scientific reasoning develops over years, rather than weeks or months.

To provide a sense of the kind of development we are alluding to, we next briefly present a series of examples at different grade levels. These examples sketch the developmental trajectory of students' thinking about a set of concepts central to both mathematics and science, namely, those in which students use data and statistics to model ideas about growth. After this brief survey across school grades, we turn to a more extended discussion of classrooms at the same grade. We compare the reasoning of students in two comparable fifth-grade classrooms trying to settle an argument about "the best way to remember things." As the fifth graders conducted an investigation to answer this question, they first defined attributes and collected data on distributions of student performance, and then confronted the challenge of how to compare distributions. In one of the classrooms, this investigation served as the capstone to an entire year's sequence of inquiries involving reasoning about both the inscriptions for representing distributions and their mathematical underpinnings. Students in the other class had a much more abbreviated history with these ideas. Close inspection of the reasoning in these classrooms aptly illustrates the close interrelationships between representational competence and conceptual growth (cf. Lehrer, Schauble, Carpenter, & Penner, 2000).

BRIEF EXAMPLES: REASONING WITH DATA TO MODEL GROWTH

As we have studied the developmental trajectory of students' thinking about data and statistics, we have noted the importance of anchoring classroom work in children's inquiry, their decisions about what is worthy of investigation (that is, how they come to regard objects and events as being constructed of attributes), and their collective work to structure, organize, and visualize data (Lehrer & Romberg, 1996). In our participating classrooms, students in the primary grades work in repeated cycles of invention and revision to aggregate and display data and to evaluate attributes and conventions for displays that can support their descriptions and explanations. Students in the upper elementary grades extend and build on this knowledge to reason about (and with) distribution and statistics.

First-Grade Inscriptions

First graders decided to compare the heights of plants grown from different flowering bulbs: amaryllis, narcissus, and hyacinth. To preserve a record of plant growth, they cut out paper strips to depict the plant stems at different points in the growth cycle. Consistent with our claim that young children prefer representations that preserve resemblance, they insisted at first that all the strips be green and that each be adorned with a "flower," as illustrated in Fig. 7.1. However, the teacher repeatedly focused students' attention on using the strips to make and justify comparisons: for example, between the heights of a plants on different days, as shown in Fig. 7.2, or the heights of different kinds of plants (amaryllis vs. paperwhite narcissus), or the heights of plants grown under different conditions (e.g., in soil or in water), as shown in Fig. 7.3. As the strips were increasingly recruited to settle claims about the plants, children began to make the conceptual transition from thinking of the strips as "presenting" height to "representing" height.

An important step in this direction occurred when a partner class sent over a note carried by an emissary: "Whose amaryllis is growing faster, yours or ours?" The first graders fired back a question of their own: "How big is yours?" They were somewhat perplexed at the reply: "Our amaryllis is two pencils high." "Well," the first graders demanded, "How big are

FIG. 7.1.   Height strips adorned with flowers.

your pencils? Do they have erasers? And are they sharpened, or not?" This series of queries eventually developed into several lessons in which children explored the need for standard units and procedures of measure, first so that they could settle questions about "Which plant is bigger?" and eventually to support more mathematically interesting questions, like, "How *much* bigger?" These lessons were guided by previous characterizations of the growth and development of children's thinking about length, area, and volume measure in classrooms designed to support development of these forms of mathematics (see Lehrer & Chazan, 1998).

Next, the teacher reminded the class about their original question concerning *changes* in plant height: "Which plant is growing fastest?" At first, children looked at their displays and chose the plant represented by the longest strip as the one growing fastest. However, one child objected that the question could not be answered without looking at successive *differences* in the lengths of the strips (on the videotape she can be seen indicating what she means by "differences" with her thumb and forefinger). As they inspected the differences in heights of the strips, children identified times when their plants grew "faster" and "slower," discussions that needed to

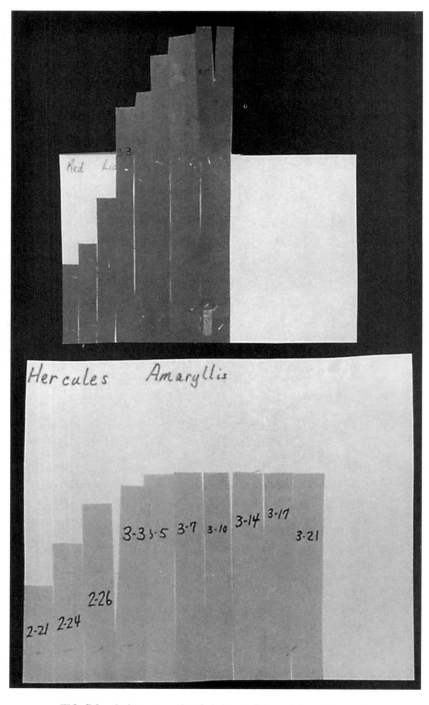

FIG. 7.2. Strips comparing heights at different days of growth.

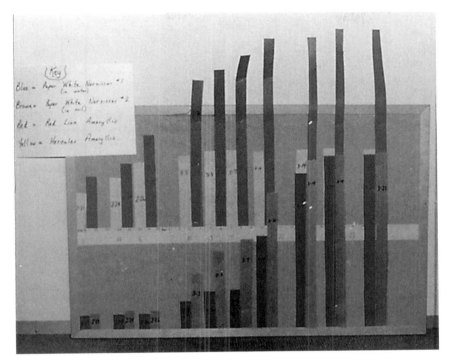

FIG. 7.3. Strips comparing heights of plants grown under different conditions.

be firmly grounded in their prior conversations about what counted as "tall" and how to measure it reliably.

Third-Grade Inscriptions

In the third grade, children also "mathematized" change (in this case, of Wisconsin Fast Plants™) in a variety of ways (see Lehrer, Carpenter, & Schauble, 2000, for more details on this example). However, because their mathematical resources were more considerable than those of the first graders, this series of inquiries was not just another instance of "measuring plants." Instead, students were able to pose a series of more sophisticated questions about growth and to resolve them in a satisfying manner.

The third graders developed "pressed plant" silhouettes that recorded changes in plant morphology over time, coordinate graphs that expressed relations between plant height and time, sequences of rectangles representing the relationship between plant height and canopy "width," and various three-dimensional forms to capture changes in plant volume.

Drawing on mathematical knowledge that they had developed in an extended study of geometric similarity (e.g., Lehrer, Strom, & Confrey, 2000), they conjectured that plant volume would change according to principles of geometric growth (e.g., "growing" cylinders of constant ratio of circumference to height). They made rectangular and cylindrical prisms to model the increasing volume of the plants and observed—counter to their expectations—that after the first several days of growth, their models of the plants did not appear to be geometrically similar. They first debated whether the violations of the conjectured pattern should be attributed to measurement error. However, they eventually concluded that the ratios of measures (i.e., height and circumference of the cylinders) were changing over time, not constant, as they had initially expected.

As the diversity of students' representations increased, new cycles of inquiry emerged. They asked, "Is the growth of roots and shoots the same or different?" By comparing the height and depth of shoots and roots, as illustrated in the graph shown in Fig. 7.4, students agreed that at any point in a plant's life cycle, the differences in measure were apparent: Roots and

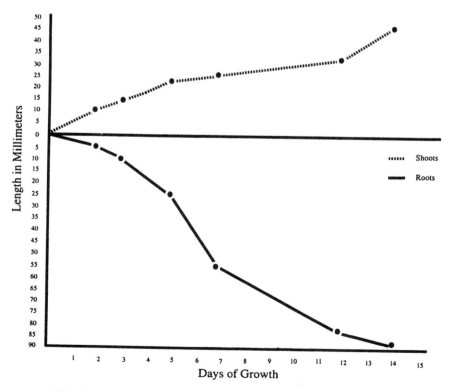

FIG. 7.4. Graph showing the "shape" of growth for roots and shoots.

shoots do not grow at the same rate. However, they also noted that graphs displaying the growth of roots and shoots were characterized by similar "shapes," S-shaped (logistic) curves. Observing these similarities in the form, but not the measures or rates of growth, students wondered about its significance. Why might growth of different parts of the plant have the same form? When was growth fastest for each part of the plant, and what might be the functional significance of these periods of rapid growth? Note that these are questions that were provoked by qualities of the graphs; it is difficult to see how they would have come to light if the inscriptions of plant growth had not been developed. In turn, the new questions that the inscriptions raised then elicited opportunities for children to invent new inscriptions. In that way, children's inscriptions and conceptions pushed each other forward in a spiraling cycle.

The variety of inscriptional forms that children either invented or used provided many opportunities for these third graders to develop meta-representational competence (diSessa, Hammer, Sherin, & Kolpakowski, 1991). For example, students discovered that coordinate graphs of two different plants looked similar (e.g., equally "steep"), yet actually represented different rates of growth. The class inspected these two graphs closely to try to determine how this could be. They solved the paradox when one boy discovered that the children who generated the graphs had used different scales to represent the heights of their plants. The discovery that graphs might "look the same" yet represent different rates of growth tempered the class's interpretations of coordinate graphs in other contexts throughout the year.

Fifth-Grade Inscriptions

In the fifth grade, children again investigated growth, this time of tobacco hornworms (*Manduca*). As students' attention shifted from individual organisms (e.g., Sally's hornworm and Peter's hornworm) to populations (e.g., groups of hornworms reared under different conditions), their mathematical ideas expanded to touch on ideas about distribution and sample. Students explored relationships between growth factors (e.g., different food sources) and the relative dispersion of characteristics in the population at different points in the life cycle of the caterpillars. Questions posed by the fifth graders focused on the diversity of characteristics within populations (e.g., length, circumference, weight, days to pupation), rather than simply on shifts in central tendencies of attributes. As the inscriptions focused students on variation, they began to raise new kinds of questions: Why was more variability in growth observed in the hornworms fed by the Department of Entomology's "recipe" than in those fed green pepper? One child proposed that perhaps the "recipe" formula was not homogeneously mixed. Another suggested that perhaps the hornworms fed "recipe" grew faster and therefore were moved earlier to larger containers—a change that might in its own right affect growth. Thus, as children's representational repertoires stretched, so, too, did their considerations about what might be worthy of investigation and how to investigate it.

In summation, over the span of the elementary grades, we observed characteristic shifts from an early emphasis on literal depiction (paper "stems" in models of change in plant height) toward representations that were progressively more symbolic and more mathematical in character. Diversity in representation and meta-representational competence both accompanied and produced conceptual change. As children developed a variety of representational means for characterizing their data about growth, those representations elicited increasingly sophisticated questions. By pursuing these questions with increasingly powerful mathematical means, students eventually came to understand biological change in more dynamic ways.

The examples presented here are just a few of the inquiries about data and statistics that our collaborating teachers have undertaken with students. Focusing on the development of big ideas requires teachers to identify points where primary grade students can profitably begin consideration of these ideas (e.g., the identification of attributes, considerations of what and how to measure, how to display data to address questions) and also ways to "push on" and beyond these entry points so that older elementary students can continue to be challenged (e.g., in describing and comparing distributions, simple statistics). We next describe in greater detail how two fifth grade classrooms—with different bases of mathematical experience—addressed the challenge of conducting an experiment that produced distributions of data which needed to be compared.

REASONING ABOUT DISTRIBUTIONS

As students begin to consider distributions as opposed to single cases, they encounter the need to find ways of representing typicality and variation. They debate ways of deciding whether distributions are "the same" or "different" and struggle with intuitions about sampling. We ensure that these ideas arise and are resolved in multiple contexts, so students come to understand that satisfactory solutions to these questions cannot be foreclosed simply by applying a procedure or an algorithm. Instead, what counts as a good solution depends on the questions being pursued and what is at stake, given different answers. We describe how these issues were negotiated in two fifth-grade classrooms where students designed and conducted an investigation to resolve debates about "how people remember things."

This project was instigated by the authors, J. R. Levin, a university researcher who studies the development of mnemonic strategies, and two fifth-grade teachers, Mark Rohlfing and Larry Gundlach. Both teachers had participated in previous studies to investigate students' thinking about data, in general, and distributions, in particular. In previous years, Mr. Rohlfing's students had developed data classification models and debated ways of finding satisfactory "typical values" to represent a range of measurement values. However, similar discussions had not been conducted with the class that participated in the current study. In contrast, Mr. Gundlach's class had worked all year on studies involving data and distributions, most notably on the project about tobacco hornworms, and many of his students were participants in the third grade study of root-shoot growth described previously. Thus, Mr. Gundlach's students provide a window to potential trajectories of thinking about distribution when students have had prolonged opportunities to model data.

In the hornworm project, which lasted for several weeks in the fall, Mr. Gundlach's class developed attributes to operationalize their ideas about what it means to "grow better," tracked changes in measurements of these attributes over time, and constructed various kinds of data displays. On the basis of these displays, the students debated about the conditions that fostered "better growth." These arguments evolved into discussions about issues such as measures of center and of variation of distributions. The class, for example, noticed that hornworms fed one kind of diet tended to be "clumped together" on a frequency graph (showing less variable growth in the population over the course of the life cycle). In contrast, hornworms fed a different diet tended to be somewhat larger, but in addition, the distribution was more "spread out," illustrating more variable growth in the population over the life cycle.

Mr. Rohlfing's and Mr. Gundlach's classes, therefore, provided a natural comparison—one with limited experience in reasoning about statistics and distribution, and one with more extensive experience. We were interested in how these differences would play out in the context of the memory study. To pursue this question, we traced the evolution of student thinking about distribution and comparisons among distributions in Mr. Rohlfing's class of novices and in Mr. Gundlach's class of more experienced students. We summarize the progress of students in Mr. Rohlfing's class rather briefly to focus more intensively on a culminating discussion in Mr. Gundlach's class that occurred at the end of the experiment.

The researchers and teachers agreed that the two classes would design and conduct a study to compare methods for memorizing the United States and their capital cities. One method, to be developed by the participating students, would be compared to an interactive picture method developed by a university researcher for previous studies of mnemonic strategies (e.g., Levin, 1983). Consistent with our overall interest in students' thinking about distributions and statistics, our intent was to generate a context in which students would have reason to judge whether two distributions are the same or different.

Overview of the Study

Before introducing the idea of a study to students, the teachers first conducted two administrations of a pretest. The purpose of the pretests was to serve as baselines for deciding whether the experimental treatments for "remembering" had resulted in learning. The identical pretest was administered on two occasions, 2 weeks apart. Students were given neither prior warning nor subsequent explanation that the results would later be used in a classroom study of memory. Because the fifth graders knew that they were to be held accountable for knowing the states and capitals, they did not question these "tests." At each pretest, students were asked to produce a list of as many of the United States (in any order) with their capitals as they could recall. Results from these pretests were charted on large frequency plots displaying the number of students who got each number of states/capitals correct. Figure 7.5 shows the display for one of these pretests.

Several weeks afterward, Mr. Rohlfing asked his students to consider "how people remember things." The ideas that students proposed ranged

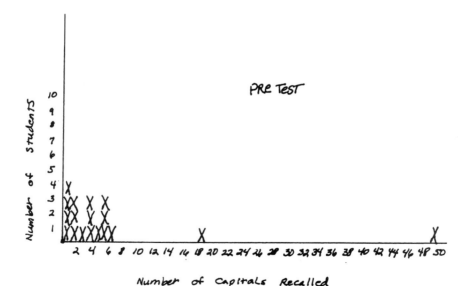

FIG. 7.5.   Pretest data from the memory study.

widely, and debate was lively. One student insisted on a simple copy theory of memory: "You just hear things and they go into your brain. Then you remember them." Others pointed out that you don't always remember things you hear; instead, sometimes you have to hear them over and over. At various points in the discussion, students proposed that memory is enhanced when the material to be recalled is organized or familiar.

This discussion eventually led to debates about the most effective ways of enhancing recall. Mr. Rohlfing challenged the class to generate their best strategies for enhancing memory of the states and capitals and mentioned that they would have the chance to test their "best method" against a method developed by a university "memory expert."

In a subsequent class, students generated and listed different candidate methods for "remembering things" and evaluated the probable effectiveness and feasibility of each of the methods. Methods proposed by the students included setting the material to "a catchy tune," using various means of cueing and association, and employing several variants of rehearsal strategies. After discussing the candidates and voting on their favorites, the class agreed that Sean's proposed method, a form of cumulative rehearsal, seemed most promising. Mr. Rohlfing then introduced the university "memory expert" (Levin), who explained that he had developed a method for remembering that was very successful. The students listened respectfully as Levin explained his "mnemonic method," one that involved studying interactive pictures illustrating objects whose names "sound like" the target state and capital. However, many students remained convinced that "Sean's method" would outperform Levin's in a fair test. The following class was devoted to debating ways to compare learning with "Sean's method" to learning via the "mnemonic method" advocated by the "memory expert."

The study eventually proposed by the students required participation from students in both of the fifth-grade classrooms, Mr. Rohlfing's and Mr. Gundlach's. The two classes were split in half, and two new composite classes were assembled that included members of both classes. Each composite class participated in two different memory conditions. In one condition, they memorized a subset of the states and their capitals, organized by geographic region, under "Sean's method" of cumulative rehearsal. In the other, they learned a different subset of states and capitals under the mnemonic method. The order of conditions was counterbalanced, so that every student participated in both conditions (one group used Sean's method first, the mnemonic method second; the other used mnemonic first, Sean second). The composite treatment groups diligently applied the assigned methods for equal periods of time. After each of the learning sessions, the groups repeated the recall test that had originally been administered at baseline. Although students generated many questions about the results, those that came to dominate the inquiry were: (a) Does studying matter?, (b) Which method is better for studying?, and (c) Does order of method matter? Although there were ways in which their experimental design was not as unconfounded (and hence, as fair) as they anticipated, we decided to background issues of design and foreground issues of distribution and comparison among distributions.

First Encounters with Distributions

Students were reconfigured into their original classes to discuss the results of the pretests and the posttest. In Mr. Rohlfing's class, much of the time in the beginning discussion was devoted to deciphering the convention of the frequency graphs that were used to display student performance. Several of the students were very concerned with being able to identify each X on the graph with a particular participant. For example, pointing to Fig. 7.5, Brian said, "Here's me," pointing to one X. "Here's Sean and here's Adrian." We have noted in earlier studies (e.g., Hancock, Kaput, & Goldsmith, 1992; Lehrer & Romberg, 1996) that when they begin to work with data, students often tend to over-focus on particular cases at the expense of thinking about aggregates, a "bug" clearly shown in Brian's thinking. Anchoring one's understanding in cases is important because it serves to ground data analysis in a search for meaning and interpretation. However, students also need to coordinate their rich understanding of cases with observation of the patterns in distributions. Frequency graphs, like those used by Mr. Rohlfing to display the class results, highlight some aspects of information (e.g., the number of students who received each score on the test), but also hide information that is usually not relevant to consideration of distribution (e.g., the identity of particular students). This hidden information was supplied by students to anchor their interpretations to the particular, although they saw little need to identify more than one or two cases.

In Mr. Rohlfing's class, the discussions revolved around typicality. To decide whether the two study methods improved learning, and if so, which method produced the most improvement, students struggled to find a way to characterize the distributions that summarized their recall performance. Given a distribution, what number of correctly recalled states and capitals could be identified as "typical" for the class? Mr. Rohlfing asked students to look carefully at the graph in Fig. 7.5 and consider how they would fill in the blank in the following sentence: "Most people in our class know _____ states and capitals."

Responses included proposals about the range (Sarah: "I think most people know 2 to 7"), the middle of the "clump" (Nicole: "Most people know about 5"), and the mode (Megan: "I'd consider that people would know 1 state, because there are most Xs by 1"). However, two of the students described senseless algorithms for finding the typical value. For example, one explained, "I'd consider 9, because there is 18 people divided by 2." We conjecture that these procedures were distortions of an algorithm for finding the mean, probably instructed in an earlier grade.

When asked to decide whether improvement had occurred on the second administration of the pretest, students vacillated between attending to the upper and lower tails of the distributions. For example, we observed one girl counting the number of students who had recalled more than 8 states and capitals (8 was the highest value in a "clump" of data points). She argued that because the number of especially high values dropped on the second pretest, ". . . we aren't really improving." A different student compared the number of individuals who recalled only one state and capital (presumably, Wisconsin/Madison). Because the frequency on the low end of the distribution had decreased somewhat on the second administration of the test, this student was willing to argue that "we improved a little bit."

Mr. Rohlfing asked, "What would convince you that most people are learning the states and capitals?" Charlie proposed that ". . . the big clump has to come out toward the middle." Sarah added, "I think the chunk has to be at least past the 7." Turning attention to posttest frequency displays, Mr. Rohlfing's students concluded that there was indeed a virtue to studying. Eventually, Mr. Rohlfing's students found ways of characterizing typical values for each posttest. By comparing these values to those of the pretests, they concluded that studying mattered. However, when they compared methods of study, they also tended to rely exclusively on the "typical values" for the distributions. Many students suggested that whichever typical value was greater "showed" that one method or the other (it varied with display) was "better" (although the differences between these values were small). However, we saw little evidence that students were coordinating their ideas about measures of center with observations about variability of measures. Comparing distributions was a new challenge for these students, and they appeared to lack important mathematical resources (e.g., ratio, sampling, and prior experience with variation) for successfully meeting the challenge. Although Mr. Rohlfing skillfully assisted students in thinking about "typical" values, he was uncertain about effective means for pushing simultaneous consideration of variation and center. (This episode served as a catalyst for further professional development. Mr. Rohlfing is revisiting these issues this year in collaboration with one of our colleagues, Anthony Petrosino).

Drawing on Experience

Mr. Gundlach's class also participated in the experiment and, at its conclusion, also gathered to consider the implications of the displays. The claims and rationales generated in this discussion provide a contrast to those made by their less experienced counterparts in Mr. Rohlfing's class. The class discussion also provides a window to how Mr. Gundlach's class capitalized on their work earlier in the school year on ideas about distribution.

Capitals and Critters.   Mr. Gundlach initiated the discussion by asking the class to consider the charts from Mr. Rohlfing's room. Peter immediately noted, "These are like frequency graphs, kind of like what we used with the critters" (a reference to the earlier displays generated in work with the tobacco hornworms). "For each person who got 10 [i.e., recalled ten capitals], they put an X there." After briefly reviewing the nature of frequency graphs and discussing what they hide (the identity of individual cases) as well as what they reveal (a display of the aggregate), Mr. Gundlach asked: "So what does the pretest show you? Why do you do pretests?"

Clumps, Ranges, and Cases.   Katie suggested that pretests ". . . show you how well somebody [i.e., the participant] did before they start to do it. A pretest and posttest tells you how they improved." Mr. Gundlach then asked the class to consider Fig. 7.5. Ross focused on two extreme values in relation to a cut-point, noting that ". . . only two (students) actually had more than 10 right." Amanda attempted to identify a characteristic range: "I see that there's a big clump in between 8 and 2 and 1." Picking up on the extreme values noticed by Ross, Amanda went on to suggest: "That kind of tells me either kids were studying before or knew what was going to happen in their room" (i.e., that they would be tested on states and capitals).

After Mr. Gundlach clarified and expanded Amanda's notions of the clump and its potential meanings, another student, Marc, drew an analogy between their previous experience with hornworm growth (now 5 months earlier in the school year) and the potential "growth" of recall in the memory experiment. "Um, this kind of looks like our critter data, because, um, I know at first they were all clumped together like that" (indicating data on the pretest chart). "And then here . . ." (gestures to Figs. 7.6 and 7.7 showing the posttest performance under each of the methods) ". . . they became all spread out, like the critters."

Analogies to Growth.   As other students chimed in about similarities to the hornworm displays, Mr. Gundlach asked, "Why would eating and growing be like studying capitals with Sean's method and taking a test on it?" Jenna suggested a clear parallel: "It's kind of like they eat and grow, and we study and learn." Mr. Gundlach probed this notion of a parallel between physical and mental growth by asking children to generate a counterexample. "Can anyone give me an example where starting out, at the starting out time you wouldn't expect to see clumping?" Elliot pro-

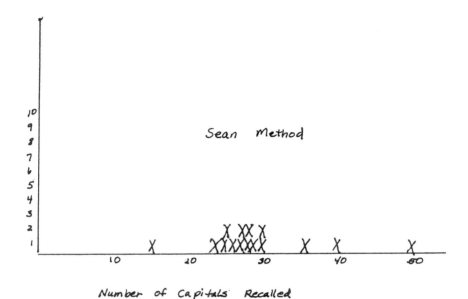

FIG. 7.6.   Second posttest after studying with Sean's Method.

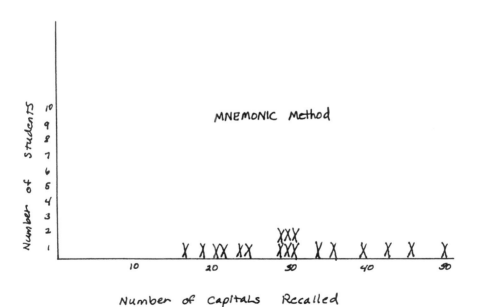

FIG. 7.7.   Second posttest after studying with the mnemonic method.

posed that testing young children on math facts would probably result in a "spread out" display, because ". . . kids don't know them well at the beginning," but as facts became mastered by older children, the displays of performance would eventually become "clumped."

A "Typical" Number. "Who sees something else worth mentioning?" asked Mr. Gundlach, returning the class's attention to Fig.7.5. Brit pointed out, "The average number correct is about 4. There's a big clump. If the 19 and 50 were not there, I'd think the average score would be a 4."

Mr. Gundlach followed up on Brit's comment, meanwhile subtly shifting the focus from average to typical. (We find that mention of "average" tends to elicit the kind of procedural manipulation that we observed earlier in Mr. Rohlfing's class and accordingly tends to cut off more thoughtful consideration of best measures of typicality.) He asked the class: "If you're gonna pick one number to represent the word 'typical' in this clump, what number would you pick? How well is the 'typical' [Mr. G gestures 'quotation' with his hands] kid doing?" This shift to typical elicited a variety of proposals, ranging from trimmed means to modes and medians. Because of time constraints, Mr. Gundlach decided to leave investigation of the implications of these various senses of typical for another day, and switched attention back to the original question: Which method, Sean's or the mnemonic method, "was better?"

Comparing Distributions. Students turned their attention to Figs. 7.6 and 7.7, the two distributions that displayed recall performance on each of the memory conditions (Sean's and mnemonic). To compare the two distributions, students proposed a variety of contrasts. Most of these involved selecting a cut-point and then comparing the number of students above or below that cut-point. We believe the cut-points came to dominate discussion partly because they were consistent with the students' characterization of the distributions by ideas like "bunches" and "spread."

The first cut-point proposed was 30: "Um, with the Sean method, there are more of them clustered around a little less than 30. The mnemonic method is more spread apart, and the Sean method is more clumped together." This first use of cut-point, therefore, focused on relative variability, and the teacher followed up by trying to relate variation to mechanism: "So there's something about the mnemonic that unbunches things?" Rob responded, "Here are more kids in the higher numbers [in Sean's method] than in the mnemonic method." This remark subtly shifted the conversation away from variability back to consideration of better as "better than what?"

Kyle disagreed with Rob's claim, proposing that if 30 were the cut-point ("That's where the clusters just about ended"), it was evident that the mnemonic method was superior: "Like after 30, there's 6 on the mnemonic and only 3 on the Sean. So it doubles how many after 30." Amanda immediately disputed Kyle's claim by pointing out that there was a difference in population sizes on the two graphs (18 vs. 15). We will revisit this issue of population size in a moment but will first review other cut-points and rationales generated by students.

Brit suggested that a better cut-point would be the midpoint of the entire interval (25), invoking the notion of "middle." Many students disputed this approach, because it ignored the location of "clumps" in the data and instead focused merely on the scale. Another student proposed that clumps should be identified and the middle of the clumps should serve as fulcrums for comparing the number of cases above the fulcrum in each distribution.

After this long period of considering the virtues of counting the number of cases above a cut-point, one student referred to Fig. 7.8, which combines the results for both methods at the first posttest. Nathan suggested that perhaps the number of people who scored "lower" (i.e., below a cut-point) should also be taken into account.

This proposal led to a discussion of the need to consider *both* tails of the distribution. Brian, for example, suggested, "So, I think Sean's method looks better for starters. You can see six people there [above the cutpoint

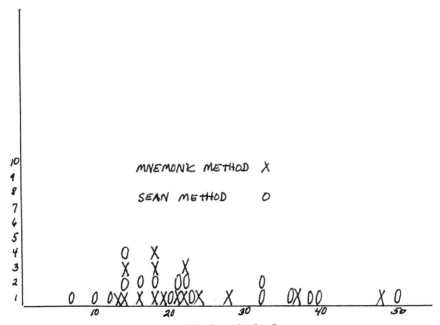

FIG. 7.8.   Combined results for first posttest.

of 30 in Sean's method] and only 2 Xs [mnemonic method] higher [than 30]." Brian then objected that things look different if one focuses on the lower tail of the distribution: "But then there's also less than 10 [a second cut-point], and there are 2 people there, both on Sean's method [and none below 10 in the mnemonic condition]." Nicole elaborated: "When you look below 10, there isn't any mnemonics, so in a way they're doing better, but in another, if you look above 30, they're doing worse." The up-shot of this portion of the discussion was a more nuanced appreciation of what "doing better" might mean, with a class consensus that the apparent virtues of one method were apparently canceled by virtues of the other.

Accounting for Differences in Populations.

As mentioned, at varying points in the conversation students noted the difference in sizes of the populations (for example, 18 vs. 15 in Figs. 7.6 and 7.7). Amanda challenged Kyle's claim of the apparent superiority of the mnemonic method by suggesting that the difference in counts (6 mnemonic students vs. 3 "Sean" students above a cut point of 30—referred to by Kyle as "dou-bling") were simply the result of the difference in size of the populations. Kyle responded by pointing out that if three more people were somehow to be added to the Sean population, "It's still pretty hard to catch up, be-cause they'd have to have all those three people get over 30" (get more than 30 states and capitals correct). Although Kyle was appealing tacitly to notions of sampling, Amanda objected, "What if they did get up there and they caught up?"

Mr. Gundlach followed up by asking, "What are the chances of that happening?" Mr. Gundlach's informal appeal to chance sparked further debate. Focusing their attention again on the entire display, students pro-posed that unless it were a person "who studied a lot," the most likely score for any single "new" student would be between 20 and 30, or near the "typical" value of about 26. Therefore, the class reasoned, it would be highly unlikely that all three "new" students would receive scores over 30, scores that were highly atypical for the distribution.

Once the class resolved that differences in population sizes need not make it impossible to compare the distributions, Michael suggested that a preferable solution might be to "use percent instead of numbers." Marc noted that percent ". . . solves the [problem of] less people in the class. `Cause, for percent, it's for every hundred. So, anyway, you turn 18 kids into 100 [and similarly, 15 into 100]."

To find out whether other students in the class were following these ideas about percentage, we probed their understanding by interjecting a hypothetical situation involving cut-points. Specifically, we asked students to judge the likelihood of recognizing 30 or more faces in a memory test, given two different memory methods—one with a sample of 100 and one with a sample of 20. In the sample of 100 (method A), 10 people recognized 30 or more faces (the analogy to the most frequently employed cut point for the capitals), and in the sample of 20 (method B), 5 people recognized 30 or more faces. "Which method," we asked, "seemed to help people remember better?"

Jenna preferred method B: "I think 20, because the fraction 1/4 is 25 percent, and the fraction of the hundred is 1/10, or 10 percent."

Kyle elaborated: "I'd say 5 out of 20, 'cause it takes 5 twenties to get to a hundred . . . so it's 25 hundreds (compared) to 10 hundreds."

Marc, however, suggested that there might be more to this situation than proportion. Building on Kyle's proportional reasoning, he proposed that perhaps the 5 out of 20 (who used method B) might be the smartest people in the school, so that if others tried it, they might fail to achieve similar levels of proficiency. Marc was sensitive to the possibility that the samples might be drawn from different populations. Mr. Gundlach seized on this claim to again look more carefully at the assumptions made in both this hypothetical situation and in the recently completed experiment. "Is that possible?" he asked. "Yeah, it's possible. But would we say it's likely? Probably not." Here Mr. Gundlach tacitly endorsed the notion that the samples were drawn from the same population and appealed to the likelihood that both would be similar, even as he acknowledged that they might differ substantially. These conversations suggest the possibility of exploring ways to couple intuitions like these to properties of sampling, issues that we are now pursuing with teachers and students.

Researchers Studying Kids Engaged in Studying Kids

Ironically, of course, we researchers and teachers are currently engaged in similar kinds of analyses, grappling with the conundrum of distribution and chance in our own work to understand students' learning. As designers, we are concerned with building a robust understanding that can support effective instruction about distribution and statistics, as well as other ideas in mathematics and in science. Therefore, like the students in Mr. Gundlach's class, we also are engaged in interpreting and evaluating the performances that we observe as students work with new forms of mathematics, classroom practices and activity structures, tools and notations, and forms of argumentation. How will we know if students are learning more under these new forms of instruction? As we make progress on this question, tracking student reasoning longitudinally across the years of their elementary schooling, we note that this is the same question the students were investigating in the memory study!

Accordingly, the forms of reasoning that we use in our work as researchers are reflected in the practices of the fifth graders and their teachers. We identify the beginnings of these ideas, for example, as they

emerge in the first and third graders growing plants and in the inexperi-
enced fifth graders in Mr. Rohlfing's classroom, and try to understand
what it takes to foster further development, as in the more experienced
fifth graders in Mr. Gundlach's class. The contrast between the two fifth-
grade classes illustrates most clearly how inscriptional competence and
mathematical resources can support forms of model-based reasoning that
otherwise would not be possible. With our teacher collaborators, we are
working to construct a broad picture of the early origins, typical developmental trajectories, and points of acceleration and stasis in the growth of
modeling. In this enterprise, the conduct of research and the invention of
instruction cyclically inform each other. From our long term perspective
on development, we observe that students' inscriptions and mathematical
understanding are both inputs to conceptual change and its products.
They serve both as the basis for initial communication and as tools for
pushing communication forward. In light of the substantial differences in
the modeling practices of different disciplines, we are especially mindful
of the need to investigate which forms of modeling prove most fruitful and
accessible to young students over time.

CONCLUSION

We are not suggesting that inscriptions are a magic road to conceptual development, because meta-representational competence does not come
"for free." Even inscriptional systems that are well tuned to both children's
thinking and the task at hand have "costs." Sometimes these costs entail
the dangers of misinterpretation. For example, one group of students inspected a textbook diagram intended to illustrate changing proportions of
human head height to body height from infancy to maturity. To make the
head/body proportions evident, the figures were all drawn the same size.
Probably for that reason, students misinterpreted the diagram as showing
that ". . . as you get older, your head shrinks." It was only after extended
analysis of an actuarial database obtained from a medical insurance company (the database displayed changes in head size with age) that they re-
linquished this idea. As the explanation of one student shows, some of
them continued to find it plausible (we speculate that this might be an idea
that is naturally attractive to preteens): "We know at least that your head
does not shrink up to age 40. Maybe after then it might start shrinking a
little bit." This example underscores that inscriptions have the potential
not only to communicate, but to miscommunicate. Their meaning and entailments must be carefully unpacked and shared if they are to be effective
tools in the classroom.

Another cost of inscriptions is in learning to understand and use them. Our research suggests that teachers may routinely underestimate the complexity of mastering symbolic systems such as maps, number systems, and Cartesian graphs. Even though students may appear to understand how to interpret these conventions, thinking with inscriptions requires developing enough facility and familiarity so that they become "transparent" (Nemirovsky, Tierney, & Wright, 1998) and their user is thus able to see the world "through" the inscription. For this reason, our teachers carefully avoid abruptly dropping symbolic systems into students' laps. Instead, they aim toward helping students first understand the problem that the representation has been developed to solve, an approach that emphasizes the long term development of what diSessa et al. (1991) called meta-representational expertise; that is, wide familiarity with symbolic systems, including their uses and purposes. To develop representational competence, teachers encourage student invention and revision of their own inscriptions to resolve problems. Inscriptions are built on a common history of experience (observing and talking about flowers, plants, and hornworms), and much of the classroom conversation focuses on identifying the attributes that are worth capturing. Therefore, from the start, inscriptions communicate shared understandings. Over time, inscriptions evolve as students agree on the need for increased clarity and precision: Inventions evolve into classroom conventions. Students come to assume that symbolic systems must always be grounded in common meaning. Of course, we are not claiming that all representational systems need to be reinvented by students. However, we do believe it is essential to help students grasp the entailments of those conventional forms, like the coordinate graphs used here to represent growth, that they appropriate.

As our examples demonstrate, it is possible to "see" things through inscriptions that cannot be observed by looking directly at the world. One does not "see" that root and shoot growth have the same general shape unless an inscription makes it apparent. One does not "see" rates of growth in ways that permit quantification unless growth is represented and fixed in a way that permits it to be measured and compared. It is possible to "see" that an organism is different from another one, but variation in two populations is difficult or impossible to compare without inscriptional support. Inscription pushes inquiry forward, so that conceptual and inscriptional development bootstrap each other.

If inquiry is sustained and if tasks are designed to provide feedback (as modeling problems do), inscriptions evolve. Early on, children tend to prefer representations that copy aspects of the represented world. Often these copied aspects are not central to the problem at hand, as in the case of the flowers placed carefully at the top of the strips used to represent plant height in the first grade. The student is faced with the problem of deciding which of many possible mappings to preserve and of these, which can be made more functional, even at the cost of losing easy reference between representation and world. To resolve these problems, good teachers provoke evaluation and revision of representations. What do our graphs (diagrams/maps/rules) communicate? Do they communicate clearly and effectively? How will an individual who was not a member of the original investigation interpret them? Working systematically to help students develop a sense of "audience" is a familiar goal for literacy, and it is equally important in contexts of mathematics and science.

Are there new and interesting questions that can be investigated if we turn up the representational power? When a teacher shifts the question about plants from "How big?" to "How *much* bigger?" she provokes an interesting problem for first graders: How can you emphasize differences between the heights of flowers with a representational system that was developed to look as much as possible like real flowers? In our first-grade example, this challenge provoked a revision of the representational system to emphasize precision of measure and ease of comparison over copy. Children become increasingly willing to "leave things out" as they focus increasingly on emphasizing what is central. But as Olson (1994) noted, such parsimony is also accompanied by augmentation. A mathematical description of growth adds information about mathematical objects to one's conceptions, so that growth itself is reconceived, much in the manner in which Europeans reconceptualized the globe when they mathematized it. Eventually, children come to explicitly consider ideas about residual and degree of fit, as did one of our fifth-grade classes. Children in this class argued about the best placement on a graph for a line drawn to represent a relationship between measured values of mass and volume (Lehrer, Schauble, Strom, & Pligge, 2001). Consideration of residual is not reserved for older students, as evidenced by students in a first grade class who considered the geometric form that would best model fairness in configuration of players in a game of tag (Penner & Lehrer, 2000) or students in a third grade class who progressively refined models of the workings of their elbows (Penner, Lehrer, & Schauble, 1998).

Both our stance as educators and our long term view of development—in this case, the 5 years of elementary education—require us to carefully consider relationships between the evolution of valued forms of thinking and the practices that promote this evolution. We have argued that modeling is fundamental to science, and that modeling practices develop from children's inscriptional and mathematical rendering of the world.

ACKNOWLEDGMENTS

We thank the teachers and students who participated in this study and the research project students and staff who contributed. This research was supported by the James S. McDonnell Foundation and a grant from the

U.S. Department of Education, Office of Educational Research and Improvement to the National Center for Improving Student Learning & Achievement in Mathematics and Science (R305A600007-98). The opinions expressed herein do not necessarily reflect the position, policy, or endorsement of the supporting agencies.

REFERENCES

Bazerman, C. (1988). *Shaping written knowledge. The genre and activity of the experimental article in science.* Madison: University of Wisconsin Press.

DiSessa, A., Hammer, D., Sherin, B., & Kolpakowski, T. (1991). Inventing graphing: Children's meta-representational expertise. *Journal of Mathematical Behavior, 10,* 117–160.

Giere, R. N. (1992). *Cognitive models of science.* Minneapolis: University of Minnesota Press.

Grosslight, L., Unger, E. J., & Smith, C. L. (1991). Understanding models and their use in science: Conceptions of middle and high school students and experts. *Journal of Research in Science Teaching, 28*(9), 799–822.

Hancock, C., Kaput, J. J., & Goldsmith, L. T. (1992). Authentic inquiry with data: Critical barriers to classroom implementation. *Educational Psychologist, 27,* 337–364.

Kline, M. (1980). *Mathematics: The loss of certainty.* Oxford, England: Oxford University Press.

Latour, B. (1990). Drawing things together. In M. Lynch & S. Woolgar (Eds.), *Representation in scientific practice* (pp. 19–68). Cambridge, MA: MIT Press.

Lehrer, R., Carpenter, S., Schauble, L., & Putz, A. (2000). Designing classrooms that support inquiry. In R. Minstrell & E. Van Zee (Eds.), *Inquiring into inquiry learning and teaching in science* (pp. 80–99). Reston, VA: American Association for the Advancement of Science.

Lehrer, R., & Chazan, D. (1998). *Designing learning environments for developing understanding of geometry and space.* Mahwah, NJ: Lawrence Erlbaum Associates.

Lehrer, R., Jacobson, C., Kemeny, V., & Strom, D. (1999). Building upon children's intuitions to develop mathematical understanding of space. In E. Fennema & T. R. Romberg (Eds.), *Mathematics classrooms that promote understanding* (pp. 63–87). Mahwah, NJ: Lawrence Erlbaum Associates.

Lehrer, R., & Pritchard, C. (2000, April). *Building on experiences of large scale space to develop coordinate geometry.* Paper presented at the annual meeting of the American Educational Research Association, New Orleans, LA.

Lehrer, R., & Romberg, T. (1996). Exploring children's data modeling. *Cognition and Instruction, 14*(1), 69–108.

Lehrer, R., & Schauble, L. (2000). The development of model-based reasoning. In R. Glaser (Ed.), *Advances in instructional psychology, Vol. 5* (pp. 101–159). Mahwah, NJ: Lawrence Erlbaum Associates.

Lehrer, R., Schauble, L., Carpenter, S., & Penner, D. (2000). The inter-related development of inscriptions and conceptual understanding. In P. Cobb, E. Yackel, & K. McClain (Eds.), *Symbolizing and communicating in mathematics classrooms: Perspectives on discourse, tools, and instructional design* (pp. 325–360). Mahwah, NJ: Lawrence Erlbaum Associates.

Lehrer, R., Schauble, L., Strom, D., & Pligge, M. (2001). Similarity of form and substance: From inscriptions to models. In D. Klahr & S. Carver (Eds.), *Cognition and instruction: 25 years of progress,* pp. 39–74. Mahwah, NJ: Lawrence Erlbaum Associates.

Lehrer, R., Strom, D., & Confrey, J. (2000). *Developing understanding of similarity.* Manuscript submitted for publication.

Levin, J. R. (1983). Pictorial strategies for school learning: Practical illustrations. In M. Pressley & J. R. Levin (Eds.), *Cognitive strategy research: Educational applications* (pp. 213–237). New York: Springer-Verlag.

National Council of Teachers of Mathematics: Commission on Teaching Standards for School Mathematics (1991). *Professional standards for teaching mathematics.* Reston, VA: NCTM.

Nemirovsky, R., Tierney, C., & Wright, T. (1998). Body motion and graphing. *Cognition and Instruction, 16,* 119–172.

Olson, D. R. (1994). *The world on paper.* Cambridge, England: Cambridge University Press.

Penner, D., Lehrer, R., & Schauble, L. (1998).). From physical models to biomechanics: A design-based modeling approach. *Journal of the Learning Sciences, 7,* 429–449.

Penner, E., & Lehrer, R. (2000). The shape of fairness. *Teaching Children Mathematics, 7*(4), 210–214.

Stewart, I., & Golubitsky, M. (1992). *Fearful symmetry: Is God a geometer?* London: Penguin.

Chapter 8

Social Relational Knowing in Writing Development

Colette Daiute
The Graduate Center, City University of New York

Cognitive and sociocultural theories have focused on social interaction as a catalyst for symbolic development, but the nature and consequences of social relational processes have remained in the shadow of cultural cognition. The argument in this chapter is that social relational aspects of cognitive development provide explanations missing from previous theories applied to the study of writing—a major symbolic tool. Social relational knowing is described here by examining children's writing development through phases of collaboration and individual composing. Social relational knowing involves affective, imaginative, and critical processes that are missing from models of cultural cognition.

After discussing social conceptualizations of writing, I present examples from a series of studies where children's interactions with a teacher and peers draw attention to social relational dimensions of symbolic development. In particular, I examine how collaborative writing supports school-based written narrative development and how social relations among peers especially engage affective and culturally critical processes. This analysis builds on theory that situates knowing in social interaction and extends the role of social knowing beyond modeling of cultural strategies to the affective and critical responses provoked in the social world. When children interact in social situations, their knowledge is shaped by interpersonal processes and responses involved in joint attention to a problem as the basis for social critique. Differences in interactions between teacher/child and peer pairs illustrate how previous theories have accounted for social reproduction of symbolic processes, and, more uniquely, how inter-actions among peers suggest the need to account for affective and criti-cally reflective processes. Finally, I discuss how this case study of collabora-tive and individual writing applies to other symbolic domains.

WRITING AS SOCIAL DISCOURSE

During the past 50 years, writing has been characterized in terms of lin-guistic, cognitive, and cultural processes. Interestingly, the communica-tion function of writing has been the focus of research only recently. Scholars from diverse theoretical perspectives agree that writing is com-munication conforming to culturally defined tools, purposes, and prac-tices, but theorists and researchers posit different functions for written dis-course. Readers and writers must learn the code of written language, and interactions around this code are the basis for its meaning, purpose, and form. As social conceptualizations have become more accepted, debates about the *sequence* of skills has given way to conceptualizations of *co-occurrence* of skills, including decoding, encoding, inferencing, and pur-poseful communication. Assumptions that mastering basics like spelling precede social uses of writing, for example, have given way to the under-standing that spelling is a social process, situated in cultural contexts that also shape sentences and genres like narrative.

According to the view that writing is social discourse, each sentence in a text functions as an utterance in previous interactions (Bakhtin, 1981, 1986). Writing is, thus, conceptualized as a conversation between writer and reader—author and audience. Writing requires awareness of the reader, just as being involved in a conversation requires considering the point of view of one's listener. Writers must engage in perspective-taking without the benefit of actual face-to-face interactions with readers during much of the writing process, so creating stand-alone text is possible to the extent that individuals have participated in previous social interactions that create the purpose, content, and support for written communication. To be engaging, writers have to assume their readers' perspectives, offer-ing details and building suspense in the right places to help them experi-ence and understand their texts as intended. Understanding and inter-preting literature—narratives written by others—also involves recognizing the perspectives of characters in stories. The ability to identify and empa-thize with characters in factual and fictional stories is, moreover, required for successful reading (Beach, 1983; Hynds, 1985, 1989).

Writing is also social purpose. The writing process has been understood as the development of ideas to make sense of the world and one's self. Genres like narrative serve specific culturally defined purposes, like conveying a moral order. Written narrative is, moreover, a discourse form that involves reflection, which makes it more difficult than spontaneous speech and powerful as a context for development and learning. The effort involved in writing appears to engage children intensely in the ideas and practices they enact. When writing activities occur in social and intellectual contexts, writing processes and structures constitute learning rather than being transparent communication. The fact that writing enables communication across time and space also makes it a tool for thought and development. Thus, diverse kinds of social contact provide the basis for symbolic communication.

The development of written language increasingly implicates form and function—written symbols with sociocultural processes. Especially in school, where writing is the major mode for learning, the desired outcome, and assessment tool, writing can be examined as a context as well as an outcome. Like speech, writing is a recursive process requiring certain symbolic representations that in turn create the context for the development of more complex symbolic tools. As 3- and 4-year-olds imitate the actions of writing, for example, they create scribbles their parents identify as letters in their names, and after copying their names, children can analyze the letters in their names as sounds. Older children transform memories into event representations, and responses by teachers, parents, and peers indicate where these reports hold their interest, make them laugh, or challenge their views of the world.

Defining writing as social discourse highlights that writing is neither culturally nor personally neutral. Writing reproduces the social structures where it was created, unless there are deliberate measures for critique. Research has, for example, illustrated how discourse patterns used characteristically by males and females carry over into gendered writing, as do grammatical and organizational patterns from other languages and dialects. Embedding writing in peer interactions is one way of transforming hierarchical social structures. Discourse by young people working together on collaborative writing projects is sensitive to archaic language and content in gradual, transformational ways, like adding rhyme to prose patterns and remarking on hypocrisies in society (Daiute, 1993).

The view that writing is social discourse is embedded in theories of writing development.

Theoretical Approaches to Writing Development

Sociocultural and cognitive-developmental theories have, for the most part, been described as dramatically different (Rogoff, 1990), yet they are similar in their emphasis on metacognition, cultural reproduction, and the limited role they posit for psychosocial processes in cognition. Although described differently, both models also characterize interaction among participants in hierarchical relationships, such as expert/novice and adult/child relations. Both theories also describe mature or expert cognitive strategies in terms of their regulative functions like planning, although the rationale for regulation differs across these theories.

Cognitive Writing. Cognitive-developmental theory has explained that written language like oral language becomes possible as a result of the development of cognitive structures. A brief sketch of a cognitive-developmental model of writing is that it progresses through phases of circular reactions, which allow scribbling; preoperational thought, which allows one-dimensional mapping of image to drawing and speech to word; concrete operational thought, allowing more complex written language processes like reader-based techniques; and finally formal-operational thought, which allows complex conceptual development through revision (Clay, 1991; Daiute, 1995). On this view, written forms are data created by writers and symbolically enacted on by them in ways enabled by their cognitive capacities. Another tenet of this theory is that writing becomes a tool for social interaction only gradually, once a child is able to conceptualize and coordinate multiple points of view.

Consistent with this view are cognitive science models that describe the mind as modular and hierarchical, where regulative processes like planning, monitoring, and revising control the details of expression (Gardner, 1983). Cognitive studies of writing have focused on the nature and development of expert strategies, like planning and revising. Toward this end, researchers observed composing processes of experienced writers by asking them to talk aloud about their thinking as they composed (Flower & Hayes, 1979). Such studies indicated how experienced writers made decisions about text content and form based on intangible communication goals and what they imagined about their readers. These discoveries set the scene for examining composing processes of children and other beginning writers, who appeared to lack strategic control over phases of writing. Children's writing was then described as "knowledge telling," a translation from memory or speech, rather than the more strategic "knowledge transforming" (Bereiter & Scardamalia, 1987).

Cognitive-developmental theory posits an important yet circumscribed role for social interaction as a way of introducing disequilibrum at points of potential transition from one developmental stage to another (Piaget, 1970). From a cognitive-developmental perspective, social interactants differ enough in cognitive capacities so they can challenge their epistemological structures in just the right way to advance toward the next developmental milestone. Researchers have examined interactions among peers whose cognitive capacities differ only slightly on conservation assessments, illustrating the function of social interaction to challenge immature modes of thought (Perret-Clermont, 1980).

Sociocultural Writing.   Sociocultural explanations have raised serious questions about characterizations of cognition as universal capacity within individuals. In contrast, sociocultural theory argues that thought occurs in social interaction, based in Vygotksy's idea that "all thought occurs first on an interpersonal plane and then occurs intrapersonally" (Vygotsky, 1978). Sociocultural theory explains how children apprentice to cultural experts in practice and thought, offering the metaphor of scaffolding to characterize an instructional, supportive role by adults and other experts who socialize children to culturally desired values, practices, and symbols. Research has shown, for example, how parents model cultural scripts (Nelson, 1993) and problem-solving processes (Wertsch, 1991), and how teachers model and transfer effective reading strategies (Palinscar & Brown, 1984).

One approach to the sociocultural study of writing has been to focus on social processes around writing. Research has shown how social interactions during journal writing where children work near each other at small tables in primary grade classrooms shape the rhetorical forms and contents of early writing (Dyson, 1993). Another theme in sociocultural research is diversity, which has shown how children's writing is shaped by community-based practices like associative knowledge chaining and figurative language in African-American discourse (Gates, 1998; Heath, 1983), social contingency patterns in indigenous Hawaiian discourse (Au, 1979), and distributed knowing by Mexican-American families (Moll & Greenberg, 1990). Identifying cultural shaping of texts in this way has shifted conceptualizations of writing development from the idea that simpler forms progress into complex forms, to the idea that contents and forms evolve as social systems. On this view, learning language involves learning cultural forms, such as the importance of narrating for novelty rather than narrating for repetition, so culture is not only a context for writing but it is embedded in written forms and practices.

Any narrow focus on the sociocultural insight that thought is internalized through social interaction fails, however, to account for the range of diversities that emerge when children engage in every day tasks with others. Children are not transparent reflectors of culture, and we need to know more about how they transform cultural knowledge and practices. As described briefly earlier, social discourse explanations of writing and writing development have explained how children learn culturally valued modes of thought, but previous theory has not explained how each generation creates new cultures. Individual variation occurring within relationships is an untapped source of insight about such transformation.

Vygotsky's theory marks a place for subjective aspects of cultural formulations when discussing "affect," "will," "imagination," "play," and other generative phenomena, but this aspect of his theory has not yet been mined in any major way. Similarly, the notion of spontaneous concepts—concepts that begin to take meaning only through "the child's personal use" (Vygotsky, 1994, p. 358)—begs for research on how experience plays a role in development. Vygotsky argued that spontaneous thinking in the din of everyday life is the basis for scientific concepts, thus basing abstract concepts in personal aspects of play. The distinction of spontaneous from scientific concepts and the inclusion of spontaneous concepts in cognitive development leaves room for subjectivity within sociocultural theory.

The Need for Social Relational Accounts of Writing

Characterizing development in terms of the experts in a culture, such as those who use effective communication processes in reading and writing, does not take into account the wide range of resources and experiences that children and other novices draw on when making sense of the world around them. Loosening the grip of enculturation and metacognition models as particular modes of thought may identify resistances to cultural ideals of cognition. This chapter continues to explore how participants' reactions to each other in specific situations bring cultural and personal diversity to cultural norms.

These excerpts are from three collaborative writing sessions over several months in a third-grade classroom in a northeastern city. Karl, an African-American boy, and his classmate, Eduardo, an American-born Puerto Rican boy, had been asked to write stories about community life based on task prompts such as "Write a story about a time when a child was lost in the city," and to use several social studies vocabulary words in their stories. Table 8.1 presents the research design for individual and collaborative writing activities and the tasks for this classroom-based study. The following excerpts are from early phases of Karl and Eduardo's collaborative writing sessions on narrative tasks 3, 4, and 6 (tasks 1, 2, 5, and 7 were individual).

Toward the Concept of "Story Beginning"
by Eduardo and Karl—Task 3

Karl: *Once. Uh oh, I messed up this too close. An' I can.*
Eduardo: *That how we're suppose' to go.*
Karl: *Once there was a.*
Eduardo: *A.*

TABLE 8.1
Design of Study with Sequence of Individual and Peer Collaborative
Writing Around Social Studies Material

Context: Public school in small Northeastern city, mostly African-American and Latino
children from a low-income neighborhood
Participants: 14 children in a third grade class (7–9 year-olds)

				Design			
Task #	1	2	3	4	5	6	7
Situation	Individ.	Individ.	*Collab.*	*Collab.*	Individ.	*Collab.*	Individ.
Individ. N =14							
Collab. N = 7							

Task structure: Writing on computers for class booklet—Community Stories

Writing prompt:	
Write a story about a child who (. . .)	Use the words (. . .) in your story if they fit
gets lost in Beacon city	*map, feelings*
becomes principal for a day	*workers, decisions*
finds a puppy with a note saying "Take care of me"	*community, nature*
brings a new kid in town on a tour of Beacon	*adventures, important*
gets to use a motorbike for a day	*explore, favorite*
finds a bag of money	*advantages, disadvantages*
solves the case of the missing skateboard	*different, transportation*

Karl:	*A little.*
Eduardo:	*Why d'you put capital!?*
Karl:	*I know.*
Eduardo:	*Why?!*
Karl:	*'Cause / / A little. L I T two T.*

Task 4

Karl:	*Once. I'll tell you what to do. Press shift. Once. I'll tell you what to write. Once N C E.*
Eduardo:	*What is it?*
Karl:	*O N C E.*
Eduardo:	*Karl, man.*
Karl:	*Can we see that, one of those dictionaries? We might need something. We might need it. C E. Once there / / No, motocycle! There was a little boy ridin' his motor scooter.*
Eduardo:	*Once there was.*

Karl: *Was a little boy.*

Eduardo: *I know what I'm gonna write.*

Task 6

Karl: *Okay, let's go. Ready. You write about um a football player.*

Eduardo: *I know.*

Karl: *How should we start it off? Once upon a time?*

Eduardo: *How come you, Karl, man you always do it with once?*

Karl: *Okay, there. There was a little boy named.*

Eduardo: *There could be, why do we always want it a boy? Can't it be a girl or something?*

Karl: *Ah, no (chuckle). Okay.*

Eduardo: *No, no, no, no.*

Eduardo & Karl: *(Both laugh)*

In interactions that resonate more with playground banter than class-room discourse, these boys used familiar language, reflected on their own less-than-optimal performance, like "messing up," risked asking questions belying ignorance, like "Why you put a capital?," challenged and teased each other ("Karl, man why you always do it with once?"), while gleefully risking the idea of a female protagonist for their story ("Can't it be a girl or somethin'?"). Over the course of the three collaborative composing sessions, Eduardo and Karl focused on the issue of story beginnings, pro-gressing from Karl's commenting on his actions ("I messed up"), to Eduar-do's restating their text purpose ("We're supposed to . . ."), to Karl's producing initial text sequences ("Once there was a little . . .").

The boys built closely on each other's comments and actions at the same time as they maintained personal perspectives, shifting seamlessly from "we" to "I," as did Eduardo, who seemed to be modeling on Karl's as-sertive composing style at first and then eventually questioning Karl's ap-proach to beginning stories. Although a transcript does not capture all rel-evant dimensions of interaction in this discussion, such as tone of voice, pacing, concurrent talk, and mood, there are important relational mark-ers embedding production of text sequences and management of the com-posing processes in laughter and protests ("No, no, no, no"), question in-tonations (indicated by "?"), and commenting on actions ("I messed up").

Through relational aspects of their collaborative problem solving, these boys who had not previously been friends created multiple stories at the same time: the story of their own blossoming friendship, the story of creating a story with a "beginning, middle, end," as third graders are typi-cally taught to do, and the actual story of a boy who was a football player making his/her way around the "community." Although not all interactions progress in such a friendly manner, the majority of same-sex dyadic peer collaborations have found ways to collaborate productively (Daiute & Dalton, 1993; Daiute & Griffin, 1993; Daiute, Campbell, Griffin, Reddy, & Tivnan, 1993). Moreover, social relational interactions like those by Eduardo and Karl involved examinations of text form and content that led to improved individual writing over time.

Eduardo's first two individually written texts in response to the series of tasks on Table 8.1, are brief reports more than stories. The first of Eduardo's texts is a sequence of conjectures about what a child who had been asked to show a newcomer around his/her town might do, and the second is an endearing description of how the author cares for his puppies—his interpretation of how the city has "nature," which was the focus on the task.

Eduardo, Task 1

A police will take a child on adventure. And a parent would to. If a new kid name in town I would take him on a tour.

Eduardo, Task 2

In my community there are not that much nature. And I have five puppies and my brother has one pup. I have little beds for them and I have bowls for them. And I take good care of them.

Whereas the previous stories are good examples of early writing, there was a dramatic difference in the way that Eduardo responded to similar invitations to write after he had collaborated with Karl twice (on Tasks 3 and 4). After interactions with Karl like those excerpted here, Eduardo wrote more classically structured stories, with rhetorically marked beginnings, "Once there was . . . ," a third-person main character, details about this character's actions, relations, and possessions, all consistent with the task requirement to write about a time when a child in the city found a skateboard.

Eduardo, Task 5

Once there was a boy named Dan Mario and his skateboard was missing. One day he got up and he got out of the house but his mother got him so he had to eat breakfast. And wen he ws don he got his toyota mr2 and he trnsported to San Fanfisco and he found his skateboard and he was 19 years old. And wen he got home he aet dinner and then he went to sleep.

Interestingly, after the pivotal interaction with Karl on Task 6, excerpted previously, Eduardo maintained a similar story structure, so it seems that the critique, "Karl, man how come you always do it with once?" served as a recognition of the textual object, perhaps allowing him a frame for creating stories rather than journal entries.

Eduardo, Task 7

Once there was a boy names Eric Johnson and he motorbike and he explored Florida. He was looking for something it was called the Dimond of Florida. And two weeks later he found the jewal.

Eduardo and Karl's interactions raise questions for both the cognitive and sociocultural explanations of writing development. Absent explicit scaffolding on effective cognitive composing strategies, like plans that consider audience, what theory explains such interactions that are part of the process of becoming a better, more fluent writer?

In the absence of metacognitive strategies, which have been well documented, children work together to get a job done by sharing knowledge, skills, and guiding each other toward a goal, which they establish by restating their assignment.

This chapter argues that affective processes are a major part of the content of social interaction, social critique, and social development. The chapter addresses the question "How do social relational processes play a role in cognitive development?" "What characterizes social relational knowing?" and "How does it constitute writing development?"

Collaboration as a Context for Writing Development

Examples in this chapter come from studies originally done to examine diverse contexts for the social construction of written narratives. In this series of studies, social contexts were varied to examine details of social construction processes among expert/novice dyads and peer dyads (Daiute, 1993; Daiute & Dalton, 1993). A strict Vygotskian theory would pair an adult or a more expert peer so that the adult can explicitly enculturate the child to higher psychological processes, but the peer context allows more open interpretation of culture.

Collaborative writing is a method and a metaphor for symbolic development. A research design allowing for social and individual units of analysis around relevant subject matter provides data for children's as well as researchers' critical reflection about the nature of discursive knowing. Discourse is important not only because children must master oral and written communication skills but also because it embodies cultural, social, and personal aspects of knowing. In this study, oral and written data are conceptualized as "knowledge texts" to refer to academic writing where children were learning and displaying subject matter concepts and rhetorical skills in narrative form. Transcripts of collaborative writing sessions capture social interactions, and we examined written texts as evidence of changes related to these interactions. A major design principle was to have enough individual writing samples across the period of the study for a within-subject examination, and one study allowed for group comparisons. Symbolic development across these studies includes literary concepts that children are expected to master at this age, including features of written texts "story beginnings," "paragraphs," and "details." The method involved grounded theory to identify participants' strategies in different contexts.

The study of social relational knowing applies most directly to children aged 7 through 11. Most children make fine progress in their early attempts at writing, but by Grade 3 children are faced with the challenges of using written language to learn and to display their learning as well as to continue mastering the complexities of written form and function in extended text. The challenges older children face in developing higher orders of written language are formidable, yet they simply must do so if they are going to participate fully in academic life. Children aged 7 through 11, in Grades 3 through 5, are involved in a world where communication and learning increasingly occur in written language, and they are in a prime phase of education for developing complex symbol systems like written language. Particularly relevant to the inquiry on social relational knowing is that during these middle years, children become intensely interested in the social worlds around them, and these worlds present them with many challenges to deal with intellectually, socially, emotionally, and physically. Like any research design, this one has its own idiosyncrasies, but the most important feature is that it allows us to observe at least some aspects of the history of written language symbol use.

Seven- to nine-year old third graders wrote on their own, with a teacher, and with a peer, allowing us to explore different types of social support in their third/fourth grade open classroom in a desegregated urban school (Daiute et al., 1993). Tables 8.1 and 8.2 illustrate the research design, in which a sequence of individual and collaborative writing activities occurred as part of the social studies curriculum and embedded in a socially situated written communication task to create a newsletter that would be shared with parents, classmates, and other members of the school. Each of the 16 third graders in the class participated in writing nine stories for the *Time Traveler News*, reporting on class study of historical periods across Medieval and Renaissance Europe, European exploration of the Americas, and the Mayan Civilization during the same period, as well as classroom events including musical performing arts events and an event when a child in the class broke his leg.

The task prompted for a narrative that cast the authors as newswriters given event headlines subject-matter related vocabulary words to include

TABLE 8.2
Design of Study With Teacher/Child and Peer Collaborative Writing

Context: Urban public school in Northeast, children from diverse sociocultural backgrounds

Design								
Writing Tasks	*1*	*2*	*3*	*4*	*5*	*6*	*7*	*8*	*9*
Group 1 N = 8	I	I	*T coll.*	*T coll.*	I	*P coll.*	*P coll.*	I	I
Group 2 N = 8	I	I	*Pcoll.*	*Pcoll.*	I	*T coll.*	*T coll.*	I	I

Note. I = Individually written; T = Collaborate with Teacher; P = Collaborate with Peer.

Task structure

In the context of 2-year study of different cultures and their impact on "history" *Time Traveler Newsletter* reporting on activities related to studying past and present cultures.

Renaissance Tasks (example)

Imagine that you are a chronicler living in Italy in 1438. A patron of the Medici family has hired you to report on an important event:
Merchants meet to discuss what to do about the city garbage and smells.
In your report, write about the event; tell why the event was important.
Try to use the words *trash* and *aroma* if they fit.

Current Tasks (example)

The editor of the Open School Newspaper has hired you to report on an important event:
Third and fourth graders from the Langston Hughes School go on a field trip to the Gardner Museum.
In your report, write about the event; tell why the event was important.
Try to use the words *explore* and *artist* if they fit.

in the article. For example, as shown in Table 8.2, each task was set in a context of the Renaissance: "Imagine that you are a chronicler living in Italy in 1438. A patron of the Medici family has hired you to report on an important event: *Merchants meet to discuss what to do about city garbage and smells.*" Or the present: "The editor of the Open School newspaper has hired you to report on an important event: *Third and fourth graders from the Open School go on a field trip to the Gardner Museum.*" Task order was randomized across pairs and individuals. Because the Renaissance subject matter had always been enacted through theater, art, music, or literature, it seemed to be accessible.

Grounded theory served for generating codes including the social structure of interactions in each utterance across the teacher/child and peer collaboration transcripts. These codes included initiating, repeating, and contesting text sequences, topical lexical connections, personal references, and partner comments, negative/positive evaluations, as well as laughing and other utterance augmentations. Analyses of frequencies and proportions of each code per transcript, per pair, and per cultural pairing (teacher/child, child/child) revealed patterns of interaction characteristic in the diverse situations. Across 32 sessions in which the teacher collaborated twice with each of the 16 third graders in her class, the teacher's approach was similar to that described of experts in sociocultural studies but very different from interactions among the same children when they worked on similar tasks with peers.

Codes accounted for all interactions around writing, and they were subsequently organized into groups of "social relational discourse," "cognitive control discourse," and "text production." Codes that involved regulation and pedagogy around content and process were grouped as "cognitive control discourse," including planning, instructing, asking questions, and initiating text sequences. Another set of codes was grouped as social relational based on assumptions about potential pragmatic function, including evaluating positively and negatively (which are likely to garner positive and negative reactions), disagreeing, directing (which could be described as bossing because it occurs in the command form), and its converse, indirect directing (which could be experienced as manipulative). Other codes explicitly engage affect, such as making personal connections, including emotion words and affects like laughing, sighing, and playing. Production discourse is the speaking of literal sequences in the texts being created.

These 17 codes were applied by turn, and several different types could co-occur, such as in the sentence: "Let's do, let's do a part where the Medici's decide to put a statue of their dog (giggle) like their dog is soooo important too. Yea, that's cool. (Gently teasing:) Better than your idea, huh?" This turn includes planning ("let's do a part where. . . ."); play ("sooo important too"; "Better than your idea, huh?"); and positive evaluation ("that's cool"; "better than . . .").

Frequency analyses indicate how much each code occurred across contexts and participants, thus offering a measure of the relative degree to which a partipant's discourse in a context intermingled cognitive control and social relational orientations. Table 8.3 presents percentages of each code among all codes applied to the teacher's and child's discourse during teacher/child collaboration and to each child's discourse during peer collaboration. The mean number of words per participant per context is also included for information about the amount of talk, and the mean number of codes applied per context is the basis for percentages of each applied. As shown in Table 8.3, the teacher spoke almost four times as much as her

TABLE 8.3
Percent Social Discourse Codes by Teacher, Children With Teacher,
and Children With Peers During Collaborative Writing

	Teacher (32 Sessions)	Child With Teacher (32 Sessions)	Child With Peer (16 Sessions)
Mean Words Spoken	1901.8	571.8	865
Mean Codes Applied	306.6	118.6	194.3
Percentages of codes by type			
Social relational discourse	*27.97*	*17.42*	*45.71*
Evaluating positively	2.83	1.01	1.28
Evaluating negatively	.65	.42	2.05
Disagreeing	1.04	1.93	5.60
Playing	1.53	1.93	11.68
Directing	5.47	1.18	10.91
Indirect directing	5.12	.59	1.18
Posing alternatives	7.10	6.23	5.14
Making personal connections	.78	2.19	5.35
Emotion words in text prop.	.88	1.01	.72
Affects	2.57	.92	1.80
Cognitive control discourse	*53.68*	*34.11*	*25.61*
Planning	12.8	2.86	3.91
Asking questions	22.4	12.81	12.50
Instructing	7.69	1.51	2.93
Initiating text sequences	10.6	12.47	6.12
Initiating on request	.19	4.46	.15
Text production	*18.22*	*48.39*	*28.60*
Proposing text sequences	10.53	30.52	18.47
Repeating partner's proposals	7.69	17.87	10.13

young partner during the teacher/child interactions, and a mean of 306.6 codes were applied to her talk; and although the children spoke much less than the teacher, 118.6 codes were applied to their talk. As also shown on Table 8.3, children spoke considerably more when they worked together, but the mean number of words per child in those peer collaborative writing sessions was still less than half of the teacher talk.

Development as Cultural Reproduction. The teacher who participated in the study of teacher/child and peer collaborative writing was a White woman known in the district as highly experienced, successful, and compassionate, and using a process approach to teaching writing in ways that helped a wide range of students in her combined third/fourth grade classroom. In interviews before collaborating with her students on the writing tasks for this study, the teacher had said that she wanted to use the opportunity to work with children to improve in their writing, but she also wanted them to be able to develop ideas and to lead the discussion. After the series of collaborations for the study, this teacher, Ann, said that she felt the collaboration had been useful because she was able to help children focus on complex composing processes, but she had also felt a tension between wanting to give students what they needed to succeed in school and wanting them to have the freedom to express themselves. Data analyses indicated that Ann did tailor interactions to individuals, but she also had a fairly consistent script in which she guided everyone to create the news genre based on certain writerly values, like keeping the needs of the potential audience in mind and reporting truthfully.

Analyses showed that the teacher's discourse was goal-directed, analytic, efficient, and grounded in the curriculum topics, which she labeled in interactions with the children. In the following excerpt, the teacher guides Lisa in analytic and strategic approaches to writing a narrative. The task was to write a news story about the day "Room 200 invited parents and friends to view a classroom art show."

Teacher: *And how about and the, we talked about the paintings, what else?*
. . .
Lisa: *The dioramas.*
Teacher: *Give me an adjective.*
Lisa: *And the wonderful dioramas.*
Teacher: *You don't have to use that word!!!! Okay, now we can maybe say something . . . about how the parents walked around and looked at everything or . . . (pause) . . . What did they do?*
Lisa: *Hmmmm. . . . They gave feedback of the pictures.*
Teacher: *What kind of feedback? Positive feedback, negative? Parents gave, how about pos . . . won . . . gave great feedback.*
Lisa: *Okay.*
Teacher: *Gave . . .*
Lisa: *Gave great feedback.*
. . .
Lisa: *And at the breakfast . . .*
Teacher: *Would you like to do some typing now?*
Lisa: *Okay. (long pause) Oops.*
Teacher: *What about at the breakfast? What are you thinking? Hmmmm? (pause, typing) You're not sharing your thoughts. What are you thinking? At the breakfast we had a lot of . . .*
Lisa: *Medieval . . . things. They would have in the medieval times.*

Teacher:	*You did? Food? I don't think we did. Are you getting confused with the Renaissance thing?*
Lisa:	*Yeah.*
Teacher:	*You could just say . . .*
Lisa:	*Had a lot of foods.*
Teacher:	*Or you could just say food.*
Lisa:	*We had a lot of food. Hmmmm. (Pause)*
Teacher:	*What . . .*
Lisa:	*Wait, and we had too much food that we had leftovers.*
Teacher:	*Okay, I don't think that that's, would that be in the newspaper?*
Lisa:	*Nah.*

The teacher directed the composing session purposefully toward creating an exemplary mainstream narrative that could appear in the newspaper. In the process, she emphasized the importance of telling what happened, getting the facts right, and being descriptive by using adjectives. The interactions were efficient yet cordial, and although Ann explicitly assumed the role of co-author with her student, she established a directive question-answer-response frame typical of instructional discourse (Cazden, 1988; Nystrand & Gamoran, 1991).

Discursive markers like questioning, labels ("adjective"), and uses of pronouns are consistent with metacognitive strategies of cognitive and sociocultural approaches. For example, the teacher often used commands, "Give me an adjective," suggestions, "Or you could just say food," and questions requesting specific text content or strategies, "What kind of feedback?" "What about the breakfast?" In this way, questions served planning functions rather than relational functions like gaining information or creating solidarity. Similarly, the teacher's use of "we" seemed to suggest important areas of compliance around text sequences or understandings about text rather than to express intersubjective experience or intention.

As shown in Table 8.3, much of the teacher's discourse was described by cognitive-control codes. Cognitive-control discourse codes accounted for over 53% of the teacher's talk, with most of that involving asking questions (22.4%), followed by another relatively large amount of discourse devoted to planning (12.8%) and initiating text sequences (10.6%), and some of explicit instructing (7.69%). The next most frequent coding was social relational discourse (27.97%), with text production the least (18.22%).

Cognitive control discourse is consistent with approaches described in cognitive science and sociocultural theories because they are strategies typically used by experts and as such modeled in explicit writing instruction. Also consistent with a sociocultural approach, the teacher used this collaborative writing context to "apprentice" her students to these effective strategies. Thus, 34.11% of codings of children's interactions when writing with the teacher were cognitive control, compared to 25.61% of their codes when working with peers. Children's cognitive control discourse was predominantly asking questions (12.81%) and initiating text sequences (12.47%), with a relatively small amount of planning (2.86%). Although the teacher engaged children in planning as indicated by her relatively extensive planning discourse, her engagement of students in the planning process could be characterized as scaffolding because the teacher did more planning than the children, and she guided students to initiate text sequences (12.47%) and to produce text sequences (30.52%) rather than to take over the majority of the planning themselves. Such engagement in the process as guided by an expert has also been described as procedural facilitation which occurs in cultures where children learn trades like weaving (Rogoff, 1990), in classrooms where children are learning math (Newman, Griffin, & Cole, 1989), and in reading classes (Wertsch, 1991).

The teacher used social relational discourse more selectively, indicated by analyses showing that she used positive evaluation and play with only a few children. Analyses indicated, for example, that with the highest achieving students in the class, two girls from European-American backgrounds, the teacher joked during collaborative writing sessions. In the following excerpt, for example, Ann played along with Roberta's tangent about a statue of a spitting frog. Ann directed Roberta and revised her suggestions toward classic narrative form, but she also interpersonally engaged this high-achieving student quite differently from other children in the study.

Teacher: *Okay, maybe as guests, as the guests leave the great hall they enter the garden where there's a beautiful fountain.*

Roberta: *They walk into the garden. A frog spitting water into a fountain.*

Teacher: *(laughs) (typing sounds) To the (typing sounds) and instantly . . . see a beautiful sculpture.*

Roberta: *And see a beautiful sculpture of a spitting frog.*

Teacher: *(laughs).*

Roberta: *That's how some of them are.*

Teacher: *(same time as above) I know. A beautiful—how 'bout a beautifully carved fish, frog, what.*

Roberta: *Frog.*

Teacher: *Spitting (laughs).*

Roberta: *(laughs) Spitting in towards the water.*

Teacher: *Spitting water.*

In spite of this use of social relational talk with Roberta, Ann still organized the composing process around the a plan to create a structured news
article with a striking opening, lots of facts from class, and a conclusive
ending. The quality of Ann and Roberta's playful and evaluative talk, however, differed from the playful talk among student peers.

With the lowest achieving children, the teacher tended to offer supportive comments appearing to encourage their perseverance and enhance
self-esteem, as in the following interaction with Brant. The personal connection to Brant differed from the one with Roberta in that the teacher
worked hard to analyze a strange suggestion by Brant rather than simply
correcting him by restating his suggestion or saying, "No," and in her con-
gratulatory note.

Brant:	*You know them on trading carts with the wheels on them?*
Teacher:	*Carts?*
Brant:	*Mm hm. That they had horses.*
Teacher:	*Yeah.*
Brant:	*And they couldn't even drive through it, use that.*
Teacher:	*Okay, okay, we could say that. So the trash is taking up so much of the street the carts, horse and carts can't even get through.*

. . .

Brant:	*Trading cart couldn't get through.*
Teacher:	*Trading cart.*
Brant:	*With three horses.*
Teacher:	*With one horse, maybe.*
Brant:	*With three. Three in a file.*
Teacher:	*Oh, Oh so it . . .*
Brant:	*Even three horses, they couldn't get . . .*
Teacher:	*I see. Even though it's probably wider and it would need more space, you're saying because it's so powerful they couldn't even push through all the garbage?*
Brant:	*Mm hm.*

. . .

Teacher:	*Okay. Of the—you're really trying.*

Ann's social relational orientation with Brant predominantly involved
affirming, agreeing, and affective comments, "You're really trying." As
mentioned previously, such interpersonally focused comments were, nevertheless, much less frequent than cultural modeling via cognitive control
discourse.

Whereas children's individual writing after working with the teacher conformed to aspects of the narrative script she had emphasized, their writing was also reduced in certain ways. For example, a number of children wrote highly stylized narratives after working with the teacher, but these texts tended to be much less detailed and expressive than those the children had written before collaborating with the teacher and than the texts they wrote after collaborating with a peer (Daiute et al., 1993; Daiute & Nelson, 1997).

Table 8.4 includes examples of two children's individual writing before and after working with the teacher. As illustrated in this table, rhetorical strategies that had been labeled and practiced in the teacher/child co-authoring sessions had an impact. Lisa, for example, included many more facts in Task 5 than she had in Tasks 1 or 2, consistent with the teacher's emphasis on telling what happened. Sticking to the facts, Lisa defined "Renaissance," described people's actions, and used a word from the task, "celebration." She also remained factual as well as "sharing her thinking" by describing her own indisputable preferences, "I like to play the paino & I like to play the recorder. I like alot of instruments." Thus, the sessions with the teacher did not seem to change Lisa's approach to the *Time Traveler News* tasks, but it reinforced certain aspects of it and did not encourage other aspects that were evident in the Danny's Leg piece.

Examination of writing by Shara, another African-American girl, illustrates how the teacher tailored some composing focus to children's individual needs but also maintained the overall script to create a structured news report. Shara, with whom the teacher had emphasized the concept of "paragraph," was especially attentive to this feature as well as to categorizing the information she was giving. Previous theory is sufficient to account for the teacher's approach to the task, but it is not sufficient to account for the children's approaches nor for the relative effectiveness of the peer interactions in spite of their more interactive and playful approach.

Development as Relation, Imagination, and Critique.   Children's interactions varied depending on whether they were collaborating with the teacher or with a peer. Although children followed the teacher's lead in their collaborations with her, their interactions with peers differed dramatically on the same types of tasks. Children's peer composing was interdependent, experiential, grounded in the interpersonal moment, effortful, playful, and personal. The following excerpt by Lisa and Kay illustrates the predominance of social relating as a strategy to propel creation of the narrative as well as the narrative context.

Kay: *The Brunelchki family (typing) . . . so happy that they were going to move.*

Lisa: *They were moving?*

TABLE 8.4
Writing by Lisa Before and After Collaborating With her Teacher

Task 1. Danny

When Danny outside playing football with his friends. A kid slipped on the ice. Then Danny slipped on the ice then another kid fell on top of Dannys leg. And Danny had to go to the hospital and they had to x-ray his leg to find out if he broke it or not. It was really difficult for Danny to walk with a broken leg. Dannys leg weighs 20 pounds with the cast on. Everyone was worried about Danny because he was really hert.

Task 2

All of the people think it was important because of the bad smell that the trash left. And people kept throwing their trash out the window. So they had to put perfume up to their nose or smelled it. And they put cinnamin and spices down their backs to keep the plauge away from everyone.

Tasks 3 and 4: Lisa collaborated twice with her teacher

Task 5. Music

I played the recorder for the "Renaissance Fair." the word Renaissance means rebirth. In the "Renaissance Fair Sue played a song on the recorder & Ian juggled. Eric played a song on the recorder & after he played the song we had a feast. I play the piano and I play the recorder. I like to play the piano & I like to play the recorder. I like to play alot of instruments when we had the "Renaissance Fair we had a celebration!

Tasks 6 and 7: Lisa collaborated twice with her peer, Kay

Task 8. From Rm 200!

FILIPPO'S DOME!

There are alot of archects in the whole world. But in the "Renaissance" like these people & they are: Donatello, Laonard, Michelangelo, Rapiel, Ghiberti & Filipp. One day the judes thought Filippo couldn't finish the dome by his self so they let Ghiberti help Filippo finish the dome. But the judes didn't know that Ghiberti didn't know what Filippo as doing. Filippo knew Ghiberti would be helping so Filippo pretended he ws sick and when the judes came back to the dome it wasn't finished. And the judes said "Hey you didn't do anything and Ghiberti said" Ididn't know what to do. And then Filippo was all better & filippo finished the dome all by his self. And the juges said hey what do you know Filippo did finish the dome & they never did that again to Filippo all the time he was alive. HE FINISHED THE DOME!

(Continued)

212

TABLE 8.4
(Continued)

Writing by Shara Before and After Collaborating With her Teacher

---

Task 5. After collaborating twice with peer and before collaborating with teacher

About one mouth ago the ghird and fouth graders went on a field trip to the gardner museeeum. When they got there they saw a lot of broken stauchus. we saw a lot of pichers from famus artist. then are guild gave the tore it was a little bit spcooky. because the spirt of miss gardner was on the fouth floor. we explored the museum there was a piucher called the reape of eroopy. it was about a god who trured him selve in to a nice bull because if is wife saw him he would and on the roof there was a big piucher of all the gods. Then we saw a woel of fuchine were a man would stand outside and when somebody was dieing they would brien the prson there to see if they would go to heven or down under. then we went back to the garden then we went in to grops and saw so other things. then in about ten miuts we went back to are cars when we came back to the lhschool it was time to go home then robins mother fixst my walk man then I went to after school it fun there but im not to talk about that so what when I got to after school I told rosa about my day she said that we wish we was in my class at 5:30 I went home.
THE END

Tasks 6 and 7. Shara collaborated with the teacher

Task 8.

The dome of stint marry of the flower was build by filippo brunleskey it took about ten years he sarted to build the dome when he was 24 years old.
filippo travled to rome
to and stued the coulmes nd the archs and the masterpices. When he came back he met a man named miclanglo
he told him him about the dome. Filippo died but the dome was still build now
the domje his still standing in florecs.
THE END

Kay:	*They were moving . . . into this new palace, 'cause maybe their house was getting overloaded, or something (typing). They were so happy that they were going to move into, a new palace.*
Lisa:	*New palace. (long pause). I'm pooped. I am, wait, wait, I'll do it A. Palace. P – A – L – A –C –E? (giggles) The Brunelechki family was so happy that they were moving into a new palace.*
Kay:	*I'll write if you don't want.*
(typing)	
Kay:	*But sometimes they felt like they missed their old house, or something.*
Lisa:	*Hmmm?*
Kay:	*But sometimes.*

Lisa: *Huh?*

Kay: *Until . . . what are you doing?*

Lisa: *Thing. (sigh) (typing)*

Kay: *See, look at it.*

Lisa: *Wait.*

Kay: *Look, it dissolved, look.*

(Pause)

Lisa: *Wait, let me see what happens.*

Kay: *It will go away.*

Lisa: *What? If you press this?*

Kay: *No. Wait (pause). Well, now it's.*

Lisa: *Wait, let me fix it.*

Kay: *No, I know how to (pause).*

Lisa: *But the Medici.*

Kay: *That'll go away (pause) . . . C – O – N – O – A. It's right there, look, won't go away.*

Lisa: *Where, right here?*

Kay: *Ya, just put it right there (pause). But, but just leave it like that and keep typing, maybe if you type a little bit.*

Lisa: *- Tron the Medici family.*

Kay: *See, what I did, that's funny. Type some more and maybe it will go away (laughter).*

Lisa: *Wait, let me backspace it one more time (pause).*

Kay: *And then press.*

Lisa: *Oh, wait, wait, wait, okay, wait.*

. . .

Kay: *Okay, but I don't think the Medici fff (typing).*

Lisa: *Fam—wait, don't move it. This isn't very funny . . . family (typing).*

Kay: *How come the Medici family isn't so.*

Lisa: *I don't think the Medici family is so happy.*

Kay: *Where are you, oh, ya.*

Lisa: *'Cause they, 'cause they're moving in without the Medici family's permission, that's why. Okay . . . oh, I've got . . .*

Kay: *Want me to type?*

This interaction differs from the interaction by Lisa and her teacher in many ways. In comparison to the teacher's focus on classically structured news article around social studies topics covered in class, Lisa and Kay played with their words, word processing commands, and each other, shifting abruptly to the Medicis. Rather than carrying out a plan, the children progressed contingent on each other's comments, and when they returned to focus on the Medicis and their move to the palace, they explored an ethical issue of interest, which never occurred in the interactions with the teacher, who kept children focused on the content as it addressed rhetorical goals of creating a well-formed narrative. In spite of such explorations, which would be considered "tangents" by many teachers and researchers, the children wrote at least one paragraph on all the tasks.

The children's peer interactions are characterized by relatively long sequences of reciprocal questioning/answering, collaborative thinking, play, critique as wonder and discovery, and interpersonal attention. Lisa and Kay, for example, grounded their text production in the task, in each other, and in the environmental medium of the computer screen, rather than in a plan about how narratives should be written. Whereas the teacher guided interactions toward a model, explicitly stating rhetorical devices and strategies to achieve narrative ends, the children built reciprocally on each other's comments and text sequences.

Particularly interesting was the children's imaginative engagement of the task content. Rather than trying to report plausible facts, peer pairs tended to imagine the lives and perceptions of the characters in their stories. In the example just given, the girls pondered the feelings of the Medici family on moving into a new grand palace. After initially and evidently automatically stating that the family was "happy" to move in to the palace, Kay introduced the idea that they missed their old home, which Lisa pursued later by conjecturing that the family was not happy because they had not asked permission of the previous inhabitants to move in. Such embellishments occurred often among the peers, beyond the text, as these wonderings created content and perhaps motivation. Such explorations beyond the topic did not typically wind up as specific sequences in the text, but they served another function.

In this way, the young collaborators spent considerable effort to create meaningful frames for contexts and texts. Like Lisa and Kay, most of the pairs I have observed over a number of years have needed to create common social scenarios, which the teacher appeared to take for granted, whether these interpretive frames were about motivations behind texts or processes involved in creating texts, like features of word processing commands. Interestingly, in a study comparing processes and texts by best friends and acquaintances, acquaintances spent more time creating social frames for the creation of text, whereas best friends, not surprisingly, progressed more quickly to generating text sequences (Daiute, Hartup, Sholl, & Zajak, 1994).

Children also used the peer context to externalize their needs through talk, as they often express their emotional states and needs, "I'm pooped";

confusions, "Why are we doing this?"; enjoyment, "This is fun"; including excitement, frustration, and anger. This embeddedness in the context extends to children's focus on the media for writing, including the writing instrument, physical arrangement of the words and page, and each other. Such focus on the here and now might be considered from the perspective of Piagetian theory as evidence of concrete operational intelligence or, from the perspective of cognitive science, typical novice orientation, but neither theory accounts for the precision of interpersonal framing nor its interaction with the generation of narrative purpose, structure, and detail. Playing imaginatively with the task, process, and content creates interpretive contexts that are often assumed in adult/child interactions, and, because of these assumptions, wind up being reproductions of specific cultural values.

In contrast to the teacher who asked questions to elicit bits of information to address a narrative and to engage Lisa in expert composing processes, Lisa and Kay asked questions in at least two ways that differed from the teacher's questioning. Lisa and Kay, like other students, posed questions to inquire about something they did not know or that they wanted to engage as a topic of inquiry, as when Lisa asked Kay, "Why do you say Brunelscky?", which resonates with self-posed questions that serve an egocentric function to introduce a thought socially so it could be considered at all. Like adult teachers, children also posed questions that are neither to inquire, to demonstrate, nor to reify—but to suggest. Kay, for example, asked Lisa several times about exchanging typing roles. At first, Kay asked an interpersonal question, "If you want to type, just tell me," followed later by a question "Want me to type?," which seems more like a suggestion in the face of a period where Lisa lapsed into a more individual mode. Kay later responded to Lisa's saying that she was "getting hot," by asking this time as a combination of question/suggestion if she should type.

Another example of an important social indicator: is the use of "we." Peers tended to use "we" in solidarity to express joint focus on a game, text sequence, or idea. In this excerpt, the girls did more sharing of personal perspectives, via reciprocal interchanges of subjectivities like "I think . . . ," "I keep trying . . . ," "I don't think . . . ," and so on. This use of "I" is more inclusive than willful or egocentric. The use of "we" by both the teacher and child in the teacher/child interactions is an authoritative one marking a cultural idea and perhaps even a cultural injunction. It is important to acknowledge that peers' interpersonal interactions are also, in part, responses to previous interaction experiences, which set up anticipations, defenses, and hopes for any current interaction. Thus, when children like Karl and Eduardo readily revise their mode of operation in response to the teacher's correction but they resist a peer's suggestions, they are using each context differently and adaptively. Children seemed to use interactions with peers to invoke personal experience—how things are—

and how it feels to act in familiar ways. Both contexts offer opportunities to differentiate personal from other knowledge. Strange and familiar ways of knowing, however, determine the nature and extent of an interaction as a learning experience. This proposal that personal meaning is the bridge between ideal knowledge, potential knowledge, and actual knowledge suggests that the nature of the relationship in which knowledge occurs is crucial to its development.

Qualities of social relational knowing among the children were also evident in data analyses contrasting teacher/child and peer interactions. For example, peers interacted more in social relational ways including playing (11.86% compared to 1.53% by the teacher and 1.93% by the same children working with the teacher) and making personal connections (5.35% compared to .78% by the teacher and 2.19% by the same children working with the teacher). Disagreeing and negative evaluations were also more common among children working with peers indicating intense and critical interactions. With peers, 5.6% of children's interactions were disagreements, compared to 1.93% when working with the teacher and 1.04% by the teacher. Negative evaluations by peers was 2.05%, compared to .65% by the teacher and .42% by children working with the teacher.

Changes in children's writing after collaborating with peers offer insights about how social relational interactions might play a role in writing development. In addition to presenting children's writing after collaborating with the teacher, Table 8.4 presents Lisa's writing after writing with her peer, Kay. Like other children, Lisa wrote longer, more descriptive, and evaluative texts after working with her peer partner.

These comparisons also underscore the impact of personal relations and power relations as functions of social interactions around symbolization. Although the teacher is kind, personable with all of the children, nurturing with one, and playful with another, her discourse involved children in master narratives—culturally valued practices and knowledge—achieved through purposeful interactions questioning, suggesting, and appealing to her young partners. In contrast, the children, although they could be brusque, competitive, and even mean to each other, engaged each other to create meaningful contexts for narrative writing as well as to create meaningful narratives. In terms of social relations, the teacher/child interactions are characterized by implicit power structure—with teacher claiming authority and children typically avoiding conflict or deferring when disagreements emerge—as they do only in hints. In addition to the interactions in these examples, data analyses on Table 8.3 indicate the discursive form of a power differential.

Theories that account for interactions among cultural representatives—teachers/students, parents/children, peers—can be broadened by paying attention to such interactions among specific people who connect, compete, control, dissent, and feel happy or sad as a result of their interactions in real time and space. It may also be that social relational strategies like those we see by children during collaboration have been as underrepresented in adults' novice and spontaneous interactions, as well as among those who are being enculturated to those specific metacognitive strategies. If social relational grounding is not only effective but essential, one reason for the apparent failure of many children (and adults) to develop school-based knowledge and skills is that social relational strategies play a much more foundational role than has been recognized. Consistent with this possibility is one that some cultures value social relational processes in ways that support their development and use through mature intellectual work.

TOWARD A THEORY OF SOCIAL RELATIONAL KNOWING

Theories not typically applied to cognitive development can help account for vicissitudes of social discourse and, thus, cognition in context. Drawing on social development, psychodynamic, and critical discourse theories, I propose social relational knowing as a process that explains how affective aspects of interpersonal interactions play a role in symbolic development. The process of social relational knowing as illustrated during collaborative writing occurs in situated discourse (whether it is explicitly collaborative or not), and the motivations and reactions to interpersonal interactions confirm or challenge the culturally salient knowledge and strategies emphasized especially in sociocultural models of cognition. I argue, thus, that the experience of social interaction involves affective responses that operate in a range of ways.

Social relational knowing is a phase of the process of cognitive development that is constituted by interdependency, subjective experience including affect and personal meaning, and critique, such as defense, disagreement, competition, and resistance. Social relational knowing is a concept that accounts for the intense interactions by Eduardo and Karl and by Lisa and Kay as illustrated in the excerpts cited. The young people contingently built on each other's comments; rather than planing ahead, they explored ethical issues and other tangents; they teased each other; they challenged outside forces; they laughed as they gradually externalized the texts they were writing and gained new understandings about it. In terms of the emphasis on writing as a mature strategic process in previous models, these interactions are stark reminders that there is much more to explain. These children are clearly working with cultural models and modes, but the interpersonal engagement of cultural meanings is an aspect of its transformation as well as its embodiment.

After outlining major features of social relational knowing and explaining how these integrate previous theory, I apply a psychodynamic concept as an illustration of how social relational knowing can expand understandings of writing development.

Interdependency and Mutuality

Emotional interdependence of thought has been described mostly among infants and those with psychosocial problems. Nevertheless, openness, trust, interest, and motivation must be an aspect in the knowing processes. From an infant's first interactions, responsiveness and affection support symbolic development as mothers and babies share their intersubjective gaze and joint manipulation of objects and bodies (Stern, 1993). Mothers and other caregivers have been conceptualized as transitional objects for their children's perception, interaction, and participation in the world, with their loving interactions creating a base for action, understanding, and adjustment that make the world manageable and analyzable (Winnicott, 1989).

Studies of emotional development around the issue of how mother and infant's joint focus on a toy, body part, or a sound offer insights about how such intersubjective focus is constituted in discourse (Stern, 1993), and, later in childhood, affective focus shifts from mothers and other adults (potential caregivers) to peers (Hartup, 1995). The excerpt of Lisa and Kay's interaction, for example, involved establishing collective focus around the activities, tools, and ideas of their writing task. They engaged each other to create an intersubjective focus on the writing machine, the words, and the nature of characters' psychological states embedded through the course of their interpersonal relations. They took intellectual risks together, making up the game of having words "dissolve" from the word processing screen when they toggled a switch to turn off the automatic wrapping function. Lisa and Kay played off each other in making and listening to different pronunciations of "Bruneleschi," taking turns saying the name, evaluating how it sounds as the partner speaks it, attempting to spell it, and interestingly, they settle collectively on an incorrect spelling. In this way, most of Lisa and Kay's planning, inquiry, and production to create text was interdependent, with relatively short turns, idea generating, questioning, interpersonal connecting, role shifting, and, for the most part, directly responding to the content of their partner's comments. Even though they do not always agree or take perfectly equitable turns, peer pairs, like Lisa and Kay, Eduardo and Karl, typically interact with each other, constantly checking affect ("are we both having fun here"), power relations ("gee she's being nice but I'm not getting my turn to type"), and collaboration ("what should we do next?") as well as in terms of cognitive tasks.

The importance of becoming other-oriented is another foundation for social relational knowing. Central in the development of social understanding and action are perspective coordination, interpersonal negotiation, and personal meaning-making (Schultz & Selman, 1998). Social perspective coordination is the increasing ability to understand one's own actions, understandings, and identity as they occur in social contexts (Mead, 1934; Piaget, 1970; Selman, 1980; Sullivan, 1953). Interpersonal negotiation is the ability to consider others' perspectives in conflicts and to find ways of bringing diverse perspectives into some mutually desirable account. Pespective-coordination is an essential aspect of social relational knowing because intersubjectivity creates the motivation and material for symbolic communication. In addition, as discussed later, social mutuality enables externalization of intellectual objects as well as self-constructs.

Interdependency as discussed here in peer relationships is an untapped aspect of symbolic communication theory. Given the salience and importance of peer relationships, it seems that a broad range of resources involved in relational dynamics influences cognitive processes and knowledge development during childhood, yet social interaction is often noted as distracting and potentially harmful, as "peer pressure." The cultural critique often involved in peer relations can become major resistance or aggression against adult society, but the positive aspects of this inevitable social force are crucial to the processes of knowledge, identity, and social change. One function of reciprocal social gaze is the development of self-concept. Social interaction around academic tasks must also be examined as opportunities to create and enhance self-representations as well as to create representations of subject matters. Because much of the process of social/identity development apparently involves questioning and resisting cultural norms, it seems important to examine how interpersonal skills interact with knowledge and how the specific course of relationships influences cultural reproduction.

Subjectivity and Imagination

Developing a theory of social relational knowing requires conceptualizing "subjectivity" in ways that are consistent with "intersubjectivity." Social relational knowing is a process of real-time discourse, accounting for subjectivities that are typically abstracted away in conceptualizations of higher order thought. Although subjectivity has been identified as primitive and vague by most cognitive theories, it has become a major focus of discourse and critical psychological theories.

Theorists who posit ordered stages of development moving toward increasingly explicit, regulative thought, have used the term "subjectivity" to represent the private, emotional self-perspective, connoting internal psychological life in a dual, sometimes oppositional, relation to social life. For example, Piaget discussed subjectivity as "autistic thought, creator of personal symbols, which remains essential to each of us throughout life" (Piaget, 1970, p. 59). Piaget went on to say that "In the child autism is everything. Later, reason develops at its expense, but—and this is the real problem—does it ever extricate itself entirely? Apparently not. There remains therefore an extremely instructive psychological task to be undertaken in order to determine in each individual the relations between the state of his intelligence and the state of his autistic or unconscious life" (Piaget, 1970, p. 59). Extending the notion of subjectivity to the social realm, Winnicott referred to "subjectivity" as "the inner, interpretive, bodily, unconscious orientation," but through social interaction, in particular with the mother who mirrors reality to an "infant's hallucinations," subjectivity can move to object relations, as is discussed later.

Embedded in recent theory on the social nature of discourse is the notion of personal discourse as an aspect of intersubjectivity. "The word in language is half someone else's. It becomes 'one's own' only when the speaker populates it with his own intention, his own accent, when he appropriates the word, adapting it to his own semantic and expressive intention . . ." (Bakhtin, 1981, pp. 293–294). Bakhtin did not offer much description of this aspect, but this theory is consistent with the explanation that knowing is inextricable from the interdependencies in which it occurs. Bakhtin has been interpreted mostly in terms of cultural abstractions, yet the affective aspects of his idea are evident in his emphasis on "intention," "accent," and "semantic" meaning.

Personal meaning has been proposed as a mechanism for the management of problems of social life, with a particular emphasis on risky behaviors and relationships in preadolescents and adolescents (Levitt & Selman, 1996). This concept entails the explanation that knowledge about what is right to do in terms of substance abuse and violence, for example, becomes operational only when linked to personal needs and desires. Personal meaning involves comparing one's own experience with others' actions and statements, like, "Just say 'No!' to drugs" or " 'Talk it out' when someone insults you." How a young person connects self, other, and society in such deliberations has a major role in how he or she interprets specific cultural injunctions as privileged abstract knowledge. An individual's experience with drugs and violence, according to this concept, mediates the meaning of the cultural knowledge about ideal behavior, self-control, and abstinence.

The evaluative phase of narrative has also been explained as a personal meaning-making function. Narrators express affective states in their use of evaluative linguistic markers (Bamberg, 1991; Labov & Waletsky, 1967/1997; Peterson & McCabe, 1983), in particular as they mark significance and emotional stance toward events, characters, and other aspects of the story being told. Individuals weave their experiences into an ongoing implicit story about life based in their subjective experiences, thus most discursive accounts rely at least in part on narrative rather than on objective truth (Spence, 1982). Narrative truth is a way of making sense of the world—an interpretive frame for understanding situations, knowledge bases, and interpersonal relationships, and this sense making is essential to survival. People's previous issues and traumas (Freud, 1900/1965) play a role in their perceptions of the world and the story one creates to explain it. Not all issues play the same role in all contexts, but unconscious processes must have more of an impact in academic knowledge and skills than has been recognized, especially among school-aged children who have not developed deliberate control over their unconscious processes. In this way, children's subjective experience is at the center of knowledge development.

What some have referred to as narrative truth, others have described as imagination. Rather than dismissing imagination as irrelevant fantasy, theorists and researchers describe imagination as interpretation grounded in social contexts. Just as distinctions between narrative truth and historical truth move objectivity into symbolic realms, relating imagination to interpretation emphasizes the intentional, meaning-making aspects of fiction. If culturally shared notions like gender and race (Walkerdine, 1984) are, at least in part, fictions, then fictions are socially situated. Imagination is a process that can be used to escape, but it is also used to create common reference points (deRivera & Sarbin, 1998). On this view, Lisa and Kay's imaginative extension of the Medici's state of mind around moving to their new palace and their imaginative play with the word processor create a meaningful context for their writing about the Renaissance. As with the need for a personal-meaning connection to make sense of drug prevention messages, the girls created a virtual reality for the Renaissance exploration. Similar social and symbolic communication occurs in pretend play among preschoolers (Goncu, 1999). Like fiction, play is not a literal representation of reality; rather, literal and extended representations are the material of symbolic communications with self and others.

Critique

Committed social relational processes include dissent, which is an important aspect of analysis and thus symbolic development. As illustrated in examples of peer interaction, banter, questioning, and challenge can lead to gradual transformation of a concept like *story beginning*. In addition to commitment, trust, and motivation, such interpersonal dynamics hinge on equality of power, status, and understanding. As shown in Table 8.3, Lisa, Kay, and all the other children challenged peers around symbolic development, but not the teacher, as evidenced in the peers' relatively high percentages (compared to the peer with teacher) of disagreeing, negative evaluation, and playing, which included extensive posing of alternatives, teasing, and other types of challenge.

In addition to interpersonal dissent, children challenged classroom conventions by their relatively extensive forays into tangents relating to moral issues, which some of them managed to draw the teacher into as well. Although moral significance is an aspect of narrative, children's focus on moral issues emerged as critique because moral deliberations about truth, justice, motivations, and social problems are typically implicit in classroom practice and subsumed in teaching about behavior and structure (Heath, 1983; Walkerdine, 1984).

In contrast to theories that posit subjectivity as private, primitive, and something to outgrow, discourse and feminist psychological theories posit a subjectivity that is always operating for meaning-making and social regulation in society. The idea that subjectivity forms as a function of societal injustices is an old one that has been revisited for understandings of social cognition. In particular, social interactional contexts reify power relations that can work for or against knowing grounded in experience (Walkerdine, 1984, 1996). Harre and Gillet (1994) put it this way: "A person's subjectivity is defined in a situation and their positioning in relation to certain discourses is implicit in that subjectivity. Subjectivity thus occurs in the process of signification embedded in sociopolitical situations, which is the active role of meaning in structuring the interaction between person and context" (Harre & Gillet, 1994, p. 24). In addition to linking subjectivity and symbol, these theories point out that subjectivity is impacted by power relations as well as personal relations.

The struggle for power and strategies to do so are obviously ones children have learned in their cultures from adults, but peer relationships are carried out with more breadth and negotiation. When children feel entitled to question, disagree, congratulate, and take risks, they have a broader base of data and strategies with which to do symbolic work. As we have seen, different social situations allow or suppress dissent, so critique is not a capacity in any absolute sense. Of course, the perils of anarchy are also present all the time, and disagreement may become mean-spirited criticism without the conventions of politeness maintained by a teacher or some peers.

Collaboration as Transitional Space for Symbolic Objects

One concept from psychodynamic theory is particularly useful in offering insights about how and why social relational discourse may be a powerful addition to sociocultural theory of symbolic communication. Collaborative writing can be characterized as a transitional space (Winnicott, 1989) where the quality of social interactions determines whether and how the symbolic object of focus can be externalized and thus crafted. As transitional spaces, collaborative writing sessions are particularly supportive of symbolic development when interactions involve object relating and object use. Whereas teacher/child, like mother/child interactions, could be optimum contexts for object relating and object use, affective aspects of school settings belie such interactions. In contrast, peer interactions tend to be highly affectively oriented both negatively and positively, so they possess certain features for object relating and object use even though young peers may be ill-equipped as cultural cognition guides or caretakers for peers.

Winnicott (1989) described object-relating in terms of experience of the subject. A capacity to use an object—an intellectual object like a written narrative—is more sophisticated than relating to the object. Using the object in a theoretical sense implies that the object is part of external reality. If a symbolic communication is the abstraction of a symbolic form that merges purpose and form, then that symbolic function is external in several ways. The ability to use written narrative communicatively and persuasively is external in that it serves social and cultural purposes as well as personal, expressive purposes. Narrative writing ability in desirable cultural forms is also external to the extent that children can reproduce the discursive form over time and contexts.

Peer interactions like those by Lisa and Kay, Eduardo and Karl, and others are object relational in several ways. Interactions between peers include a wide range of the types of object-relating that lead to object use. The broader range of affective interactions among children than teachers is not surprising given children may be less likely to constrain their interactions to specific forms. Characteristic object relations including cathexis, feeling depletions, destructions, and externalizations were evident in the peer interactions, which may explain how peer interactions led to often dramatic changes in written narrative forms.

The relatively large number of affectively charged interactions indicated in the comparison in Table 8.3 is evidence of the extensive "cathexis" or concentration of emotional energy on the object of the texts the children were creating together and the specific narrative news story form they were using for the first time. Even though the children expended considerable energy with the teacher, the relatively high incidence of playing, disagreeing, negative evaluation, directing, and personal connecting among peers suggests a more intense emotional interaction. This tool of cathexis, thus, integrates extensive sections of children's peer discourse that seem like noise without such insight.

Peer interactions were also more likely than teacher/child interactions to include explicitly critical qualities, which are essential to externalizing ideas. In terms of object relating, these qualities are described as depletion and destruction. As shown in Table 8.3, children were more likely to offer explicitly negative critique during their peer collaborations, including negative evaluations, disagreeing, and directing. Such challenge is likely to capture imagination, whether through defense or inspiration, as indicated when Eduardo teasingly critiqued Karl's repetitive use of "Once" as a story opener and boys as main characters, and as in Lisa's challenge to Kay about what might be bothering the Medicis. It is also intriguing to consider whether such a challenge, even if temporarily destructive of an idea or an ego, extends beyond specifics of the immediate task to broader social concerns. In the examples given, for example, the girls' interactive banter about activity at the Medici household led to considerations about ethical aspects of the characters. Such probing beyond the surface to social consequences related to the task was almost exclusively introduced and pursued by young peers rather than with the teacher. Interestingly, the teacher's evaluations were more explicitly positive than the children's, but children's relatively taciturn contributions during teacher/child collaborations compared to their extended peer interactions may indicate that the children understood the teacher's more subtle negative evaluations, embedded in indirect directing and cognitive control discourse.

Relational processes around writing include creating contexts for interacting and knowing, such as establishing a quest to figure out a good story opener and doing this in a way that is fair. Creating socially responsible interactions typically occurs as participants establish interpersonal accountability, follow up on negotiated rules for co-participation, and revise these rules as they progress. Children seem to establish a social modus operandi fairly quickly, with the background of classroom practice and the assistance of certain rules like the requirement that they alternate control of the keyboard every 15 minutes. Most pairs, like Eduardo and Karl, worked consistently over several collaboration sessions and then began revising social interaction practices as they became better acquainted with their working styles in this context. Although each pair's social organization activities do not usually occur in any explicitly organized manner, the codes to account for social interactions included a stable list applied fairly consistently across pairs, including stating purpose and approach by repeating, asking questions, responding to questions, building on each other's comments, and competing, including interrupting, one-upping, being mean, taking resources, and shocking. Children's academic interactions involve taking intellectual risks together, engaging in fantasy, exaggeration, humor, possible worlds, and what ifs.

Implications

Further development and research about theories of social relational knowing are important for research and practice. As a proposal, this argument raises many questions about social relational knowing in symbolic communication. Future research can examine the nature and influences of social relational knowing in contexts other than writing with preadolescents, who may be at a particularly optimum time for working with peers. Social relational processes are, however, likely to play a role across age groups, and these processes may play a particularly salient role at early phases in the development of new symbolic systems. To examine the issue of developmental maturity, research on social relational knowing across age groups engaged in relatively familiar and unfamiliar symbolic systems would be invaluable. The research design described here of practice-based examinations of individual work and social interactions with experts and comparable novices is one that offers insights given a social discourse model of thought.

Another implication of these findings is the need for more interdisciplinary theory and research explaining how children engage a range of cognitive, cultural, and affective resources with their oral and written discourse. Social development and narrative psychologies, in particular, have been useful as the basis for extending previous explanations of symbolic development.

The qualities of social relational knowing are most evident in explicitly social cognitive contexts, like collaborative writing, and among certain participants, like young peers, but the processes could apply more generally to augment cultural cognition.

CONCLUSION

In summary, studies on the nature of interaction and changes in written texts across different social contexts offer several insights about the function and influence of interpersonal relationships in the symbolic work of writing academic narratives. Across the studies described here, children engaged a full range of discourse when interacting with peers. Young writers beginning to deal with extended knowledge texts did not approach writing tasks predominantly with metacognitive strategies, as had previously been shown in many studies comparing expert and novice writers and readers. Instead, social relational knowing involves symbolic content in ways that externalize it and thus engage it as critical social discourse rather than just expression. This insight loosens what is sometimes a de-a deterministic application of sociocultural and cognitive theories positing regulative strategies as the primary organizers of cognitive development.

Whether they simply embellish existing theories or change them more dramatically, the earthly details of social and personal interaction and reaction must be addressed. If nothing else, issues of mutuality, subjectivity, imagination, and critique offer insights about how knowing among those outside the cultural elite differ from those whose symbolizations represent cultural ideals. More significantly, attention to knowing as it occurs in interpersonal contexts can offer insights about how cultures change; how children think off center to create new perspectives and influence the "adults and more able peers," whom Vygotksy posited as the social origins of thought. Given insights about how cognition is situated in culture, we are freer to explore how personal perspectives interpret, resist, and transform culture as well as enact it in predictable ways.

REFERENCES

Au, K. H. (1979). Participation structures in a reading lesson with Hawaiian children: Analysis of a culturally appropriate instructional event. *Anthropology in Education Quarterly, 11,* 91–114.

Bakhtin, M. M. (1981). *The dialogic imagination: Four essays by M. M. Bakhtin* (M. Holquist, Ed.). Austin: University of Texas Press.

Bakhtin, M. M. (1986). *Speech genres and other late essays.* Austin: University of Texas Press.

Bamberg, M. (1991). Narrative activity as perspective taking: The role of emotionals, negations, and voice in the construction of the story realm. *Journal of Cognitive Psychotherapy: An International Quarterly, 5*(4), 275–290.

Beach, R. (1993). *A teacher's introduction to reader response theories.* New York: Teachers College Press.

Bereiter, C., & Scardamalia, M. (1987). *The psychology of written composition.* Hillsdale, NJ: Lawrence Erlbaum Associates.

Cazden, C. (1988). *Classroom discourse: The language of teaching and learning.* Portsmouth, NH: Heinemann.

Clay, M. (1991). *Becoming literate: The construction of inner control.* Portsmouth, NH: Heinemann.

Daiute, C. (1993, September). Youth genres: Links between sociocultural and developmental theories of literacy. *Language Arts,* 402–416.

Daiute, C. (1995). What is writing development? Invited critique of D. McCutchen. Cognitive processes in children's writing: Developmental and individual differences. *Issues in Education, 1*(2), 185–191.

Daiute, C., Campbell, C., Griffin, T., Reddy, M., & Tivnan, T. (1993). Young authors' interactions with peers and a teacher. In C. Daiute (Ed.) *The development of literacy through social interaction* (pp. 41–63). San Francisco: Jossey-Bass.

Daiute, C., & Dalton, B. (1993). Collaboration between children learning to write: Can novices be masters? *Cognition and Instruction, 10,* 281–333.

Daiute, C., & Griffin, T. (1993). The social construction of written narratives. In C. Daiute (Ed.). *The development of literacy through social interaction* (pp. 97–120). San Francisco: Jossey-Bass.

Daiute, C., Hartup, Sholl, W., & Zajac, R. (1993, March). *Peer collaboration and written language development: A study of friends and cquaintances.* Paper presented at the Society for Research in Child Development Convention, New Orleans.

Daiute, C., & Nelson, K. A. (1997). Making sense of the sense-making function of narrative evaluation. *Journal of Narrative and Life History, 7*(1–4), 207–215.

De Rivera, J., & Sarbin, T. R. (1998). *Believed-in imaginings: The narrative construction of reality.* Washington, DC: American Psychological Association.

Dyson, A. H. (1993). *Social worlds of children learning to write in an urban primary school.* New York: Teachers College Press.

Freud, S. (1900/1965). *The interpretation of dreams.* New York: Avon Books.

Freud, S. (1961). *Beyond the pleasure principle.* New York: Norton.

Gardner, H. (1983). *Frames of mind.* New York: Basic Books.

Gates, H. L., III (1988). *The signifying monkey: A theory of Afro-American literacy criticism.* New York: Oxford University Press.

Goncu, A. (Ed.). (1999). *Children's engagement in the world: Sociocultural perspectives.* New York: Cambridge University Press.

Harre, R., & Gillet, G. (1994). *The discursive mind.* Thousand Oaks, CA: Sage.

Hartup, W. W. (1995, March). *The company they keep: Friendship and its developmental significance.* Presidential Address at the Society for Research on Child Development, Biennial Meeting, Indianapolis, IN.

Heath, S. B. (1983). *Ways with words.* Cambridge, England: Cambridge University Press.

Hynds, S. (1985). Interpersonal cognitive complexity and the literary response processes of adolescent readers. *Research in the Teaching of English, 19,* 386–404.

Hynds, S. (1989). Bringing life to literature and literature to life: Social constructs and contexts of four adolescent readers. *Research in the Teaching of English, 23,* 30–61.

Labov, W., & Waletzky, J. (1997). Narrative analysis: Oral versions of personal experience. In J. Helm (Eds.), *Essays in the verbal and visual arts* (pp. 12–44). Seattle: American Ethnological Society. (Original work published 1967)

Levitt, M. Z., & Selman, R. (1996). The personal meaning of risk behavior: A developme: tal perspective on friendship and fighting in early adolescence. In G. G. Noam & K. W. Fischer (Eds.), *Development and vulnerability in close relationships* (pp. 201–233). Mahwah, NJ: Lawrence Erlbaum Associates.

Mead, G. H. (1934). *Mind, self, and society.* Chicage: University of Chicago Press.

Moll, L. C., & Greenberg, J. B. (1990). Creating zones of possibilities: Combining social contexts for instruction. In L.C. Moll (Ed.), *Vygotsky in education: Instructional implications and applications of sociohistorical psychology* (pp. 319–348). Cambridge, England: Cambridge University Press.

Nelson, K. N. (1993). Events, narratives, memory: What develops? In C. A. Nelson (Ed.), *Memory and affect in development, Minnesota Symposium on Child Psychology: Vol. 26* (pp. 1–24). Hillsdale, NJ: Lawrence Erlbaum Associates.

Newman, D., Griffin, P., & Cole, M. (1989). *The construction zone: Working for cognitive change in school.* Cambridge, England: Cambridge University Press.

Nystrand, M., & Gamoran, A. (1991). Instructional discourse: Students' engagement and literature achievement. *Research in the Teaching of English, 25,* 261–290.

Palinscar, A. M., & Brown, A. (1984). Reciprocal teaching. *Cognition and Instruction, 1,* 117–175.

Perret-Clermont, A. N. (1980). *Social interaction and cognitive development in children.* New York: Academic Press.

Peterson, C., & McCabe, A. (1983). *Developmental psychology: Three ways of looking at children's narratives.* New York: Plenum.

Piaget, J. (1970). Piaget's theory. In P. Mussen (Ed.), *Carmichael's manual of child psychology* (3rd ed.). New York: Wiley.

Piaget, J. (1977). Psycho-analysis and its relation with child psychology. In H. Gruber & J. J. Voneche (Eds.), *The essential Piaget*. London: Routledge & Kegan Paul.

Rogoff, B. (1990). *Apprenticeship in thinking: Cognitive development in social context*. New York: Oxford University Press.

Schultz, L. H., & Selman, R. L. (1998). Evaluating pairs: The assessment of developmental process and risk-taking status. In R. L. Selman, C. Watts, & L. H. Schultz (Eds.), *Pair therapy: Toward intimacy and conflict resolution through the development of close relationships* (pp.). New York: Aldine de Gruyter.

Selman, R. L. (1980). *The growth of interpersonal understanding*. Orlando, FL: Academic Press.

Spence, D. (1982). *Narrative truth and historical truth*. New York: Norton.

Stern, D. N. (1993). The role of feelings for an interpersonal self. In U. Neisser (Ed.), *The perceived self: Ecological and interpersonal sources of self-knowledge* (pp.). Cambridge, England: Cambridge University Press.

Sullivan, H. S. (1953). *The interpersonal theory of psychiatry*. New York: Norton.

Vygotsky, L. (1978). *Mind in society*. Cambridge, MA: Harvard University Press.

Vygotsky, L. (1994). The development of academic concepts in school-aged children. In R. Van der Veer & J. Valsiner (Eds.), *The Vygotsky reader* (pp. 335–370). Cambridge, England: Blackwell.

Walkerdine, V. (1984). Developmental psychology and the child-centered pedagogy: The insertion of Piaget into early education. In J. Henriques, W. Holloway, C. Urwin, C. Venn, & V. Walkerdine (Eds.), *Changing the subject: Psychology, social regulation, and subjectivity* (pp. 153–202). New York: Routledge.

Wertsch, J. (1991). *Voices of the mind: A sociocultural approach to mediated action*. Cambridge, MA: Harvard University Press.

Winnicott, D. W. (1989). Critical notice of "On not being able to paint." In C. Winnicott, R. Shepherd, & M. Davis (Eds.), *D.W. Winnicott: Psycho-analytic explorations* (pp. 390–392). Cambridge, MA: Harvard University Press. (Original work published in 1951)

Part IV

CONCLUSION

Chapter 9

Symbolic Communication and Cognitive Development: Conclusions and Prospects

Eric Amsel
Weber State University

James P. Byrnes
University of Maryland

INTRODUCTION

The purpose of this chapter is to review the previous chapters and find the common themes regarding the nature, origin, and acquisition of symbolic communication and its function for cognitive development. As presented in the preface, our broad goal is to identify the cognitive developmental consequences attributed to communicating symbolically. As previously defined, symbolic communication means understanding others or expressing oneself with symbols, whether that involves communicating linguistically, mathematically, or through another symbol system expressed in speech, gesture, notations, or through some other means.

Although all the chapters focus on symbolic communication, we have found the task of finding common themes among them to be both challenging and fascinating. The challenges emanated from the fact that the authors examined different phenomena, used different methods, and made different theoretical assumptions about development. These differences are in addition to the one mentioned in the preface regarding the nature of communicative media: the difference between, on the one hand, spontaneously arising communication systems such as gesture and speech and, on the other, formally developed and taught notational systems. We begin this discussion by detailing the three ways the chapters differ (i.e., phenomena, methods, and theoretical assumptions) as a first step in making clear their underlying contribution to the issue at hand.

The Ways Chapters Differ

To begin the comparative analysis of the chapters, consider the range of phenomena through which the authors sought to examine the relation between symbolic communication and cognitive development. These phenomena differ in multiple dimensions, including the *specific acquisition* studied, the *contexts* in which the acquisitions were studied, the *populations* to whom the phenomena were generalized, and *ages* of children who were studied. Most significantly, there is a wide enough breadth of phenomena covered in these chapters that no one will mistake the present book as an examination of a single "foundational" domain (Wellman & Gelman, 1992). This is an important point as we try to find general relations between symbolic communication and cognitive development, not those that are embedded in a specific domain.

The specific *acquisitions* examined by the authors of the chapters range from children's theory of mind (Budwig) to children's acquisition of literacy and writing skills (Olson); from their processes of categorization and memory of biological and other entities (Gentner and Loewenstein) to their scientific and mathematical reasoning (Lehrer and Schauble). In addition to the wide range of acquisitions being examined, the *contexts* in which these acquisitions are studied are different, ranging from parent–child dyads in the home environment (Nelson and Kessler Shaw) to peer collaborators in school (Daiute) to classroom discussions and debates (Lehrer and Schauble). These differences are microsystems in Bronfenbrenner's (1979) scheme of sociocultural contexts. But there are also mesosystem, ecosystem, and macrosystem differences across the chapters associated with the authors' attention to very different populations. The *populations* examined in the chapters included majority groups of predominately White Americans but also such unrepresented groups as deaf children (Goldin-Meadow) and minority children from inner-city schools (Daiute). Finally, the phenomena studied address development in children of a range of *ages*, from toddlers learning language (Nelson and Kessler Shaw, Budwig) to preadolescents inferring the properties of the evidence by which to determine the most effective memory strategies (Lehrer and Schauble).

Not only do these chapters vary in the phenomena through which the relation between symbolic communication and cognitive development was investigated but also in the methodologies employed by the researchers to study the relation. In chapters that report recently or unpublished research, the designs reflect a range including experimental (Gentner and Loewenstein), quasi-experimental (Goldin-Meadow, Lehrer and Schauble), observational (Nelson and Kessler Shaw, Budwig), and ethnographic (Daiute) studies. The time designs by which development was assessed also vary across the chapters and include cross-sectional (Gentner and Loewenstein), microgenetic (Budwig), short-term longitudinal (Lehrer and Schauble), and longitudinal designs (Daiute).

Finally, the chapters vary in terms of the theoretical assumptions of the authors regarding the nature of change and development. A number of chapters include references to Vygotsky and other sociocultural theorists, for whom development involves a socialization into cultural forms of thought. Olson aptly describes this process as an "outside-in" account of development. In these chapters, Vygotsky's account of development is extended to focus on the nature and significance of individual subjectivity and imagination in the socialization process (Daiute). Also, the semiotic context is carefully scrutinized to examine how the child's relations between words, objects, and concepts become coordinated with a parent's relation (Nelson and Kessler Shaw).

In addition to Vygotsky's notions of an outside-to-inside view of the developmental process, many of the authors examined the inside-to-outside constructivist processes of development championed by Piaget and others. For example, Olson refers to the role of inside-to-outside constructivist processes in accounting for development of writing as a notational system. He writes, "I am enough of a Piagetian to hold that the outside-to-inside view of 'internalization' is flawed; rather, the child has to construct his or her own knowledge, even if that knowledge is already present in some sense in the culture." The framework is extended to examine the factors associated with the process by which symbolic communication skills are acquired. For example, Budwig investigated parent–toddler dialogues to understand the nature of the inferences children make about the forms and functions of mental state expressions. Gentner and Loewenstein demonstrated the role played by acquiring domain-specific linguistic and conceptual knowledge in the development of memory and categorization processes. Finally, Lehrer and Schauble discussed the role of inferential processes not only in constructing a socially accessible notational system for coding data but also in exploiting mathematical properties of the notational system for analyzing the data.

The diversity of chapters in this book demonstrates that a focus on the nature, origin, and acquisition of symbolic communication and its function for cognitive development need not specify a particular acquisition to be studied, a methodology to be employed, or theoretical assumption to be adopted. However, the breadth of the contributions raises the possibility that the only common themes about symbolic communication and cognitive development that can be identified may be empty platitudes about how symbolic communication influences all aspects of cognitive development. To avoid mere platitudes but to respect the variability in accounts of children's development found in the chapters, we first review a number of conceptual issues associated with the role of symbolic communication in cognitive development. These issues concern (a) the nature and function of symbols used in communication, and (b) how forms of symbolic communication impact thought. The authors' arguments on these matters are reviewed and the commonalities between the positions identified. Performing this exercise involves reviewing psychological processes alluded to by the authors in their account of children's acquisition of various symbol systems and ways of communicating with them. Traditional theoretical accounts of the nature and development of these symbolic communicative systems (cf. Byrnes & Gelman, 1991) are discussed as are alternative models proposed to account for how symbolic communication impacts cognitive development.

With this preliminary work completed, we co-opt Scholnick's metaphor of "partnerships" between language thought and notation to further explore the different ways the authors account for cognitive development through symbolic communication. In particular, we examine different kinds of partnerships that children form in different communicative contexts. We take these different contexts to be associated with and categorized by different forms of representational "partnerships." Central to our analysis is that different partnerships are forged in these different communicative contexts. Although not meant to be exhaustive, distinguishing between these communicative contexts is central to our account of how and why symbolic communication influences cognitive development throughout life.

In summary, to find conceptually interesting commonalities between the chapters, the authors' positions on the nature, origin, and acquisition of symbolic communication and its cognitive developmental significance is analyzed and synthesized. The analysis is based on central philosophical, psychological, and developmental issues associated with communicating symbolically. The synthesis draws on Scholnick's analysis of development in terms of a metaphor of partnership: relations between representational systems among agents who communicate symbolically in particular contexts. The partnerships born in these communicative contexts, we believe, are the fertile ground in which cognitive development flourishes.

Issues in the Study of Symbolic Communication

Although symbolic communication was a topic of discussion in each chapter, there were a variety of ways in which authors characterized the nature of symbols and symbol systems. The same holds true for the impact of symbolic communication on thought. In this section we review these different characterizations. The goal is to find a common language for comparing and contrasting the various proposals as well as to provide a framework for understanding the different accounts of the processes of acquiring and contexts for communicating with symbol systems.

The Nature of Symbols and Symbol Systems.   At the heart of any account of symbolic communication must be a recognition of precisely what is meant by symbols and communicating with them. A review of each chapter reveals both agreements and disagreements in this regard. To highlight these agreements and disagreements and to develop a common language for talking about symbols we use the semiotic theory of C. S. Peirce (1897/1955; Deacon, 1997; Hawkes, 1977), to whom a number of authors made reference. To Peirce, semiosis is the process of communicating with signs, that is, the process by which a sign signifies. "A sign or *representamen* stands for something (its *object*); it stands for something *to* somebody (its *interpretant*); and finally it stands for something to someone *in some respect* (this respect is called its *ground*)" (Hawkes, 1977, p. 126–127). For Peirce this relation captures the underlying logic of thought itself. Deacon (1997) wrote that "Peirce . . . . rephrased the problem of mind in terms of communication, essentially arguing that all forms of thought (ideas) are essentially communication (transmission of signs), organized by an underlying logic (or semiotic as he called it) that is not fundamentally different for communication processes inside or outside of the brain" (p. 70).

Essential in Peirce's notion of thought is that the elements through which communication is carried (i.e., signs) are distinct from the concepts or ideas that are communicated. Peirce further distinguished between three types of signs based on the *ground* or the relation between the sign and the object: An *Icon* functions as a sign by virtue of features of itself that physically correspond to its object; an *Index* functions as a sign by virtue of a having a factual, correlative, or causal relation with its object; and a *Symbol* functions as a sign by virtue of an arbitrary but habitual or conventional association between itself and its object. Piaget (1951) and many other scholars have relied heavily on this seminal analysis. Deacon (1997) noted the sign–object relations considered by Peirce are an exhaustive inventory of the classic accounts of the processes by which ideas are associated: similarity for icons; contiguity or correlation for indexes; and law, causality, or convention for symbols. In this sense then, the trichotomy between icons, indexes, and symbols is based on the act of interpreting signs and objects, not on intrinsic or formal properties of the signs themselves.

Peirce's semiotic theory can be used to understand and synthesize the range of views about the nature of the sign–object relation discussed by the authors of the chapters. For example, according to Nelson and Kessler Shaw's account of language acquisition, words become symbolic for the child when they are used "to represent a state of the world that is not present in the immediate environment, and when they are used with the intention of communicating that representation to another." This point emphasizes what Peirce claims is unique about symbolic communication: It is the communication of a state of affairs *as represented*. It is not possible for a state of affairs *as represented* to be the topic of a conversation when communicating with iconic or indexical signs. Such nonsymbolic signs do not represent states of affairs, only serving to remind one of (iconic signs) or be associated with (indexical signs) the states that are the topic of communication. As a result, the topic of conversation in these cases may be a sign itself or the state of affairs itself, but it is not the state *as represented*.

According to Nelson and Shaw, to communicate about a state of affairs as represented, a symbol must relate not only to objects in the world (reference) but also to concepts (denotation) and other symbols (sense). They labeled these relations between the symbols, objects referred to, and concepts denoted as the "semiotic triangle." These relations serve to account for constraints on the meaning of a given symbol imposed by other symbols in sentences or semantic fields. It is important to note that only symbolic signs can be so constrained (see Deacon, 1997). There is more to say about this in the next section, but suffice it to say here that communicating about a state of affairs *as represented* opens up the world of conventional representations that could not be opened unless one was communicating with symbols. In this way symbols are social, shared, and form a system, as Nelson and Shaw emphasized in their chapter.

Nelson and Shaw's examination of sign–object relations in oral language parallels Olson's and Daiute's analyses of sign–object relations in written language. The meanings carried by written and oral signs are *social* in the sense that they are about the social-cultural world, interpersonally *shared* in the sense that they are used for communicating with others, *symbolic* in the sense that they are about states of affairs *as represented*, and form a *system* in the sense that they derive from relations to other symbolic signs. However, it is important to note that written, unlike oral, language is a notational system. Notational systems are intentionally created external inscriptions or depictions that stand for and communicate about aspects of reality. Notational systems are both a *medium* for the expression of meaning and an *outcome* of material human activity (i.e., a cultural artifact). Whereas songs and spoken words are not examples of notational systems, musical scores and written words are. However, not all notational systems are symbolic in the sense that they are about states of affairs *as represented* (see Tolchinsky-Landsmann & Karmiloff-Smith, 1992, for a discussion of the distinguishing factors that make notational systems symbolic). Notably, drawing fails the symbolic notation test, thereby creating a challenge for children to distinguish characteristics of symbolic and nonsymbolic notational systems (as seen in one 5-year-old who insisted that he was drawing a "lower-case heart").

The agreement between Nelson and Kessler Shaw, Olson, and Daiute regarding the nature of the sign–object relations, despite their focus on oral or written forms of symbolic communication, points to the fact that specification of sign–object relations may remain the same when different forms of symbolic communication are examined. However, it is also true that sign–object specifications may be different when the same symbolic communication forms are examined. This is precisely a source of contrast between Budwig and Nelson and Shaw. The sign-object relation in oral language is treated as symbolic to Nelson and Kessler Shaw but as indexical to Budwig. Budwig's indexical view of the sign–object relations in oral language allows for expressions to be treated as literally linking or pointing to a situation, not symbolically referring to it. To Budwig, " . . . language does more than refer to the world; it also suggests that there is a specific linkage between various language functions and linguistic forms." It is Budwig's point that an indexical view of language makes form–function linkages explicit in a particular context such that language development can be viewed as "changing relations between linguistic forms and language functions." Thus, to her, the indexical view of language is central for "routine communicative practices" to become "grammaticalized."

Although we do not intend to deny any differences between Budwig's and Nelson and Kessler Shaw's theories of children's language acquisition, the difference associated with how the sign–object relation is conceptualized may be more apparent than real. Returning to Peirce for a moment, he did not claim that there is necessarily a mutual exclusivity between signs whose ground is iconic, indexical, or symbolic. Rather the set is considered by Peirce (Hawes, 1977, pp. 129–130, italics in original) as

> . . . three modes of a relationship between sign and object, or signifier and signified which co-exist in the form of a hierarchy in which one of them will inevitably have dominance over the other two. As Jakobson observes, we can have symbolic icons, iconic symbols, etc., and the nature of a sign's ultimately dominant mode will depend on its *context* . . . Thus a traffic signal may, in terms of epistemology, be said to combine *index* (pointing to a situation and calling for immediate causally related action) and *symbol* (red in our society signals 'danger,' 'stop'; green signals the opposite, and these arbitrarily related colours are binarily opposed by the traffic signaling system, as *symbols*).

So, it may be the case that Nelson and Kessler Shaw and Budwig only differ in their recognition of this power of the context to elicit signs' dominant modes. The indexical mode of a sign may be dominant in contexts when new grammatical forms are first being learned, as when toddlers first learn mental state expressions. Budwig gave an example of a child's dialogue with her mother in which the signs served to index rather than to represent a state of affairs.

Child: (tries to open container, fails) *My* open that
Mom: What?
Child: *My* open that, mommy (handing container to mom)
Mom: Wanna open that?
Child: Yeah
Mom: (opens container)

According to Budwig, the expression "*My* open that!" invoked a desire to bring about change in the situation rather than a genuine reference to desire as a mental state. That is, her communication indexed a situation, but did not refer to a state of affairs *as represented*. Nelson and Shaw identified the latter but not the former as being essential to a symbolic use of words. In response, the mother rephrased the expression, clarifying it so there would be a genuine reference to the represented mental state. In this sense, the dialogue was *quasi-symbolic* as one partner in the dialogue (Mom) symbolically interpreted the other partner's non-symbolic communication (Child). As Nelson and Kessler Shaw might characterize it, the mother sought a correspondence in the semiotic super triangle relation between her own and the child's symbols, concepts, and objects.

Thus, it seems that a sign's status as symbolic depends on contextual factors that permit its symbolic mode to dominate. One such factor is whether a grammatical form is sufficiently developed to permit the symbolic mode to dominate. Unless the child has learned a grammatical form, the signs used in the expression are not symbolic. Such a contextual constraint on symbolic signs is often short-lived and local, being specific to the particular grammatical form to be learned. In contrast, other contextual factors influencing whether the symbolic mode dominates may be more general and permanent in scope, that is, extended in time and across situations. For example, Goldin-Meadow examined gestures as signs and argued that the sign–object relation is grounded differently depending on whether gestures were used as a primary communicative outlet (as they are by congenitally deaf children whose hearing parents did not expose them to sign language) or as a secondary outlet (as they are by hearing children of hearing parents who have oral language as their primary outlet).

Gestures used as secondary communicative outlets convey information iconically by resembling their objects (as a hand gesture depicting the eastern seaboard of the United States), or indexically, by literally pointing to their objects. According to Goldin-Meadow, such gestures served to give "voice" to thoughts that may be "inchoate or untamed" and inexpressible through the conventional (i.e., primary) communicative outlet.

In contrast, when gestures are used as the primary communicative outlet (by deaf children of hearing parents who were not exposed to sign language), the evidence suggests that their dominant mode is symbolic. Goldin-Meadow found that, when appropriated for communication, the iconic gestures have "language-like" properties, including morphological, semantic, and grammatical properties that, for most of the children she studied, were consistent with ergative oral languages. The dominant mode of these gestures is symbolic in Nelson and Kessler Shaw's sense in that they intentionally communicate actions and objects *as represented* (i.e, gesture-to-world relations) and form systems with other gestures (gesture-to-gesture relations). The gestures of deaf children unexposed to sign language and living with hearing parents are also social and shared, but not in the same way as Nelson and Shaw characterized the signs of hearing children living with hearing parents. Goldin-Meadow notes that because their hearing parents use gestures nonsymbolically with their deaf children, the children are producers but not receivers of language-like gestures. Indeed, it is likely that no one in the children's social world uses language-like gestures to interpret the social world for them. Nonetheless, the deaf children's language-like gestures may be social and shared in the sense that the gestures are not the child's own, but are refinements of the ones they first encountered from their parents or others in their social environment. Moreover, as suggested by Goldin-Meadow, the message that hearing parents express with nonsymbolic gestures are encoded symbolically by the deaf children. The parent–child interaction described by Goldin-Meadow parallels the interaction described by Budwig between hearing parents and their children who are learning a grammatical form. In such cases, one person in the dialogue (i.e., the hearing parent or the deaf child) is interpreting symbolically the nonsymbolic expressions of the other (i.e, the hearing child learning a grammatical form, the hearing parent using an iconic gesture). Such an interaction was characterized as quasi-symbolic and as a consequences of such an interaction is a growing coordination of the child's and parent's symbols, concepts, and objects in the super semiotic triangle (Nelson and Kessler Shaw). From this analysis, it seems that when signs are the *primary communicative outlet* for a person, whether expressed gesturally or orally, the signs have similar properties; they not only become symbolic and form a system but also they are social and shared.

The dominant mode of a sign can be affected by two types of factors: (a) those that have a shorter term, less stable, or less permanent influence (i.e., learning to use a particular grammatical form), and (b) those that have longer term, more stable, or more permanent influence, (i.e., a sign's use as a primary or secondary communicative outlet). These factors affecting the dominant mode of signs apply not only to oral and written language but also to other types of symbol systems as well. Lehrer and Schauble found that young children initially intended to create inscriptions (which they define as drawings, diagrams, physical models, read-outs from instruments, and mathematical expressions) that were iconic in nature, sharing the physical properties with the object being inscribed. For example, they found that first graders created inscriptions for plant heights at different times by, at each time, cutting green paper strips to the exact height of the plant stem. The iconicity of the inscriptions lies in the inscriptions being the same color, shape, and height as the object being inscribed. They also found that some older children treated histograms indexically, as correlated to the objects being inscribed. Some fifth graders sought to determine the correspondence between individuals and their inscription in the histogram (marked with an "x"). The indexicality lies in the identity the students sought between individual markings in the histogram and the individual students whose performance was being depicted.

Nonetheless, in both cases Lehrer and Schauble report that when the symbolic mode of the inscriptions became dominant, the children were able to conceptually appreciate and interpersonally communicate about the more abstract properties of reality represented by the inscriptions. In the case of the younger children, the children began to discuss occasions where their plants grew faster and slower by computing the size of the difference between the lengths of green paper. This shift in dominant mode took trial and error, scaffolding by a talented teacher, and the insight of a student, but was accomplished over a relatively short time period. In the case of the older children, those with practice and experience with histograms over the course of their schooling were able to shift from iconic to symbolic mode of inscriptions and even entertain ways to measure central tendency and spread. They were eventually able to work out techniques to compare different histograms representing different experimental conditions; in essence, they ran an "intuitive t-test." But students without previous school-based experiences with histograms of distributions had much more difficulty gleaning information from it. Children proposed "senseless algorithms" for computing central tendency and were selectively considering only aspects of the data. Lehrer and Schauble note that, conceptually, these students lacked mathematical resources to fully exploit symbolic aspects of the inscription.

To summarize this section of the review, signs can bear a number of different kinds of relations to objects, including iconic, indexical, and symbolic. There appears to be nothing about the physical properties of the signs that specifically constrain the nature of the sign–object relation. Speech was presented as indexical and symbolic, gestures as iconic and symbolic, and inscriptions as iconic, indexical, and symbolic. A symbolic sign–object relation is necessary for communicating about state of affairs *as represented* because nonsymbolic signs do not represent states of affairs, but rather serve to be reminiscent of or associated with the states. But, as noted earlier, there is no exclusivity of a sign's ground as iconic, indexical or symbolic, and any given sign may shift in its dominant mode. Contextual factors constrain whether the symbolic mode of a sign becomes dominant. Some of these factors may be short-term and easily overcome, whereas others are more permanent.

This review offers an alternative, perhaps more tractable question that can be asked about the nature and origin of symbolic communication. Instead of asking static questions about when children use symbols or demonstrate symbolic thought, we can ask dynamic ones about factors influencing how signs' symbolic mode becomes dominant in a context. The dynamic questions suggest that signs, plentiful in children's environments, can have a variety of different types of meaning for them. Indeed, a number of the authors in the present volume warn us not to jump to conclusions about a person's use of particular signs in a context, as the signs' meanings can vary. For example, Nelson and Shaw caution that the mere fact that children use words in a context should not lead to the conclusion that they are being used symbolically; they may be used by children nonsymbolically, either without meaning or as indexing a situation. A similar warning is issued by Goldin-Meadow in that similar-looking gestures may be used to communicate iconically or symbolically. Posing the problem of symbol use dynamically, as one of identifying a shift in dominant mode, makes analyses of children's nonsymbolic uses of signs more pertinent and relevant to understanding their symbol use. Nelson and Shaw's and Budwig's analysis of the sequences in the development of linguistic expressions are cases in point, as is Lehrer and Schauble's analysis of the sorts of misunderstandings students had in coming to understand inscriptions as symbolic signs.

The work of many of the authors in this book offers insight into factors influencing the shift in interpreting a sign's dominant mode from nonsymbolic to symbolic. But much more work is necessary to examine whether and which kinds of factors influence symbolic dominance across the sign types of words, gesture, and inscription. It seems likely that biological-evolutionary, cognitive-developmental, and sociocultural influences are at work together to realize the interpretative shifts. For example, although the creation of some elemental grammatical categories, essential to communicate symbolically, seems to be brought by the child to the language learning situation (Goldin-Meadow), the comprehensive system of linguistic forms created must assuredly be related to sociocultural factors (Goldin-Meadow, Olson, Budwig, and Nelson and Kessler Shaw). This may be the most productive consequence of asking dynamic instead of static questions about the nature and origin of symbolization: Factors that have been treated as antagonistic when the problem of symbolization is treated statically are seen as interrelated and interactive when treated dynamically.

The Significance of Symbolic Communication for Cognition.   In this section, we review the authors' specific claims about the cognitive and developmental significance of communicating symbolically in hopes of arriving at general conclusions regarding its impact. As previously discussed, the chapters in the book represent a range of different phenomena, methodologies, and theories, so the conclusions will have a great deal of territory to cover. For example, the conclusions will have to capture the cognitive consequences of all the forms of symbolic communication considered by the authors (e.g., oral and written language and other notational systems) on various levels of cognition, from lower level perceptual and memorial functioning to higher order reflective and metacognitive processes. The conclusions will also have to apply to symbolic communication about a range of different types of represented states of affairs, be they concrete or abstract, real or imagined, having existed in the past, existing in the present, or possibly existing in the future. Finally, the conclusions will have to address the theoretical significance of symbolic communication for theories of cognition (i.e., Sapir–Whorf and other theoretical views on language and thought) and development (i.e., Vygotsky and other theoretical views on cognitive development as internalized language).

As noted previously, communicating symbolically involves intentionally communicating states of affairs *as represented*. To Peirce, the formation of symbolic signs to represent objects implicates the more sophisticated of the classical mechanisms for the association of ideas, including law, causality, and convention. The development of these mechanisms is a necessary condition for symbolic communication, so they cannot themselves be cognitive consequences. However, when successful, symbolic communication involves simultaneously communicating the states of affairs as represented and the status of the states of affairs as being represented by conventional symbols. For example, a parent–child dialogue about a *school bus* involves both participants intentionally communicating about a state of affairs as represented (i.e., the word *school bus* designates the concept of school bus and refers to school buses in the world) and an appreciation that the states of affairs are ones that can be referred to with conventional symbols.

This latter point is as unique about communicating with symbolic signs as is the former one. When communicating successfully with iconic and indexical signs, states of affairs are brought to mind by virtue of the signs' correspondence (iconic) or connection (indexical) to the states. In such cases, states of affairs are brought to mind without necessitating an additional appreciation of the sign's relation to the object or the object's relation to the sign. In contrast, successful symbolic communication involves the sender and receiver understanding not only that symbols designate concepts and refer to states of affairs, but also that states of affairs that are referred to are ones that can be conventionally symbolized.[1]

Nelson and Kessler Shaw make this point about what gets expressed in symbolic communication in even the simplest cases of a child comprehending and expressing common nouns that name objects in the world (e.g., understanding or using the word "dog" in referring to new instances of dogs and not other things). Although the child may have had experiences with—and even a preverbal (i.e., non-linguistic) concept of—dogs prior to her production and reception of the word "dog," learning the label adds something to children's conceptual understanding: Dogs are objects that can be referred to by a symbol. According to Nelson and Kessler Shaw, such a symbol serves as the pivotal point by which the child's denoted conceptualization of dogs is refined to correspond to the adult's conceptualization. Nelson and Shaw invoke the semiotic super triangle relation between the parent's and child's word (symbol), the concept it denotes (conceptualization), and the object to which it refers. A common word (i.e., "dog") is the basis for aligning the entire super triangle so that the same word expressed or comprehended by child or parent will denote the same concept and refer to the same object. By virtue of being the topic of communication with symbolic signs rather than with nonsymbolic signs or no signs at all, the child's world of dogs becomes more conventional, stable, continuous, and context-general.

From the foregoing discussion, we can discern that use of symbolic signs as object labels (basic level object category terms) has at least two cognitive consequences. First, there is an expansion of the child's understanding of the parts of the world that can be conventionally symbolized and conceptualized. That is, more of the basic objects of the world have a name. Second, the child can now select from systems of symbols the one(s) that would allow for more precise and effective communication. Many more symbols are available to choose just the right one with which to communicate about a particular aspect of the world. These two consequences are related; by expanding the world as symbolized and conceptualized, children are better able to be more effective and precise in communicating about a given aspect of the world.

These cognitive developmental consequences appear to be unique to symbolic communication as they are not associated with nonsymbolic com-

---

[1]Claiming that symbolic communication involves communicating that states of affairs referred to are ones that can be symbolized does not necessarily assume that the sender or receiver has an explicit theory of the representational process itself (cf., Perner, 1991). The only assumption is that the receiver and sender understand something about the referent of communication (i.e., it can be "symbolized") and not about the process of representation.

munication. Goldin-Meadow outlined the cognitive significance of the gestures produced by hearing children who otherwise use oral language as a primary communicative outlet. Such gestures are nonsymbolic and function to (a) communicate thoughts or strategies on tasks that are not or cannot be verbally expressed, (b) support memory for expressed ideas (although whether at encoding, retrieval, or both is unclear), and (c) lower the cognitive demands on the primary communicative outlet. Although expressing thoughts, supporting memory, and offloading cognitive demands may well be cognitive consequences of the use of any type of sign (i.e., iconic, indexical, or symbolic), they are not unique to communicating with symbolic signs. Indeed, the cognitive consequences of nonsymbolic gestures support neither of the consequences we claim accrue by virtue specifically of symbolic communication.[2]

The two consequences of symbolic communication previously alluded to go beyond merely improving the process of communication itself. Communicating with symbols has the general cognitive consequence of offering a new way to represent the world, one that is organized around a system of shared symbols with conventional meanings. The communicative function of such conventional representational systems requires not only that symbols be distinguished from and related to each other within a given system but also that the symbols are distinguished from and related to those of other representational systems. This latter point was made by Nelson and Shaw with regard to basic level object nouns and concepts; there is a coordination between young children's prelinguistic conceptual representations and semantic representation during language development.

An emphasis on the communicative function of representational systems, with its focus on coordinating shared symbols within and between multiple representational systems, can provide a new perspective with which to challenge traditional views of language. For example, an alternative to traditional claims of an autonomous and innately constrained grammar holds that its acquisition is just a case of the child's socialization into communicative practices of a community of speakers (Tomasello, 1998; Budwig, this volume; Nelson and Kessler Shaw, this volume). By virtue of rejecting an autonomous and innately constrained grammar, this communicative perspective could also be a basis for challenging traditional views of cognitive processing. Instead of the traditional assumptions that cognition is the rule-governed manipulation of mental symbols (i.e., rules of grammar operating on "words"), the present communicative view

---

[2]Goldin-Meadow argues that nonsymbolic gestures sometimes serve to unintentionally express a sender's conceptual volatility, with the gestural channel expressing thoughts that are inconsistent with thoughts expressed in the verbal channel. This function of expressing conflicting ideas is opposed to the functions we are proposing for symbolic communication that would result in more coherent and consistent communication.

of language may be compatible with Connectionism, which holds that mental rules do not actually exist but are immanent in the processing of nonsymbolic (i.e., phonemic) content (Collier, 1998).

Despite its compatibility with alternative accounts of language and cognition, acknowledging the importance of symbolic communication for cognitive development does not necessitate the rejection of traditional assumptions. Indeed, even the two cognitive consequences being claimed for symbolic communication (expansion of the world as conventionally symbolized and conceptualized and precision in the aspects of the world communicated about) may arise without true symbolic dialogues; that is, dialogues between partners who are both expressing themselves symbolically. Budwig notes that hearing parents symbolically interpret their hearing children's indexical expressions and Goldin-Meadow points out that deaf children (unexposed to sign language) symbolically interpret their hearing parents' iconic gestures. In both cases there is a quasi-symbolic dialogue in which one of the two partners in a dialogue interprets symbolically the nonsymbolic expressions of the other partner. The consequences of quasi-symbolic dialogues according to Budwig is that the child learns appropriate linguistic forms for particular functions, which Nelson and Kessler Shaw characterize as involving the coordination of the semiotic super triangle between objects, words, and concepts of parents and children. From this perspective the quasi-symbolic dialogues promote both linguistic and cognitive growth. Goldin-Meadow concludes that even these quasi-symbolic dialogues are not required for deaf children's cognitive achievements as inventing semantic and grammatical categories. According to her, these achievements must arise "de novo," without support of a conventional language model in the environment.

Whereas we acknowledge that some cognitive consequences of symbolic communication may arise without true symbolic dialogues, we wish to explore what consequences fall out of such dialogues. We propose that true symbolic dialogues are important to conventionally symbolizing and conceptualizing abstract or hypothetical aspects of the world and precisely communicating about those aspects. This is not to suggest that the deaf children studied by Goldin-Meadow do not symbolically communicate about abstract and hypothetical aspects of the world or that prelinguistic children cannot conceptualize abstractly or hypothetically. Our claim is only that without engaging in true symbolic dialogues such communication may be particularly difficult. Gentner and Loewenstein and Nelson and Kessler Shaw argue that the more concrete aspects of the world are stable and salient, and concepts about them are readily learned and communicated about. In contrast, abstract or hypothetical aspects of the world are less stable and salient, requiring symbolic dialogues to stabilize and highlight them in order for children to conceptualize and communicate about them.

Nelson and Kessler Shaw and Budwig exemplify this claim by pointing to the importance of symbolic dialogues (or Wittgensteinian "language games," as Nelson and Shaw refer to them) in the development of conceptualizations and expressions of mental states. In her chapter, Budwig notes the development of toddlers' conceptualization and expression of mental states, demonstrating the struggle young children have "grammaticalizing" routine parent–child communicative practices regarding desire. The functions of the forms that the toddlers expressed provide unique views of their developing conceptualization of desire. Nelson and Shaw further demonstrated that even by 3 and 4 years of age, when children learn grammatical forms for expressing such mental states as "believe" and "know," they are still working out the meanings of and conceptual relations between the terms.

Gentner and Loewenstein argue strongly that true symbolic dialogues regarding relational terms have critical consequences for children's abstract relational thinking. Gentner and Loewenstein provide evidence of four ways in which using relational words affect abstract relational thinking. First, upon hearing relational terms, children direct their perceptual and encoding processes to seek the referred-to relational patterns. Second, the relational pattern is then encoded symbolically so that the relational term preserves the pattern. Third, the relational term and the pattern it encodes may then be input for further metacognitive analysis so that a system of relational terms is forged. Finally, with a system of relational terms by which to encode new patterns, a uniform encoding and transfer of relational patterns is achieved. Thus, dialogues about new relational terms open up for children a world of conventional symbols referring to relational patterns as represented, supporting their perception, encoding, memory, transfer, and precise reference to those patterns.

Symbolic dialogues promote children's understanding of relations and mental states by providing them with tools for representing, conceptualizing, and precisely communicating about these more abstract aspects of the world. Such cognitive consequences also accrue for symbolic dialogues using notational systems for writing and reading. Written letters, words, and sentences are everywhere in a child's environment, but symbolic dialogues with a notational system are not achieved until the child plays the role of either a writer or reader, an author or audience. Olson stressed the significance of acquiring a notational system for reading and writing, claiming that it "is not just a matter of improved storage and communication of information, but a new form of representation, thought, and consciousness." As evidence, Olson discusses the consequences of a notational system for writing and reading for representing, conceptualizing, and precisely communicating about a particularly abstract aspect of the world—speech itself. For Olson, a writing system is a "notation for speech," involving children acquiring the symbols representing speech and thereby conceptually reconstructing it. Letters are learned as symbols that children use to represent, conceptualize, and communicate about their own and others' speech sounds. Sets of these letters, symbolized by the word "*word*" are also used to represent, conceptualize, and precisely communicate about segments of their own and others' speech.

Olson points to the struggle children have conceptualizing the writing system as notations symbolizing their own speech. He characterizes the process as "not a natural development; it is a consequence of learning to deal with a particular writing system." That is, as a result of acquiring a notational system for reading and writing, children have new symbols with which to represent, conceptualize, and communicate about their speech.

Olson shows that oral language is conceptually transformed as a consequence of symbolic written dialogues. In contrast, Daiute shows how written language is transformed as a consequence of symbolic oral dialogues. Daiute provides evidence of the impact of teacher–student and student–student oral dialogues on mastery of such concepts associated with written texts as "story beginnings," "paragraphs," and "details." Perhaps it comes as no surprise that teacher–student oral dialogues promoted children's writing performance; after all, the dialogues were dominated by teachers who engaged in cognitive control discourse (i.e., question asking, instruction, planning). What is more fascinating was the impact of student–student oral dialogues on the creation and composition of narratives. Although the dialogues were riddled with discourse that many may characterize as off-task (i.e., play, affect, making personal connections, etc.), they impacted narrative details. Daiute argues that such discourse, which she labels as social-relational, provides a symbolic dialogic basis for, among other things, the creation of shared fictional worlds about which a story was written.[3] Like the self-directed dialogues so important in preschoolers' sustaining symbolic play (cf. Amsel, Bobadilla, Coch, & Remy, 1996; Amsel & Smalley, 1999; Berk, 1994; Vygotsky, 1978), the third- and fourth-grade children's dialogic construction of a virtual reality was sustained so that it could become a topic of narrative composition. Thus, in the service of writing, symbolic dialogues between students supported a shared representation of a hypothetical aspect of the world—a fictional or virtual reality—and permitted children to conceptualize and communicate precisely about that hypothetical world.

Finally, the importance of symbolic dialogues in representing, conceptualizing, and communicating about abstract and hypothetical aspects of the world is further demonstrated by Lehrer and Schauble. They examine the mathematical thinking of first- to fifth-grade students who were guided in discussions about how to symbolically model or "inscribe" growth information. Rather than just being given an inscription system, they were scaffolded to develop their own. Through these discussions, students the world is further demonstrated by Lehrer and Schauble. They examine the mathematical thinking of first- to fifth-grade students who were guided in discussions about how to symbolically model or "inscribe" growth information. Rather than just being given an inscription system, they were scaffolded to develop their own. Through these discussions, students learned that an inscription system sometimes represented information that may not be readily perceived (e.g., rates of growth and central tendency) and have standard units and measurement procedures to permit communication among students in the same class and between students in different classrooms. The discussions promoted increasingly sophisticated inscriptions developed by students over time that correspond to the increasingly abstract (i.e., modeling growth rate and systematically comparing growth rates of different systems) and hypothetical (i.e., determining population means and variances) mathematical concepts they formed. The guided dialogues promoted students' inventing and refining the inscriptions to address the problem of understanding growth, supporting their representation of, conceptualization of, and communication about more abstract and hypothetical aspects of the world.

Lehrer and Schauble conclude that the relation between symbolization (inscription) and conceptualization (mathematical concepts) reflects a dynamic "reciprocal bootstrapping" process. Not only does developing more adequate and complex inscriptions for conventionally representing information promote the acquisition of mathematical concepts for understanding the properties of the information inscribed, but the reverse is also true: Developing mathematical concepts promotes the adequacy and complexity of inscriptions. This view of distinct but interrelated symbol systems for referring to and communicating information on the one hand, and conceptual understanding of the represented information on the other, accounts for many of the authors' theoretical proposals regarding the relation between language and thought. Notably, there is no strong support for the Sapir–Whorf hypothesis, which supposes that conceptualizations of the world are determined by grammatical and semantic structures of a language such that thought is relative to language variation (Byrnes & Gelman, 1991). This hypothesis is rejected by Nelson and Kessler Shaw and Gentner and Loewenstein who, like Lehrer and Schauble, argued that linguistic and conceptual structures are distinguished but connected by a dynamic pattern mapping (Nelson and Kessler Shaw) or a bidirectional relation (Gentner and Loewenstein).[4]

---

[4]The strong form of the hypothesis is also rejected by Goldin-Meadow, who demonstrates linguistic structures in deaf children who lacked linguistic models in the enviroment, although she does leave open the possibility that choices in the specific organization of semantic categories may reflect variations in language.

The dynamic reciprocal bootstrapping process proposed to relate symbol systems on the one hand and conceptual structures and processes on the other is inconsistent not only with Sapir–Whorf, but also with Piagetian and Vygotskian claims. Piaget recognized the importance of children's ability to form, think with, and think about (i.e., reflect on) symbols. However, Piagetian theory holds that such abilities are consequences of cognitive development, not an impetus for it (Byrnes & Gelman, 1991). Piaget's "cognitive determinism," which suggests that children's symbol skills are largely determined by their cognitive development, is rejected by all the authors as too narrow a view of the significance and impact of spontaneously acquiring symbol systems as primary communicative outlets (oral and gestural language) or of formally learning notational systems in school (writing and inscriptions). Whereas cognitive developmental factors were identified as affecting children's ability to interpret signs symbolically, their symbolic sign interpretation also impacts their cognitive development.

For Vygotsky and other sociocultural theorists, language and other symbol systems serve as tools to direct and control thought. Although promoting the significance of symbolic communication for cognitive development, this view of cognition is seen as too strongly and broadly controlled by symbol systems. Gentner and Loewenstein argue for the cognitive impact of *specific* relational terms, not necessarily of all symbols, and Daiute argues for the role of private subjectivity in cognitive development, instead of supposing that all of cognitive development reflects cultural practices. This criticism is not to deny the claim that the actual social practices or language games, in which parents, teachers, peers, and the like, communicate symbolic meanings that have wider social or cultural significance, provide the platform or entry point for the child's conceptual socialization. Such a process is identified specifically by Nelson and Shaw and Budwig, and elements of the claim are found in many chapters.

Specifying the relation between language or other symbol systems and thought as dynamic reciprocal bootstrapping allows for the rejection of claims denying the separation between them (Sapir–Whorf) or emphasizing primarily one direction of the relation over the other (Piaget and Vygotsky). It does allow for local and temporary relations to obtain between a symbol system and thought, which may be specific to a particular problem in a given context. One such relation includes the process of "thinking-for-speaking" (Slobin, 1996), which was referred to by Goldin-Meadow and Gentner and Loewenstein. Thinking for speaking is the form of on-line and ongoing thought that is designed to fill the requirements of a linguistic code in a communicative context. It is the thinking one does to express oneself linguistically in a particular communicative context (McNeill & Duncan, 1998). Both Goldin-Meadow and Gentner and Loewenstein are sympathetic with the proposal but offer extensions. Gentner and Loewenstein suggest that there are lasting rather than only temporary effects of language on thought, which is consistent with Nelson and Kessler Shaw's view of the effect of language and Olson's view of the effect of writing on children's conceptualization of the world. Goldin-Meadow extends Slobin's conceptualization of thinking-for-speaking by considering the significance of gestures communicating dimensions of experience that are not readily expressed linguistically, as Spanish speakers gesturally but not linguistically expressing the manner of an object's motion (e.g., wiggling). The synchrony of the linguistic and gestural expressions suggests that thinking-for-speaking may be only a part of a broader process of "thinking-for-communicating."

In summary, symbolic communication is claimed to have significance for cognitive development in two ways. First, there is a progressive expansion of children's knowledge about aspects of the world that can be conventionally represented and conceptually denoted by symbols. This expansion builds on itself with different symbol systems (i.e., from oral language to inscriptions) that are acquired in different contexts (i.e., spontaneously at home or taught in school). Second is the notion of being able to select a symbol out of a system of symbols that can be used to communicate about increasingly precise aspects of the world. Just as symbols coexist with other symbols, forming symbol systems, so symbol systems coexist with other symbol systems forming a multirepresentational network. So increasing the precision of communication refers to the selection of an appropriate symbol from a particular symbol system out of a network of such systems.

The role of true symbolic dialogues was seen as important in children accruing these cognitive consequences, particularly for their representation, conceptualization, and communication about more abstract and hypothetical aspects of the world. These dialogues came in many forms (i.e., child to himself or herself, child to parent, child to peer, child to teacher) associated with unique communicative contexts (formal learning, informal learning, writing, playing, expressing desire and agency, and others) and involve distinct kinds of symbol systems (oral language, written language, inscriptions). Despite these cognitive consequences accruing from symbolic communication, the relation between symbolic communication and cognitive conceptualization was seen as bidirectional, not unidirectional.

CONTEXTS FOR PARTNERSHIPS

Although the cognitive developmental consequences of symbolic communication are specified generally in this chapter, there are important ways in which the consequences are different for children depending on their context. To provide a more fine-grained analysis of these contexts and the cognitive consequences that result, we extend the partnership metaphor that Scholnick presented in her chapter. Her partnership metaphor was a way to account for the interrelation of the three "representational media" of language, thought, and notation. The partnership metaphor acknowledges the unique qualities of each type of representational system and how each may be implicated on the same task, refining representations of the others. The metaphor of a partnership emphasizes a dynamic and coordinated process of communicating content between and among the child's spontaneously acquired, or formally learned, representational systems. This sharing allows the child to internally represent external symbols and to externally symbolize internal conceptualizations. This "reciprocal mediation" creates new, more powerful ways of representing, conceptualizing, and communicating about the world that may not be created without it. As Scholnick suggests, each chapter points directly to this process, highlighting different computational or social aspects of it.

The partnership metaphor subsumes a number of themes presented in this review. The claim that symbolic communication has the consequence of increasing the aspects of the world that are conventionally represented and conceptualized certainly involves processes implicated by the partnership metaphor including both representing external symbols and symbolizing internal conceptualizations. Similarly, the claim that symbolic communication has the consequence of enabling communication about more precise aspects of the world involves selecting from among the already internalized symbols and appropriating the most appropriate for the purpose of communication. Finally, the partnership metaphor captures the claim of a dynamic reciprocal bootstrapping process relating symbol systems on the one hand and conceptual structures and processes on the other, and with it, the "thinking-for-speaking" account (with all of its proposed extensions) of the language/thought debate.

We conclude by considering how the metaphor of partnerships between representational systems might play out differently in different types of communicative contexts. Communicative contexts are also partnerships but ones between people in true symbolic dialogues. In this sense we are expanding the partnership metaphor to include individuals in true symbolic dialogues and the representational systems they coordinate between and among themselves in such communicative contexts. These communicative contexts are distinguishable by such characteristics as the person with whom a child communicates (i.e., parent, teacher, or peer) and the nature of the topic of communication (concrete, abstract, hypothetical). We consider four such communicative contexts, not in an attempt to be exhaustive, but in the interests in sampling an interesting range of contexts. The four contexts sampled (parent-concrete, parent-abstract, peer-hypothetical, teacher-abstract), are notable for their very different kinds of purposes and the nature of the cognitive developmental consequences that accrue. Two communicative contexts (parent-concrete, parent-abstract) are associated with informal learning environments (Schauble & Glaser, 1996), one with a formal learning context (teacher-abstract), and one with a play or discussion context (peer-hypothetical).

Parent-Concrete

Contexts in which parent–child communication centers on concrete states of affairs include the standard cases of object labeling. One notable characteristic of such contexts is that the child likely has perceptual experience of states of affairs being talked about, perhaps even having acquired a preverbal or verbal conceptual understanding of the topic. As such, the conversation would have the consequence of introducing the child to a conventional symbolic form in its appropriate linguistic frame for the state of affairs. Of course, other adults or children can also introduce the symbol. However, it is more likely that a parent would have sustained interactions with the child to both introduce the same symbol appropriately and respond to subtly incorrect uses of the symbol by the child.

With repeated appropriate presentation, the conventional symbol would serve as a pivot for the child to refine her conceptualization of the states of affairs to align it with the adults' conceptualization. This process, captured by Nelson and Shaw's semiotic super triangle, insures a correspondence between the reference and denotation of the child's and adult's symbol. This is achieved because the symbol provides a conventional means for the parent and child to communicate about the state of affairs in different contexts in which the state of affairs is physically present, absent but remembered, or absent but anticipated. In these contexts quite specific partnerships are forged. The child would internally represent the external symbol and externally symbolize his or her internal conceptualization. This partnership reflects a bidirectionality between language (external symbols) and thought (internal conceptualization) that would remain stable over time and communicative context.

Parent-Abstract

Sometimes parent-child communication is about more abstract, perhaps relational, entities such as mental state terms.[5] In this context, the child may be more likely to have no experience or conceptual understanding of

---

[5]Mental states are relational terms in the sense that they relate propositional attitudes (wanting, hoping, wishing, believing, etc.) to propositional content.

the relational pattern prior to exposure to the symbol. The introduction of the symbol, by way of parental conversations, would be the child's first encounter with the pattern. In this context, learning the symbol, a relational term, is a struggle, as documented by Budwig and Nelson and Shaw.

The relational term would serve as a "relational label" that is pivotal in the child's perception of, reasoning about, storage of, and transfer of the abstract pattern. Moreover the label may be centrally important to "stabilize" the pattern and sustain focus on the relational patterns rather than the individual properties (cf. Gentner and Loewenstein, and Nelson and Shaw). Thus, a child's conceptualization of the pattern denoted by the symbol would have arisen by way of this linguistic mediation; as Gentner and Loewenstein put it, ". . . the acquisition of relational terms provides both an invitation and a means for the learner to make comparisons and to store the relational meanings that result." In this sense, parental-abstract communicative contexts involve more of a unidirectional partnership between language and thought, with language mediating thought.

Peer-Hypothetical

In a very different communicative context, peers communicate in order to affect thought, not about the real world but about a hypothetical one. For the present purposes, the hypothetical world includes statements that are false of the real world but true of an alternative unreal world, which is imagined or presumed to exist. This may include thought about pretend, possible, or hypothetical worlds (Amsel & Smalley, 1999; Amsel, Trionfi, & Morris, 2000). In such contexts, as discussed by Daiute, children's internally represented hypothetical worlds are interpersonally shared. In order to share their subjective and unique hypothetical worlds, each participant would have to symbolize their internal representations. Out of negotiation between participants regarding their own internally represented hypothetical world would emerge a shared conceptualization that participants could then use to refine their internal representations. Thus, there would be a repeated cycle of participants symbolizing their unique and subjective internal representations and augmenting their internal representations in accordance with a shared conceptualization. This activity may be the basis for the participants writing well-developed stories (Daiute) or engaging sociodramatic play (Berk, 1994), among other activities.

Such a process may well occur with other participants rather than with peers. But in few other relationships is there the equality of status that is found between peers. This equality of status would presumably promote a dynamic negotiation process in which each participant would have contributed to the shared conceptualization. The partnership formed in this case may be very temporary as the hypothetical world created as a shared conceptualization may not be sustained with other peers or with the same peer at different times.

Teacher-Abstract

In formal learning contexts, teachers may well introduce new symbols about which the child has no experience or conceptual understanding. Paralleling the parent-abstract informal learning environments, the teacher's introduction of new symbols in formal learning environments would be the basis for the child's conceptualization of the abstract entity or pattern. Again a more unidirectional partnership obtains between language and thought. The pattern of communication by teachers in formal learning contexts, as alluded to by Lehrer and Schauble, may not be optimally structured to support children's slow process of interpreting signs that are presented by the teacher as symbolic. Such failures may be difficult to detect but critically important to correct.

Compared to parent-abstract contexts, teacher-abstract ones may result in different patterns of symbol integration and transference. Conceptualizations learned in school may more readily transfer across classrooms than those learned outside school, in contrast to the conceptualizations learned at home that may transfer more generally. Moreover, the symbols learned in school might be more readily integrated with other ones learned in school than ones acquired in informal learning contexts (McVaugh, Amsel, Joersz, & Syphus, 2001), perhaps limited only to those similarly learned in formal contexts.

What is unique about teacher-abstract communicative contexts is the significance given to children's facility with notational systems. Learning to comprehend or express the symbols notationally makes the challenge of learning the appropriate conceptualization of the symbol that much more difficult. Learning the concept of "verb phrase" while learning to read, or the concept of "paragraphs" while learning to write, or "growth rate" while learning to create histographs requires complex partnerships between thought, language, and notational systems. The child's conceptualization created from the symbolic language used by the teacher becomes symbolized linguistically and notationally, with the consequence of a forging of partnerships between thought and language, thought and notation, and language and notation. The translation of thought into language and notations provide *multiple* opportunities for externalizing thought into conventional symbol systems and provide the first chance for the child to select from among symbol systems, the one symbol that is the best for communication in a context.

In summary, the specific cognitive developmental consequence of symbolic communication depends on the context in which the child's true symbolic dialogues occur. That is, unique partnerships between thought, language, and notation were forged in each of the four communicative contexts. Perhaps the most significant conclusion to draw from all this is the one answering the questions posed in the preface about the cognitive consequences of acquiring linguistic versus notational forms of symbol communication. It seems that the communicative contexts in which language and notational systems are learned have generally parallel cognitive consequences. In both contexts, others introduce new symbols that must be internalized and conceptualized by the child. The processes for representing symbols internally and symbolizing internal conceptualizations result in new specific but stable language and thought relations being forged. Learning to symbolize thought with both language and notations provides additional learning problems and opportunities for children. These problems and opportunities arise in managing the symbol systems in order to communicate precisely. With more communicative options available, there are more and increasingly complex partnerships to manage.

There is both theoretical, methodological, practical significance to considering the parallel cognitive consequences of learning to communicate linguistically in informal environments and notationally in formal ones. Methodologically, claims of contributions to cognitive development of acquiring language or notational systems can be specifically tested. For example, Olson cited those who claimed a role of notional systems in memory. But Goldin-Meadow cited research suggesting iconic gestures have the same effect. Thus any sign, from iconic gestures to symbolic notations, may serve to improve memory. In terms of application, Daiute and Lehrer and Schauble advocate that formal learning environments should exploit the sort of communication processes that occur in informal and play or discussion ones. They propose that such communicative practices as sustained interactions, negotiations, and careful monitoring of appropriate symbol use promotes learning in classrooms. Theoretically, as the relation between cognitive development and symbolic communication is better understood, broad proposals that characterize the relation between language and thought or between notations and thought without regard to the other will be seen as increasingly inadequate. Simple and general unidirectional theories of thought and language or of thought and notional systems cannot be made to answer questions raised in the present volume about the complex interactions and interrelations between all forms of symbolic communication and cognitive development.

REFERENCES

Amsel, E., Bobadilla, W., Coch, D., & Remy, R. (1996). Young children's memory for the true and pretend identities of objects used in object-substitution pretense. *Developmental Psychology, 32,* 479–491.

Amsel, E., & Smalley, J. (1999). Beyond really and truly: Children's counterfactual thinking about pretend and possible worlds. In K. Riggs & P. Mitchell (Eds.), *Children's reasoning and the mind* (pp. 99–134). Brighton, England: Psychology Press.

Amsel, E., Trionfi, G., & Morris, N. (2000). *Children's reasoning about alternate realities: The nature and creation of pretend and hypothetical worlds.* Unpublished manuscript.

Berk, L. E. (1994). Vygotsky's theory: The importance of make-believe play. *Young Children, 30–39.*

Bronfenbrenner, U. (1979). *The ecology of human development.* Cambridge, MA: Harvard University Press.

Byrnes, J. P., & Gelman, S. A. (1991). Perspectives on thought and language: Traditional and contemporary views. In S. A. Gelman & J. P. Byrnes (Eds.), *Perspectives on language and thought: Interrelations in development* (pp. 3–27). New York: Cambridge University Press.

Collier, M. (1998). On the compatibility of connectionism and cognitive linguistics. *CRL Newsletter, 11,* 3–11.

Deacon, T. (1997). *The symbolic species: The co-evolution of language and the brain.* New York: Norton.

Hawkes, T. (1977). *Structuralism and semiotics.* Berkeley: University of California Press.

McNeill, D., & Duncan, S. D. (1998). Growth points in speaking-for-thinking. (http:// cogprints.soton.ac.uk/archi . . . 05012/doc.html/McNeill&Duncan.html)

McVaugh, W., Amsel, E., Joersz, J., & Syphus, K. (2001). *Learning classical conditioning: The interaction between prior intuitive theories and new information.* Unpublished manuscript.

Peirce, C. S. (1955). Logic as semiotic: A theory of signs. In J. Buchler (Ed.), *Philosophical writings of Peirce* (pp. 98–119). New York: Dover. (Original work published 1897)

Perner, J. (1991). *Understanding the representational mind.* Cambridge, MA: MIT Press.

Piaget, J. (1951). *Play, dreams and imitation in childhood.* New York: Norton.

Schauble, L., & Glaser, R. (1996). *Innovations in learning: New environments for education.* Mahwah, NJ: Lawrence Erlbaum Associates.

Slobin, D. (1996). From "thought and language" to "thinking for speaking." In J. J. Gumperz & S. C. Levinson (Eds.), *Rethinking linguistic relativity* (pp. 70–96). New York: Cambridge University Press.

Tolchinsky-Landsmann, L., & Karmiloff Smith, A. (1992). Children's understanding of notations as domains of knowledge versus referential communicative tools. *Cognitive Development, 7,* 287–300.

Tommasello, M. (1998). Introduction: A cognitive-functional perspective on language structure. In M. Tomasello (Ed.), *The new psychology of language: Cognitive and functional approaches to language structure* (pp. vii–xxiii). Mahwah, NJ: Lawrence Erlbaum Associates.

Vygotsky, L. S. (1978). *Mind in society.* Cambridge, MA: MIT Press.

Wellman, H. M., & Gelman, S. A. (1992). Cognitive development. Foundational theories of core domains. *Annual Review of Psychology, 43,* 337–377.

Author Index

Subject Index